THE BENGAL CONUNDRUM

THE BENGAL CONUNDRUM

THE RISE OF THE BJP AND THE FUTURE OF THE TMC

SAMBIT PAL

BLOOMSBURY
NEW DELHI • LONDON • OXFORD • NEW YORK • SYDNEY

BLOOMSBURY INDIA
Bloomsbury Publishing India Pvt. Ltd
Second Floor, LSC Building No. 4, DDA Complex, Pocket C – 6 & 7,
Vasant Kunj, New Delhi, 110070

BLOOMSBURY, BLOOMSBURY INDIA and the Diana logo
are trademarks of Bloomsbury Publishing Plc

First published in India 2021
This edition published 2021

ISBN: PB: 978-93-89714-79-1; eBook: 978-93-89812-68-8
2 4 6 8 10 9 7 5 3 1

Typeset in Manipal Technologies Limited
Printed and bound in India by Thomson Press India Ltd.

MIX
Paper from
responsible sources
FSC™ C010615

CONTENTS

AUTHOR'S NOTE

'Whatever you say, you will see, Didi will come to power!'

Mahesh Barman, a lean but able-bodied man, uttered these words with full conviction while looking straight ahead through the windscreen and holding the steering wheel of the car tightly. The words had so much power that the car full of journalists went silent. He was a farmer from North Bengal's Cooch Behar who earned a living by driving hired vehicles in and around Kolkata, and his words had silenced all of us, a pack of seasoned journalists. There were reasons for his sharp and sudden reaction.

Almost a decade ago, some of my senior colleagues from other media houses—Prasenjit Bakshi, Jayanta Chowdhury, Rabishankar Dutta and Jagannath Chattopadhyay—and I routinely met up at the end of the day on our way home. We would dissect Bengal politics and evaluate the political moves by the Left, Right and the Centre. Maheshda was generally not part of our discussions. He was privy to our political critique but never contributed unless asked. The day Maheshda spoke up, we were perhaps critically evaluating a move by the Trinamool Congress (TMC) and Maheshda could not control himself.

In 2008–09, when Mamata Banerjee was riding high on the popularity bandwagon on the back of the anti-land-acquisition-movement and inching closer to the house of power in the state, Maheshda voiced the popular sentiment of the common man in Bengal.

His 'outburst' made me ponder the sharp distinction between the popular sentiment and the underlying politics behind the creation of such a narrative.

Minutes later, we stopped by our designated roadside tea stall. As my colleagues sipped steaming hot tea from *bhanrs* (earthen cups) and I gulped my favourite boiled eggs, I seriously thought about the possibility of documenting the politics, and not just the politicking, of Bengal. I proposed to my colleagues that we should write a book on the contemporary political history of Bengal as objectively as possible, drawing from our first-hand experiences. However, the dream remained unfulfilled due to our busy professional lives.

In 2017, as winds of change seemed to be blowing once again in Bengal and the political scenario started metamorphosising, the dream resurfaced. The Left Front government was dislodged in 2011 by the Mamata Banerjee–led TMC and the BJP was gradually emerging as the principal Opposition party. At that time, I was writing a weekly column on Bengal politics, without being prejudiced or partisan, in Bengali for *Ebela Digital*. Initially, I was almost determined to compile my weekly pieces into a book.

Before the idea materialized and I transformed from a full-time journalist to media educator and freelancer, one fine afternoon in June 2019, another thought struck my mind. Why shouldn't I attempt to reach the national audience? West Bengal had made national headlines in 2019 when Narendra Modi returned to power for the second term. The BJP bagged 18 seats out of 42, decimating the ruling TMC in the state. I felt the national audience must be interested in understanding the reason behind this sudden surge in support for the saffron camp in Bengal. How could the citadel of the Left (remember, Mamata Banerjee was branded as being more Left than the original Left) suddenly change its direction?

I immediately rang Kanishka Gupta, the founder of Writer's Side, with a lot of apprehensions, wondering if he would tolerate a stranger and a first-time author from Bengal willing to write on Bengal politics. To my utter surprise, Kanishka turned out to be more excited than me about the book. Thus, the journey began.

After rejections, mentoring, restructuring the proposal and rewriting the draft chapters, finally, the idea landed in the hands of my editor, Bloomsbury's Prerna Vohra. Our long discussions on national and Bengal politics and this book boosted my confidence. They helped me find a proper direction and gave the narrative shape. I would like to thank Kanishka, Prerna and Amish Mulmi (who briefly mentored me at an initial stage) for their valuable inputs to make this book happen.

The book does not only aim to examine why the rightist force engulfed the imagination of the people of Bengal, who often boasted of being progressive, Left-liberal flagbearers of communal harmony. It is also not just about showing why Mamata Banerjee fell from grace. This book is an attempt to present a holistic view of Bengal politics over the last couple of years. With reference to the past and present political incidents, I have tried to demonstrate how Mamata Banerjee's TMC, despite enjoying popular support and implementing social welfare schemes, gave way to the BJP. I also critically evaluate the role of the Left and the saffron camp's politics of polarization. In the end, I outline how Mamata Banerjee has been trying to fight back in the face of the BJP's onslaught post the 2019 Lok Sabha elections.

The broad reasons behind this unprecedented politically pathbreaking result (as I have identified in this book) are—Mamata Banerjee's absolutism and overdependence on the administration rather than the party organization; her political, ideological and organizational weaknesses and her failure to arrest corrupt practices at the grassroots; her alleged minority-appeasement, which gave rise to Hindutva politics; the swing of the Left support base towards rightist forces; and the groundwork done by the RSS for years, the organizational restructuring of the Bengal BJP and the shift in focus of central leadership towards the East. The politics of development has gradually been replaced by identity politics.

The discussions on the above points do not maintain a strict timeline. To me, the agitation and the violence that followed in Darjeeling in the summer of 2017 in the presence of Mamata Banerjee and her full cabinet marked a turning point in recent Bengal politics, which has been dominated by Banerjee since 2007–08. This was the first direct challenge to her authority since she came to power in 2011. So, the book starts with the Darjeeling incident. I have tried to pick up such political developments, going back and forth, to explain the broad points of the book rather than chronologically narrating and analysing the change of politics in Bengal.

The most interesting chapter is perhaps the last one which highlights Bengal politics after the Lok Sabha elections. I love to compare the developments with the analogy of a seesaw. Bengal politics has been continuously changing its colour. Here, I outline the strategy Mamata Banerjee is adopting with the help of Prashant Kishor to counter the BJP after a disastrous result in 2019 and how the saffron camp is still relying more on people's anti-establishment sentiment rather than projecting a chief ministerial candidate, quelling factionalism among the state leaders or concentrating on rejuvenating the organization they were proud of during Modi's re-election.

This is not a reporter's memoir. However, I have relied more on my personal experiences and observations as a journalist who covered Bengal politics from the ground, as well as the comments of other senior journalists, researchers and commentators who gave me a 360-degree view validating most of my understandings. Many politicians across party lines have also spoken to me on the condition of anonymity. I have quoted some of them without revealing their names. Yes, I have also interviewed the first-rung leaders of the many political parties (to get their party's official point of view), including the TMC. Still, Chief Minister Mamata Banerjee's office did not reply to my request for an interview. My email to her office remained unanswered and I refused to go to her via a close associate or leader.

I would like this book to remain as a document of the contemporary political history of Bengal for generations to come. I have tried to be as neutral and objective as possible in my approach while analyzing the state's politics.

I am thankful to the colleagues I mentioned at the beginning. The idea for the book germinated with their help. I must especially thank Jayanta Chowdhury, a senior journalist, for continuously encouraging and guiding me to write this book and critiquing my manuscript. As I write this book, I remember the support I have received from my comrades-in-arms in my journalistic adventures, my video journalists, Suraj Pandey and Sudarshan Parida. I thank my friend Kamalika Sengupta for always supporting and encouraging me. I would like to express my gratitude to my former editor,

Arnab Goswami, and my former colleagues at *Times Now,* including Jayanta Bhattacharya and Hector Kenneth, and all my colleagues at the Kolkata Bureau for supporting my travels across the state to report on Bengal's socio-political issues. This helped me gain first-hand knowledge about grassroots politics. I may not name each of them, but I am grateful to the district reporters of Bengal with whom I have worked very closely. They were, on many occasions, my eyes and ears in understanding the politics at the ground level. I must mention another former editor, Ayanjit Sen, and the entire *Ebela Digital* team for supporting me to write the weekly column 'Ekka Dokka', which paved the way for this book.

I would like to thank Dr Mrinal Chatterjee, my teacher and head of IIMC, Dhenkanal, where I work now, and other colleagues for providing me a creative space to attempt such long-form writing. My gratitude to my teachers at Cardiff University, Matt Swaine, Janet Harris, James Stewart, Howard Barrell and Gavin Evans, who taught me critical long-form writing, my professors in Presidency College, especially Dr Prasanta Ray, for teaching me politics as a subject and critical thinking as a practice. My regards to my teachers at Mahesh Sri Ramkrishna Ashram and R.K. Mission Residential College, Narendrapur.

I am thankful to my parents, Kartick Chandra Pal and Maya Pal, and my elder sister Sanchita for bringing me up without any inhibition or any political dogma. They let me grow as I wanted. Thanks to my parents-in-law, M.K. Bhattacharya and Tapasi Bhattacharya, for having faith in me. Special thanks to another elder sister Madhurima Vidyarthi for her emotional support and inspiration to write a book.

And finally, also most importantly, I would like to extend my love to my wonderful wife, Deepshikha, without whom I am nothing. Without her, this book would have never happened. We have been together in our journalistic adventures, ups and downs, the emotional turmoil in life and the challenging journey this book has seen. She has been my fiercest critic and a rock-solid support. I remember how she meticulously read and corrected the first drafts of the proposal and manuscript despite her busy professional schedule.

I would like to dedicate this book to the common people of Bengal like Maheshda, who find shelter in the popular political narrative, and to those who have sacrificed their lives in political violence without being aware, most of the time, of the deep-rooted politics behind the scenes.

PROLOGUE

'Stop the car,' I told the driver. I had to get off the car to know where I was. The surroundings looked unfamiliar. The last time I had visited this place was around eight years ago, and then, neither was there a concrete bridge across the Kangsabati River nor any skyscrapers. 'Are we at the right place or even moving in the right direction?' I asked myself. The large hoarding at the start of the bridge said, 'Welcome to Lalgarh Bridge.' I was indeed at the right place.

Lalgarh, a tiny block in West Bengal's West Midnapore district (which was later divided and now belongs to the Jhargram district), dominated by tribals, was the hub of armed ultra-Left Maoist activities around a decade ago. The Maoist activities intensified in the area with a landmine attack on former chief minister Buddhadeb Bhattacharjee's convoy in November 2008 and subsequent police raids on the villages. The Maoists, who carried out the attack, mobilized the villagers to protest against police atrocities on the innocent. Soon a Maoist frontal organization named People's Committee Against Police Atrocities (PCPA) was formed and a prolonged movement was launched. The movement took a violent turn when the Maoists armed young PCPA members and launched the People's Militia. Lalgarh was akin to a laboratory for the Maoists. Not only Lalgarh, but the entire western part of the state, known as Junglemahal—because of its geographical location and forests—was supposed to be under the 'Red Army' to convert it into a 'Free Guerrilla Zone' as they had done in Chhattisgarh.

The spot I was standing at used to have a broken wooden bridge for cycles, motorbikes and pedestrians to cross the Kangsabati River. Maoists had burnt down a part of the bridge. As journalists, while covering the Maoist movement and the subsequent action by the joint forces of the central and state police way back in 2008–09, our regular drill was to reach the riverbank by car, walk down the sandy riverbed, cross the makeshift bridge made of bamboo on foot and then hitchhike on motorbikes to reach the Maoist den. Motorbikes were the best mode of transportation as most of the arterial roads had either been dug up or blocked by logs. This was done by the Maoists to delay and obstruct the movement of police vans. There was also the risk of getting blown up by landmines planted on the roads, which were triggered by heavy vehicles.

Buses, too, could not ply on these roads for a few years. Shops in the area were closed most of the time, mainly due to bandhs called by the Maoists. We had to always pre-order lunch at a small eatery known as Boudir Hotel in the morning before venturing out for 'stories' into the villages or forest or go hungry till dinner. The staple lunch comprised daal, omelettes and rice.

At that time the police station in the area was under lock and key from inside. There was an atmosphere of terror in the villages. The PCPA would hold protest marches every other day and thousands of villagers would join them. Almost every morning, a body, usually of a Communist Party of India (Marxist) (CPIM) activist, with a Maoist poster alongside it, could be spotted on the roads or fields. The Maoists apparently killed the 'spies' or the 'class enemies'.

The Maoists even egged the villagers on to demolish or torch the houses of CPIM leaders, who had been in power in West Bengal for over three decades and had allegedly terrorized or tortured the people in the locality. Schools and colleges were shut and paramilitary forces took them over to set up their camps. Lalgarh turned into a battlefield between the armed Maoists, along with the PCPA, and the security forces. Before the security forces were called in, the CPIM-backed 'harmads', or armed groups, had tried to resist the Maoists. The CPIM tried all means to reclaim the lost ground in Junglemahal, but ultimately, it failed to re-establish its rule in the area.

Ten years down the line, standing in front of the Lalgarh bridge, I could see the area had transformed. There was now a huge bridge over the river and it took a little over 30 minutes to cover a distance of around 20 kilometres to reach Lalgarh from Jhargram, the district headquarters. The roads were unexpectedly wide and smooth. There were civic volunteers managing traffic. In front of the newly built bridge, on which heavy goods vehicles were plying, there were skyscrapers and on the right side and after crossing the bridge, a cluster of new buildings painted blue and white. One was a nursing college and the other a Krishi Mandi and Technical College. Further down the road, I could see a group of students cycling to school. The cycles bore stickers of the Sabooj Sathi scheme[1] of the government of West Bengal. Packed buses were plying to the district headquarters from the neighbouring district of Bankura and West Midnapore. The market area was abuzz with customers. The police station, too, had got a fresh coat of blue-and-white paint. Central Reserve

---

[1] A West Bengal government scheme that provides bicycles to students in classes of IX to XII in government and government-aided schools to enhance their secondary education. It is being implemented since 2015. More details: https://wbsaboojsathi.gov.in/v2/

Police Force (CRPF) camps no longer had security personnel on watch towers looking out for strangers or suspicious activities.

Lalgarh was like any 'normal' rural block in Bengal. Peace had long been restored under the Mamata Banerjee government. Ultra-Left activities had been completely neutralized with the killing of top Maoist leader Koteswar Rao alias Kishenji on 24 November 2011, who was responsible for spearheading the movement in this area. Green fields on both sides of the road signalled a bountiful year for the farmers.

West Bengal Chief Minister Mamata Banerjee can most definitely take credit for restoring normalcy in Maoist-hit areas and giving them an image-makeover with her development plans. If you ask, she will be able to narrate a list of development projects she has initiated in the area without the help of any document. 'I have visited Junglemahal more than a block president [of the TMC] ever visits the area,' Mamata Banerjee claimed at public meetings.

In the same breath, Mamata also lets everyone know that she has set up three super speciality hospitals, a medical college, a university, degree and technical colleges, a nursing institute, health sub-centres, neonatal units for sick infants, a tribal development board and has launched a special scheme for kendu leaves collected and sold by the tribal population, along with sanctioning lakhs of rupees for self-help groups.

Apart from these schemes and projects, there is a long list of roads and bridges her government has constructed in this vulnerable zone. Her government also provided rice at ₹2 per kg for the residents of the area. None of these claims is false. She has poured in crores of rupees to uplift the backward area and restore peace in Junglemahal. Still, this was not enough to save the vote bank she had tried to nurture and keep intact for the future. She felt a jolt in the elections.

THE FIRST SIGNS OF DEBACLE

Despite such an aggressive and determined development pitch, Mamata Banerjee's TMC faced a debacle of sorts in the panchayat elections of 2018 in the Junglemahal districts of Jhargram, Purulia, West Midnapore and Bankura, as compared to the other parts of the state. While the TMC did win the majority of seats in the zila parishad, their performance at the grassroots level (that is, in gram panchayat and panchayat samiti) was an indicator of the resentment brewing among the people. Also, the BJP's emergence as the main Opposition in the panchayat elections less than a year before the Lok Sabha polls, especially in Junglemahal, caused a lot of concern among the ranks and files of the TMC. It showed that Mamata had failed to win hearts even after restoring peace in the area.

The TMC fared well in Jhargram Zila Parishad winning 13 seats, while the BJP could only bag three. However, in Jhargram alone, the TMC won 399 gram panchayat seats, while the BJP won 329. In Purulia, the BJP won 645 gram panchayat seats against the TMC's 863. In Bankura, the TMC was again in a better position, winning 2,138 seats against BJP's 234. In Jhargram district, BJP did get the majority of the seats in 24 gram panchayats while 10 gram panchayats were hung with no party reaching the majority mark.

Even though the win in the zila parishad polls provided a momentary respite for the TMC, the gram panchayat level results were a cause for concern. Given the fact that the TMC had won 34 per cent of the total seats in a three-tier panchayat election uncontested (the results were finalized in the uncontested seats after a long legal battle), this result in Jhargram sent a shockwave in the ruling party.

It is not difficult to analyse why this had happened. After all, there were loopholes in the TMC's organizational set-up in the area. In the beginning, when Mamata Banerjee came to power in 2011, things seemed to go well for the TMC with her government restoring peace in the region and her development pitch hitting the emotional chords of the people. 'In Jhargram district, Maoists had cashed in on the people's anger against the CPIM leaders, who treated the area as their fiefdom. For every little dispute, we had to resort to the CPIM local committee office. While the leaders multiplied their properties, we were left languishing,' says Abani Mahato, an elderly farmer from Dharampur village in Lalgarh. 'So the Maoists formed the PCPA and we rallied with them to teach the CPIM a lesson. After the 2011 elections, the PCPA members joined Trinamool.' Indeed, the Left was routed from the area after the 2011 assembly elections and most of the PCPA members who were once with the Maoists merged themselves with the TMC. There was hardly any opposition.

But soon cracks began to show. Buddhadeb Pratihari, a BJP booth level leader in Kantapahari, where the saffron party was non-existent in 2011, says, 'Those who were part of the PCPA joined the TMC and got money, posts and in some cases, they got contractual jobs as well.'

However, over time the malpractices of the CPIM engulfed the TMC as well. As Mahato says, 'They [TMC] didn't allot jobs for 100-day work. They didn't allot funds from the Pradhan Mantri Awas Yojana as we were CPIM supporters. I told them I supported no one. People vote for those who work for the people. But they didn't listen.' Thus, the TMC leaders also began to behave in a partisan manner and lost connection with the people.

This is ironic. Take the example of Dharampur, which has an interesting history. In June 2009, with the help of Maoists in the region, this village had put up a mass revolt against the CPIM leaders. It is the place where Maoist commander Bikash, brandishing his AK47, held an open-air press conference for the first time with a select group of journalists and admitted that in November 2008 they had wanted to eliminate the then chief minister Buddhadeb Bhattacharjee when he was returning from the foundation-laying ceremony of the steel manufacturing unit of Jindal Group in Salboni. The same day (16 June 2009), Bikash and his comrades led thousands of villagers to demolish the palatial house of a local CPIM leader Anuj Pandey and also set the CPIM office ablaze. Beside the office, three bodies, including that of CPIM activist Shalku Soren, lay rotting for days. Neither the police nor the family members or the CPIM leaders dared to take the body for cremation. The Maoists cut off the police and administration's access to the area. A battle between the government and the Maoists—along with the villagers aligning to PCPA—ensued. While the CPIM leaders and their supporters fled from the scene, Dharampur could only be recovered by the administration with the help of the central police force later. The TMC reaped the electoral benefits as the CPIM was thrown out of power in West Bengal in 2011.

In the 2009 Lok Sabha elections, CPIM candidate Pulin Bihari Baske secured 47.84 per cent of the votes polled in the Jhargram assembly segment in which Dharampur falls and the TMC-supported Congress candidate Amrit Hansda polled 30.13 per cent of the votes. In the same constituency in the 2011 assembly elections, that is post-Maoist insurgency when the CPIM had to retreat from the area, TMC's Sukumar Hansda polled 44.67 per cent of the total votes whereas CPIM candidate Amar Basu could poll only 34.85 per cent votes. In the 2014 Lok Sabha elections, the CPIM was further decimated as they could garner only 22.94 per cent of the votes polled against TMC's Uma Saren, who secured 55.32 per cent votes from this assembly segment. Hence, the TMC had wrested the Dharampur Gram Panchayat from the CPIM in 2013 itself, completely decimating the Left.

However, as Mahato claimed, perhaps the local TMC leaders fell into the same trap as their Left counterparts. Partisan politics in allotting government welfare benefits must have led a section of the villagers to support the BJP, which was non-existent in 2011 in Dharampur. Then, almost 10 years down the line, BJP flags were flying in front of the closed CPIM party office, with people like Abani Mahato alleging how the TMC-led panchayat deprived them of their basic rights.

There was also resentment among various tribal groups. Identity politics took centre stage once again. The Santhals were looking for constitutional recognition of their social codes and they blocked off a part of the state with various demands in June and again in September 2018. They had gathered under the banner of their apolitical organization, Bharat Jakat Majhi Pargana Mahal (BJMPM)—a social umbrella organization of tribals—at the district headquarters with their traditional weapons to hold a peaceful demonstration and blocked the state and national highways and the railway tracks. Their demands included proper infrastructure for schools, higher education in Santhali language, maintaining exclusive rights of tribals over their land, non-dilution of the Scheduled Castes and the Scheduled Tribes (Prevention of Atrocities) Act, 1989, stopping atrocities against tribals among others. During the panchayat elections, they put up independent candidates in several villages against the ruling TMC. They were upset with the way the state and the central government treated the tribals.

On the other hand, Kurmis, one of the Other Backward Classes (OBCs) in the region, were demanding their inclusion in the list of Scheduled Tribes. They were a part of the list but had been taken off it in 1931. They formed about 42 per cent of the population in Junglemahal. Mamata Banerjee had written to the Centre about their demands, but no action was taken. BJP leaders also took a delegation of the Kurmi Samaj to Delhi to appeal to the Union government to bring the necessary amendment. It yielded assurance but no concrete result. Ultimately, during the Lok Sabha elections in 2019, the Kurmis declared that they would not allow any political party to campaign in their village. They, however, did not call for a vote boycott directly, but the underlying message was 'Don't vote for the TMC'.

Mamata Banerjee, being a seasoned grassroots politician, detected the disease in her party in Junglemahal. As early as February 2018, well before the panchayat elections, in an administrative review meeting, she pulled up her party leaders in Jhargram. Naming the TMC-run Binpur II Panchayat Samiti Sabhapati, Bangshibadan Mahato, she warned, 'You all have to get rid of the attitude that what you decide is final and there can't be anyone in the beneficiary list whom you didn't select. Let me make something very clear. The government schemes are meant for the poor and no one should be left out, no matter which party he supports. Why should

I have to hear complaints that you are not available in the area? I have my own information channel and I have come to know that some people in the area need houses. Some are not getting widow pension.'[2]

Mamata Banerjee knew the ground realities in Junglemahal. She warned her party's local leaders at regular intervals. Unfortunately, she did not have any strong mechanism inside the party or in the administration to monitor these leaders and take remedial actions.

In addition to these local problems, Mamata Banerjee lacked local leaders who could mobilize the party in Junglemahal and hold the fort. This was the only district in West Bengal that did not have a district TMC president. The president of the neighbouring and parent district of West Midnapore ran the party affairs in liaison with a committee formed for Jhargram. On behalf of the state organization, the district was apparently in the hands of Youth TMC leader and Mamata Banerjee's nephew, Abhishek Banerjee, after the party's all India general secretary, Mukul Roy, left to join the BJP on 3 November 2017. Another senior leader (former MP and minister in the Mamata Banerjee government since 2016) Suvendu Adhikari was stripped off his responsibilities in Junglemahal apparently at the behest of Mukul Roy soon after the 2011 assembly elections. The point is that both Abhishek and Mukul looked at the organization from the top. They were, in a sense, 'outsiders' and failed to nurture any local leader to grow and hold the leash of the grassroots organization. The issue was not only with the local leadership but also with understanding

---

[2] Khanra, S. *Times of India*. 'Mamata Banerjee unhappy with the development work in former Red zone'. 17 February 2018.

the local sentiment to formulate administrative policies as well as political strategies.

'The problem with the mainstream political party like the CPIM or [the] TMC and for that matter [the] Congress is that they cannot understand the sentiments of the tribal population. No party has elevated a tribal leader at the helm of affairs,' says a former CPIM district committee member from West Midnapore. According to him, an outsider who has no knowledge of the terrain and its population is always entrusted with planning the governmental schemes.

Dahar Sen, a CPIM leader who was in charge of Jhargram, cites an example of lack of understanding of tribal issues by the planners seated in Kolkata. He says, '[For instance], the Lodha community does not believe in allopathic treatment and wouldn't generally go to a doctor. As I have worked with them, I have seen that they do go to ayurvedic doctors. I had proposed that four ayurvedic chambers be set up in various parts of Jhargram where the Lodha population can come and get themselves treated. Instead, the government sent a homoeopathic doctor who used to travel to these four centres and it did not yield much result.'

Mamata Banerjee too, apart from assigning organizational responsibilities to some South Kolkata-based leaders, thought that simply pouring in money for infrastructural projects and extending welfare benefits would help her sail through the elections. Even after the debacle in the panchayat elections in the tribal-dominated Junglemahal, she appointed expelled CPIM Rajya Sabha MP Ritabrata Banerjee as the head of the Tribal Development Board on 6 July 2018, overlooking the leadership at the district level. This shows the attitude CPIM leader Dahar Sen spoke about. Ritabrata who is neither from the tribal community nor has any prior experience working in tribal areas, was assigned to handle the Tribal Development Board. The critics alleged that it was difficult for the Kolkata-based leader to understand the issues haunting the tribals. This also exposed Mamata's lack of trust in the local leadership.

She was visibly upset with late Jhargram MLA Sukumar Hansda and Salboni MLA Churamani Mahato, sons of the soil who could be her trump cards. Contrary to such possibility, they were accused of not reaching out to the people. At party and administrative meetings, Mamata Banerjee asked them to improve their connection with the people. 'Sukumarda, you are senior and a doctor. The community respects you. Don't wait for getting an invite [from the people to visit them]... you reach out,' said Mamata at the administrative review meeting in February 2018. Soon after the debacle in the panchayat elections, on 5 June 2018, Mamata Banerjee dropped Churamani Mahato from her cabinet. Churamani was holding the portfolio of Backward Class Welfare department.[3]

Immediately after the TMC came to power in 2011 and the Mamata Banerjee government initiated the development projects, a section who worked as middlemen cropped up in every village. These 'middlemen' worked for their own vested interests and ignored the general tribal sentiment. They reaped the benefits of infrastructural development programmes and government schemes. Anup Mahato, a resident of Joram village in Belpahari block, the first village in Junglemahal that Mamata had visited as Youth Congress leader way back in 1992, alleges that the TMC leader in his village misappropriated government funds allocated

---

[3] PTI. *India Today*. 'Mamata removes three ministers from cabinet'. 5 June 2018.

for building homes. 'See, he has built a pucca house for himself, but we have not received funds to build our house,' he says, pointing out the TMC leader's house.

The villagers in Ramgarh's Mallapara claim that TMC leaders asked for money to release government funds. Once they knew that funds had been transferred to the beneficiary's bank account, the TMC leaders would allegedly come to the house or wait in front of the bank to extort cash. 'We had got ₹20,000 for building the house, the local TMC leader demanded ₹6,000,' says a villager in Mallapara indicating his half-built pucca house.

A section of the TMC workers and leaders were not happy with the fact that some of their colleagues were involved in the malpractice. Some were not happy as they did not get a share in the 'extortion money' and some did not like the way the office-bearers of the TMC's district committee ignored a section of the grassroots workers. The first sign of such dissatisfaction among the TMC workers and supporters was seen during the panchayat elections of 2018 when they joined the Opposition camp or contested the elections as 'independent' candidates.

TMC leaders admit that a number of party workers switched sides and joined the saffron camp. 'There were some issues with the selection of candidates in panchayats. Some wrong people had been nominated and those who were denied a ticket switched sides,' says Shyamal Mahato, the Binpur Block I TMC president.

Not only the disgruntled TMC workers and leaders, but the villagers also revolted against the ruling party to lodge their protest against the *dadagiri* of the local TMC leaders. 'We don't have any problem with Mamata Banerjee. Our grudge is against the local leaders,' says Asit Malla, an agricultural labourer from Ramgarh.

The tribal population of Junglemahal has limited needs and not many demands, but the political experience of both the Left and the TMC clearly shows that political parties must respect their tribal identity. When they see the middlemen misappropriating money allocated to them or denying them their rights, they revolt. Ironically, political establishments in Kolkata assumed that dole-and-development politics could win hearts. That was not the reality.

THE BJP GAINS GROUND

While the TMC failed to understand and act upon the ground realities of Junglemahal, the BJP gained ground in the area by filling up the Opposition vacuum created after the removal of the Left parties, which were either shunted out due to Maoist insurgencies or the aggressive politics of the ruling party. The CPIM had lost all credibility in this rural belt after they were thrown out of power in 2011. The organizational weakness further diminished their influence over the people. 'Our workers have stopped going to the villages and talking to the people. How can you rebuild the organization if you don't go to the ground and develop a connection with the people,' says a local CPIM leader who has been inactive since 2011.

The BJP saw a great opportunity in Junglemahal. Through the RSS and other fringe Hindu organizations, they penetrated the remote villages. They were on the job for a couple of years. Take the example of Shantanu Mohanto, the BJP Yuva Morcha leader in Ramgarh, about 10 kilometres from Lalgarh. The young man in his thirties left his job in Axis Bank, Kolkata, and settled in his native Ramgarh apparently to start his own business, but he wanted to raise an organizational base for the saffron camp. A former student of Midnapore K.D. College and a former activist of Chhatra Parishad, the students' wing of the Congress party, Shantanu was attracted by the RSS–BJP ideology. 'About 10 years ago, we were only two or three people from the village, mostly me and my brothers, who joined [the] BJP's meetings in Jhargram or Midnapore,' says Shantanu. 'Now, we have 8 out of 16 gram panchayat representatives. Around 400 cars passed through this road in front of my mobile phone shop to join Modiji's rally during the Lok Sabha election campaign in 2019.'

'About seven years ago, when there was no sign of [the] BJP in our village, we had set up a Bajrangbali temple here adjacent to the video hall. We organized programmes around Bajrangbali,' reminisces Shantanu. His colleagues and he visited villages and held small meetings acquainting themselves with the villagers.

The fringe organization of the Sangh Parivar, Bajrang Dal, also expanded their base by setting up Bajrangbali temples and organizing religious programmes in many villages. Anyone visiting Junglemahal now sees saffron flags (not just the BJP's but plain saffron flags) flying high in every village and there are hundreds of Hanuman temples in the district. They are not run by BJP leaders, but by Bajrang Dal supporters who worked hard to create a fertile ground for the BJP's political activities. The personal rapport built with the villagers gave the BJP political dividend in the 2018 panchayat and the 2019 Lok Sabha elections.

Another BJP activist Buddhadeb Pratihari from the same locality says, 'We used to hold secret meetings in the forest. No one identified himself as a BJP activist. But we used to field an independent candidate [in local body elections]. Many from CPIM and TMC joined our fold when they were fed up with TMC.' According to Buddhadeb and Shantanu, it was considered a 'crime' to be a part of the Opposition. The TMC leadership wanted to enjoy unchallenged power in the area. Hence, the BJP supporters had to go 'underground' to operate their organizational activities or conduct them in the guise of 'independent candidates'.

Despite the several cases, such as attacking TMC leaders and assaulting local villagers, slapped against Shantanu (he claims he has 50 cases against him) and his colleagues by the TMC, the BJP activists did not abandon the battlefield. During the panchayat elections, the locals, already angry with the TMC leaders, supported the BJP and found 'solace' in their activities, claims Shantanu. 'We travelled to villages and helped people make online applications for government schemes. We had gained the people's trust. That worked for us,' he adds.

The BJP touched a religious chord with the villagers. Their supporters organized religious festivals and involved the people to gain their confidence. Under the banner of local clubs run by BJP supporters, these villagers found a voice in the BJP cadres. Today, Shantanu flaunts tattoos on both his arms—one saying 'Jai Shri Ram' and another, 'Bharat Mata Ki Jai'. He rides a motorbike with a saffron seat cover and the image of Bajrangbali imprinted at the front. The fluttering saffron flags across Junglemahal, especially in remote villages and paddy fields, and the Bajrangbali temples here and there are reflections of the attitude Shantanu has been representing. The gathering of the supporters at Shantanu's shop also shows that BJP activists no longer need to hold secret meetings and field their candidates as 'independent'.

THE TMC FAILS TO RECOVER LOST GROUND

After a rude shock in the panchayat elections in Junglemahal, especially in the Jhargram district, Mamata Banerjee made a few cosmetic changes. She asked Partha Chatterjee, the secretary-general of the TMC, to take stock of the situation. He visited Jhargram and held meetings with the party members. Ironically, the ruling party was not prepared to accept the truth that they were losing ground in Jhargram and Junglemahal. They blamed it on the BJP's 'money power' and even disrespected the 'people's mandate'. In some villages, they even appointed/elected a TMC representative as the panchayat chief despite not having a majority. It did not go down well with the locals. 'The BJP had the majority in our village, but first, they stalled the process of forming the panchayat board and now they have forced a TMC man as the gram panchayat pradhan. Why are they not going by our mandate?' asks Anup Mahato of Joram village.

The TMC also initiated the process of luring back disgruntled workers and leaders who had contested and won the election on a BJP ticket. Soon after the panchayat election results were out, the TMC district president Ajit Maity said, 'We have lost a few seats at the gram panchayat level, but in panchayat samiti and zila parishad, people have voted for Mamata Banerjee. Those who had gone to the BJP, due to some misunderstanding, will soon come back. Some are already in touch with me.'

Despite changing their candidate in the Lok Sabha elections and putting up Birbaha Soren, wife of Robin Tudu (a leader of the tribal organization BJMPM), and dropping some leaders accused of corruption, Mamata Banerjee's dole-and-development politics could not recover the lost ground in Junglemahal. The BJP gained a footing as those angry with the TMC supported them.

Break away TMC leader Mukul Roy exerted his influence on a section of disgruntled TMC workers to work in favour of the BJP. He visited Junglemahal at regular intervals. During the panchayat election campaign, he visited former PCPA convenor Chhatradhar Mahato's house. Chhatradhar was in jail, but his influence in Lalgarh still worked (he has been let out on bail and inducted in the TMC state committee in 2020). Mukul cashed in on the sentiment and later held several small *gharoa baithaks* with the villagers to build a network. He then addressed small public meetings. The same man took the representatives of the Kurmi Samaj to Delhi before the Lok Sabha elections to assure them that the central government would look into their demands for Schedule Tribe (ST) status.

Not just in Junglemahal, but the 2018 panchayat elections indicated the fall of the TMC support base and the rise of the BJP across Bengal. In 2014, the Modi-wave might have worked in Uttar Pradesh, decimating Mayawati and Akhilesh Yadav, but it was halted in Bengal. The BJP had won only two seats and the TMC went to the Parliament with 34 seats. Its vote percentage had also increased. It was mainly due to Mamata-magic. In the 2013 panchayat elections, the same magic had worked despite the Saradha chit fund scam that had rocked rural Bengal; yet, the TMC held on to its position. In the 2016 assembly elections, the TMC had increased its vote percentage despite the Narada sting operation blighting the names of Mamata Banerjee's MLAs, MPs and ministers. In 2019, nothing worked.

In 2018, the TMC won 34 per cent seats of three-tier panchayat elections uncontested, but people witnessed large-scale violence. Between the day of filing nominations and the day the results were declared, nearly 30 people were killed in poll-related violence. TMC workers did not even spare the woman nominee of the Opposition in Hooghly district. An alleged TMC goon was caught on camera physically assaulting a woman who came to file her nomination; he did not mind that he was being filmed. There were several cases in Birbhum, Murshidabad, East Midnapore and some other districts where goons of the ruling party were caught on camera beating up Opposition candidates coming to the Block Development (BDO) office to file their nomination. The situation went to such a head that the Calcutta High Court allowed nine candidates of an ultra-Left resistance group in Bhangar, South 24 Parganas, to file nominations through WhatsApp. These candidates had been physically restrained from going to the BDO office to file their nominations.

Sharmistha Chowdhury, leader of the CPI-ML (Red Star), alleged that she and a few others of her group were held captive for hours by miscreants and not allowed to file nominations. They were leading a protest against the construction of a power sub-station and farmland acquisition in the locality.

The large-scale violence during the 2018 panchayat elections and the subsequent results created a major problem for the ruling party. 'It was competitive politics within the ruling party. They were trying to capture panchayats and show their leader that they had fared so well,' says Suvashis Maitra, a senior journalist. 'In the process, they had beaten the record of uncontested seats during the Left regime and I would say this was a huge blunder by TMC. Had Mamata allowed a free and fair election in the panchayats, she would have heard the alarm bell. She might have fared poorly, but she wouldn't have to face the disaster in Lok Sabha on this scale.'

The arrogance of the TMC district leaders also cost them people's support. Controversial Birbhum district

TMC president Anubrata Mandal had threatened the Opposition of 'consequences' in case they dared to take on the TMC in his district. 'Let them go and file nominations. "*Unnayan*" would be standing on the way,' said Anubrata without explaining what he meant by the word '*unnayan*'. In Bengali, it means 'development', but the Opposition received the hidden message—they will be intercepted if they try to file nominations.

West Bengal is the first state in the country to have had party-based direct elections to all three tiers of the panchayat (gram panchayat, panchayat samiti and zila parishad) in 1978 under the first Left Front government. 'After coming to power in 1977, CPIM retained the West Bengal Panchayat Act of 1973, but with some amendments, thus reflecting a new kind of political pragmatism. The most important innovation in the context of India that they introduced was that all tiers of the panchayats would have party-based elections and secondly, there would be direct elections to all three tiers,' writes Kolkata-based independent researcher Debraj Bhattacharya.[4] Political participation in panchayat is so widespread that it invites confrontation among the parties. 'If you calculate all the central or state or collaborative schemes and projects, a gram panchayat office deals with about ₹1 crore on an average every year,' says an executive of the panchayat in South 24 Parganas district.

So, grabbing panchayat allows a political party to grab both power and money. Its essence in implementing government schemes cannot be denied at the same time. Even Chief Minister Mamata Banerjee admits, 'We need

---

[4] Bhattacharya, D. *Academia*. 'Panchayati Raj in West Bengal: A Synthesis of Existing Research'.

the panchayats to implement the developmental projects.' Therefore, the fight over the panchayat elections is intense. If the ruling party cannot win gram panchayats, they cannot create an impact on the minds of the villagers across the state. Winning the other two tiers, panchayat samiti at the block level and zila parishad at the district level, is also crucial as these bodies are responsible for formulating plans for government schemes and projects.

In the process of grabbing power in the three tiers of panchayat and winning a huge number of seats uncontested, the TMC leadership lost track of their actual strength in the state. Before the Lok Sabha elections, it was clear that the leaders were not aware of their original support base. The party in power was supposed to have booth-wise calculations for the number of voters in their favour and against them. The TMC did not have a clear picture. Mamata could not gauge how much the BJP had invaded her bastion and how her leaders were actually performing. Now, she was paying the price for allowing her party-men to jump into the race for winning uncontested elections and prove their 'power' to the supreme leader of the party. If Junglemahal had given her early signs of disaster, exposing the loopholes of her governance and political strategies, the panchayat elections crippled her understanding of the ground realities of Bengal. The next one year was too little time to recover the lost and unknown ground before the Lok Sabha elections.

1

Mamata's Absolutism and Governance

In the summer of 2017, not many in hot and humid Kolkata had anticipated that political unrest was brewing in one of the finest tea-producing regions of Bengal, the Queen of Hills, Darjeeling. Yes, there had been signs of trouble for over a month, but no one could foresee that the lush green hills of Bengal would be engulfed in violence so soon after witnessing disturbing scenes in 2010 over the murder of a popular local Gorkha leader Madan Tamang; in 2011 over the killing of three GJM (or Gorkha Janamukti Morcha, the principal political outfit in Darjeeling demanding a separate state) activists; and in 2013 after Telangana was accorded with separate statehood over the demand for a separate state of Gorkhaland carved out of Bengal. The same demand resurfaced in a new avatar and the agitators found an alibi to rouse the sentiment of the hill residents.

In June 2017, Chief Minister Mamata Banerjee's visit, along with her cabinet, acted as the trigger for all hell to break loose in Darjeeling. For the first time in the last 45 years, a chief minister had brought her entire cabinet, about 30 odd ministers, home secretary and chief secretary, to the hills. She was about to hold the cabinet meeting at Raj Bhavan, the summer retreat for the titular head of state, the Governor. Mamata wanted to show her might in front of an ongoing agitation against her government by the GJM led by its chief, Bimal Gurung. Outside, a few hundred metres away from Raj Bhavan, thousands were gathering in front of Bhanu Bhavan, an administrative building, and chanting slogans against the chief minister. Anger in the hills was rising.

Journalists who had gone to cover the cabinet meeting got a glimpse of the simmering anger a day before the cabinet meeting. Mamata Banerjee was out on her morning walk. She was headed towards the zoo, passing by GJM's Singmari office, when a cavalcade crossed her. A furious Mamata openly chided the then director (security) of West Bengal Police, Sanjoy Mukherjee, the man in charge of her security and the protection of the VIPs in the state, for the 'security breach'. Not only was this incident irksome for her, but it was made worse by who was breaching her security. It was none other than GJM and Gorkhaland Territorial Administration (GTA, the semi-autonomous administrative body of Darjeeling) chief Bimal Gurung and his supporters; his cavalcade had passed by her and many wondered how the police could let Bimal's car on the road where the chief minister was taking a walk.

Just after the security breach, Mamata was seen exchanging pleasantries with tourists and residents in her inimitable style, which might have fooled a few into believing that things were under control. However, just one kilometre away, Gurung was organizing a protest rally against her. The battle lines between Mamata and Gurung had been drawn a few months ago when the TMC won the Mirik Municipality elections in the hills defeating Gurung's GJM. He did not like the way the TMC was gaining ground in his fiefdom. Gurung, who had once considered Mamata as close as their 'Ma' (mother), now dubbed her as their 'enemy'. Once a trusted ally of Mamata, Gurung was now gunning to take her head-on. The bonhomie between Mamata Banerjee and Bimal Gurung had long been over.

The next day, 8 June 2017, security was tightened, but while the cabinet meeting was in progress, thousands of protestors gathered outside Bhanu Bhavan chanting slogans against the Bengal government and the chief minister. Soon, the protest took a violent turn as supporters of Bimal Gurung tried to storm the police barricades. The protesters clashed with the police, hurling bricks and crude bombs at them. They even attacked the police with bows and arrows. The police had to fire tear gas shells and resort to lathi charge to disperse the rioting crowd. Tourists and other visitors became unsuspecting casualties of the violence, and many took shelter in the nearby Darjeeling Mall. Shops in the mall also started downing their shutters. A few hundred metres away from Raj Bhavan, the protestors vandalized at least 12 vehicles and torched a government bus. Mamata Banerjee and her entire cabinet were confined in Raj Bhavan.

THE FIRST CHALLENGE FOR MAMATA

This violent uprising in Darjeeling, aimed directly at the state government, was the first major political challenge that West Bengal Chief Minister Mamata Banerjee had faced since assuming power six years ago. The violence was a direct fallout of the face-off between Mamata and the chief of GJM, Bimal Gurung. The agitation broke out on the day of the cabinet meeting, amidst a call of indefinite strike in the hills.

The skirmish flared up, killing three GJM activists and an Indian Reserve Battalion commandant, Kiran Tamang, a week later.

The violence in Darjeeling was nothing new. If one looks back, it can be seen that the GJM, launched in October 2007, is the largest party in Darjeeling, which has been demanding the creation of Gorkhaland—a separate state for the area's majority Nepali-speaking Gorkha community. They have been fuelling a 100-year-old demand for a separate state on ethnic lines. In the 1980s too, Darjeeling was bloodied by a violent agitation with the same demand. In 1986, the Gorkhas, under the leadership of a retired Indian Army soldier, Subash Ghisingh, had settled for an autonomous council that promised a degree of self-rule for the hill region. Similarly, another prolonged protest led by Ghisingh's close aide Bimal Gurung was doused with the creation of the GTA in 2012. The clashes in the summer of 2017 reminded one of those earlier violent days.

There was a hope that as chief minister, Mamata Banerjee would tackle the Gorkhaland situation. It was believed that Mamata had matured politically over the years. Gone were the days when the fiery lady would take impulsive decisions without considering their long-term consequences. No doubt she had tried to temper herself after sitting on the chair of the chief minister, but what had perhaps not changed was her core style of functioning. After coming to power in 2011, on one hand she took the agitating outfits on board to resolve the crises in different regions of the state, while on the other she wanted to wrest political control over these areas when the situation cooled down. There is no denying that increasing activities of the mainstream political parties does help in dissipating existing tensions between the administration and separatist or insurgent groups. They act as a moderating factor while the native outfits always take an extreme stand. But here, it seemed that Mamata had hurried to capture the political space in those regions.

Mamata behaved like a mature politician when she resolved the Junglemahal Maoist crisis and the Gorkhaland agitation post 2011. Since she came to power, she has taken the aggrieved parties on board and that has given her dividends. In Darjeeling too, during the initial years of her tenure, she developed an understanding with Bimal Gurung. 'Mamata was accepted by Gurung and others in the hills because she was representing the anti-Left sentiment. People of the hills found an ally in her, who opposed the Left and empathized with their agitation against the Buddhadeb Bhattacharjee's government,' says Soumen Nag, a researcher and author based in Siliguri.

After assuming power in 2011, Mamata Banerjee met Bimal Gurung and the GJM leaders for an official dialogue between the West Bengal government and the GJM. Despite GJM's alliance with the BJP, she did not hesitate to offer them room for negotiations to address the demand for Gorkhaland. Her only condition was that Darjeeling could not be annexed out of Bengal. After all, Darjeeling was a proud possession of the state despite its distinct geographic and demographic difference with the rest of the state. Mamata Banerjee has often told the people, 'Darjeeling is not out of Bengal. It is a part of Bengal and it is the heart of Bengal. The state is not getting divided. Darjeeling is dear to me.'[1]

Unlike previous chief ministers like Jyoti Basu or Buddhadeb Bhattacharjee, Mamata Banerjee tried hard

[1] Dutta, A. *The Hindu*. 'West Bengal won't be divided: Mamata'. 19 July 2011.

to bridge the gap between the hills and the plains with her frequent visits and announcements of development projects in Darjeeling. She made it a point to visit the hills at least once every three months. 'I have visited Darjeeling more than 50 times in the last four years. I think nobody else [no other CM] has visited Darjeeling so many times. My Darjeeling is smiling,' she told a gathering in August 2015.[2]

Whenever she visited Darjeeling, while riding up the hills, she stopped at almost all the hamlets as the people would line up on both sides of the road and greet her with traditional *khada*. 'Mamata Banerjee enjoyed the personal rapport she had built with the local residents of Darjeeling and liked the fact that she was accepted by those who once demanded Gorkhaland,' says Vikram Rai, a professor of communication in Darjeeling. However, there were rumours that Bimal Gurung and his supporters would arrange these people at each junction to welcome the chief minister. In July 2011, she initiated the tripartite meeting with the central government led by the United Progressive Alliance (UPA), her government and the GJM. The result was the creation of the Gorkhaland Territorial Administration (GTA) in 2012. On 19 July 2011, the historic tripartite agreement was signed amid much fanfare in the presence of Mamata, Bimal Gurung and the then union home minister, P. Chidambaram. On the day of the accord-signing, local residents were seen dancing in traditional Gorkha attire, blowing bugles and beating drums. 'The GTA arrangement gave Bimal Gurung a breathing space after a long agitation. He had something to show his supporters,' says Nag.

---

[2] *FPJ Bureau*. 'Mamata launches Rs 500 cr green project for Darjeeling'. 26 August 2015.

After signing the tripartite agreement, while she was seen speaking to Bimal Gurung, both appearing happy that they could bring the violence in the hills to a halt after almost six years, the GJM supporters were dreaming of something else. With Gurung and Mamata seated on the dais, a school teacher in Darjeeling, who was among the audience to witness the historic treaty signing, said, 'We have achieved the first step. We have got GTA. Now we should fight for the next step to get the separate state.' A majority of the GJM supporters echoed his sentiment. The slogan 'We want Gorkhaland' started ringing in the air even before the ink on the dotted lines of the agreement had dried.

The bonhomie between Mamata and Gurung did not last long. The June 2017 violence in Darjeeling hills in presence of Mamata Banerjee and her cabinet ministers had a specific trigger. Things turned sour between them. State Education Minister Partha Chatterjee, on 15 May 2017, announced that the government was making Bengali a compulsory language in the school curriculum as part of their three-language teaching scheme.[3] 'From now on, it will be mandatory for students to learn Bengali in schools. The schools affiliated to other boards (ICSE/CBSE) will have to make Bengali as an optional subject from Class 1, giving students the option to choose it either as a second or third language,' said the education minister in a hurriedly called press conference at his residence. 'We will take into account the legal aspect as to whether separate legislation is needed or a state cabinet decision will be enough.'

The decision to make Bengali compulsory was in response to the presidential assent to the

[3] *The Hindu*. 'West Bengal makes Bengali mandatory in schools'. 16 May 2017.

recommendation of parliamentary committee on official languages to make Hindi compulsory from classes VIII to X in CBSE and central schools. A month ago, the then President of India, Pranab Mukherjee, had accepted the parliamentary committee report on the recommendations originally made by the earlier UPA government to popularize Hindi across the country.

On 16 May 2017, a day after the announcement, the chief minister wrote on her Facebook page, 'Bengal respects all languages and languages of all States. Our three language formula shows how we really do... Students have the freedom to take any language of their choice as a first language, second or third language. If the student chooses Bengali, Hindi, English, Urdu, Gurmukhi, Nepali, Alchiki as a first language, he/she may opt for two other languages of their choice. One of the three languages would have to be Bengali. The two other choices are completely dependent on what the student chooses. This method would enable them to reach regional, national and international standards.'

While challenging the 'linguistic imperialism' of Narendra Modi's government with her trademark 'Bengali versus non-Bengali' and 'how-the-Centre-disregarded-federalism' narratives, she never took into account the possible consequences of such a directive in her own state. Mamata's decision was a kneejerk reaction to the parliamentary committee's recommendation and she involuntarily passed on a weapon to the GJM chief in the hills. He was looking for an issue to rouse the Gorkha sentiment.

'Gurung was feeling insecure because there was a rift within the GJM. The intellectual personalities in the GJM could not adjust with Gurung. People like Harka Bahadur Chhetri, a retired teacher, a former

GJM MLA and member of Gurung's core team, broke away from GJM. At the same time the way Mamata Banerjee was trying to project her victory in Mirik Municipality [the area once dominated by Gurung's GJM] as a popular support for TMC, further made Gurung feel isolated. He did not want the repeat of his predecessor Subash Ghisingh's fate. He wanted to revive the Gorkhaland issue to avoid such a situation,' says Soumen Nag. Subash Ghisingh was the chief of the Gorkha National Liberation Front (GNLF) and had steered the Gorkhaland movement in the 1980s. He withdrew the violent agitation after an accord with the Union government and later became the chief of the Darjeeling Gorkha Hill Council (DGHC), an autonomous body that ruled Queens Hill. For the next two decades, he did not raise the demand for a separate Gorkhaland and ran an autocratic administration as the head of the DGHC. This irked the people of Darjeeling and the sentiment was used by Bimal Gurung and his associates to break away from the GNLF and relaunch the Gorkhaland movement. It was evident that Gurung, who almost followed his predecessor's path by launching a movement for a separate state (signing an accord with the state and the central governments and becoming the chief of the local autonomous administration), did not want to be another Ghisingh. He had been waiting for the right moment to assert his power and take on Mamata Banerjee. The sharp reaction by GJM General Secretary Roshan Giri to making Bengali compulsory in schools set the tone that the moment to strike back had come. 'Imposition of Bangla on Nepali-speaking residents of the hills is not accepted. Nepali is a recognized language and we will fight back against the linguistic and cultural hegemony of

Bengal,' said Roshan Giri.[4] This rhetoric touched a raw nerve and hurt the sentiments of the supporters of Gorkhaland.

Addressing his supporters at Gorkha Rangamanch Bhavan on 2 June 2017, Bimal Gurung said,[5] 'There is a limit to everything. We are not against the Bengali language or Bengali community. What we are saying is "please do not impose a language on us". Let it be a choice for those who want to study the language.' Gurung called for protests against the 'imperial decision'. People started coming out on the streets. The GJM chief tactfully blended the demand for a separate state of Gorkhaland with a move to oppose the decision to impose Bengali. He also warned,[6] 'The town is teeming with tourists and this is not because of Mamata Banerjee. The tourists have come here because we have maintained peace. I have not done anything different but it is Mamata Banerjee who is now trying to create unrest by trampling on our sentiment. If any untoward incident takes place, Mamata Banerjee should be solely held responsible.'

By the time the Mamata government realized its mistake, the damage was done. Darjeeling was on the boil again over the issue of a separate state of Gorkhaland. Mamata announced on 6 June 2017 that the hills' schools need not make Bengali compulsory. However, her assurance did little to pacify the agitators. Mamata Banerjee's missteps made in Darjeeling and subsequently the first political challenge she had to face during the summer of 2017 (as described earlier) perhaps explain her style of functioning and her

[4] *The New Indian Express*. 'West Bengal govt makes Bengali mandatory till Class 10 in all schools'. 16 May 2017.

[5] Chhetri, V. and Banerjee, B. *The Telegraph*. 'Gurung ups ante in language fight'. 3 June 2017.

[6] Ibid.

shortcomings as an administrator. She often failed to see the larger picture and lost touch with the ground realities, overconfident that her 'development-dole-division' pitch would decimate all opposition and win the hearts of the people. It was not to be, at least in the 2019 Lok Sabha elections.

THE WAY MAMATA FUNCTIONED

Soon after taking over as the chief minister, Mamata Banerjee wanted to reach out to the people across the state in her unique style. She announced a galore of infrastructure development projects and government welfare schemes for every section of the society, showcased them in the form of fairs and festivals and took up beautification projects. Simultaneously, she wanted to obliterate her Opposition and grab power at every corner of the state. To achieve her political goals, she depended more on her police and administration rather than on her party colleagues. She assumed that she enjoyed unwavering support from the people of Bengal because of her dole politics, basis the election results between 2011 and 2018. She apparently did not worry much about the consequences of any mistakes her party or the government committed. In the process, she lost touch with the masses. A grassroots leader like her ultimately failed to gauge the sentiment of the people.

'Development' has been Mamata's mantra to counter any kind of backlash. In Darjeeling too, she made a development pitch to fight the violent movement in the name of a separate state of Gorkhaland. To counter the BJP's bonhomie with Bimal Gurung during Lok Sabha elections in 2009 and 2014, she vehemently criticized former BJP MP Surindar Singh Ahluwalia's absence from Darjeeling. She knew people were sensitive about their MP's inaction during the violent period and unhappy that he seldom visited Darjeeling after winning the elections in 2014. The same allegations were levelled against the previous BJP MP Jaswant Singh. She blamed the Bimal Gurung faction of the GJM and BJP for creating trouble in Darjeeling to keep her government under pressure and halting their development process.

In a public meeting in Darjeeling in April 2019, Mamata Banerjee openly told the crowd,[7] 'I don't come to you only for elections and then vanish. I come to Darjeeling once in every three months. I ask the BJP party, after Bimal Gurung helped Ahluwaliji to win the Lok Sabha seat, have you come to Darjeeling ever?' The audience said 'No' in chorus. She added, 'They have done nothing for the brothers and sisters of Darjeeling. I had no MLA, MP or councillor in Darjeeling. Still, I have done a lot for Darjeeling. They just want to reap benefit out of the violence in the hills.'

Since becoming the chief minister, apart from her regular welfare schemes, she has announced a number of projects for the hills that include a modernized printing press at Kurseong, a basic training centre at Kurseong, a filter manufacturing plant for diesel locomotives at Tridhara, drinking water projects, a biotechnology hub in Kalimpong, skill development parks in every block, IT parks for unemployed youths and an education hub in Kurseong. She has set up committees to look into the wage structure of the tea garden workers and for providing land rights to them. In March 2018, soon after the violence died down, she held an 'Industry Meet' in Darjeeling and promised to create jobs for the people.

---

[7] AITC Official. 'Mamata Banerjee addresses a public meeting in Darjeeling'. YouTube, 11 April. Available at: https://www.youtube.com/watch?v=ss_lVXutL1w

'Ask her how many of them have been implemented properly? Where is the drinking water at every doorstep?' asked a journalist-turned-GJM activist in Darjeeling. They alleged that none of the promises have been fulfilled in their entirety. The TMC leadership countered the allegations by blaming the GJM for creating a ruckus in the hills. When Gurung resigned from the GTA a few weeks before elections to the semi-autonomous body were due, Gautam Deb, the then Darjeeling district president of the TMC, said, 'Morcha leaders are trying to enact a drama by tendering resignation. Their only intention is to divert the attention of the common people. They don't want to face unpleasant questions, which would be raised once the audit team [sent by the state] comes up with specific details of anomalies in the utilization of funds.'[8]

Still, Mamata did not want to give a free hand to Bimal Gurung in spending money allocated by the state and central governments. As Bimal Gurung confronted the ruling party and the state government, she did something none of her predecessors had dared to do even with the DGHC, which was an equivalent of the GTA, and its leader Subash Ghisingh. She asked for the audit of the accounts of the GTA. Mamata wanted a detailed account of where the state and central governments' funds amounting to ₹1,500 crore had gone.

'Earlier, the state government used to provide funds to the DGHC and never asked for its expenditure details. In lieu of that, Subash Ghisingh, Gurung's earlier boss, maintained peace in the hills. The central government also did not disturb him as it has been a sensitive area in terms of national security. It shares borders with Nepal, Bhutan and China. CPIM had an ideology and

---

[8] *The Telegraph Online*. 'GTA exit a drama: Deb'. 28 June 2017.

a long-term political game. They wanted Ghisingh to be neck-deep in corruption and, in course of time, use the resentment of the people against him. At that time, CPIM had little organizational presence there. They could not do it. Here, Mamata played, as always, an emotional politics without, perhaps, the in-depth understanding of the issue,' says Soumen Nag.

Mamata broke the tradition and earned Gurung's ire. It was one of her tactics to keep Gurung under pressure as there were already reports of misappropriation of funds in the GTA. She did the right thing as an administrator but could not manage the situation properly. 'She thought her development-drive would override the question of self-identity of the people of the hill. That was not to be,' says Nag.

Mamata also did something to keep Gurung from becoming all-powerful in the hills. She adopted the colonial policy of 'divide and rule' by forming 15 development boards in Darjeeling itself for different communities like Lepcha, Bhutia, Tamang, Gurung, and others, bypassing the GTA entirely. At the same time, she also tried to expand and strengthen her own party's organization in Darjeeling.

During the Left rule, the CPIM was happy to get Subash Ghisingh's support for their candidate in the Lok Sabha elections. Ghisingh sent his own MLAs from three assembly constituencies in the hills—Darjeeling, Kalimpong and Kurseong. Mamata broke this rule as well. In 2014, the TMC Lok Sabha candidate and former Indian football captain, Bhaichung Bhutia, lost the election to the GJM-supported BJP candidate, S.S. Ahluwalia. But, Mamata did not lose hope. In May 2017, during the municipal elections, there were TMC flags flying high along with GJM's. That the posters and flags of both the TMC and the GJM were on display side by side was a new phenomenon. It was for the first time that any political party from the plains had taken on the parties of the hills.

Along with the GJM, GNLF and Jana Andolan Party (JAP), the TMC too contested the civic body elections in all four municipalities in the hills. While Gurung fought the election with the 'Bengal versus Gorkhaland' pitch, Mamata Banerjee stressed on development issues. On 17 May 2017, the day of the results, there were unprecedented scenes of TMC supporters dancing to the beating of drums, playing with green *abir* and waving TMC flags. Out of 84 seats in four civic bodies, the GJM had won 69 while the TMC won 12. But, TMC had got the majority seats in Mirik Municipality and formed the board. The TMC's advances were a threat to the GJM. Gurung told the media,[9] 'I like the fact that I am fighting against the chief minister of Bengal. We had some problems with our candidate selection in Mirik. We have learnt the lesson for the future.' On the day of the result itself, when Mamata Banerjee thanked the people of Mirik for creating history by electing majority councillors from a party from the plains, Gurung's supporters raised the slogan, 'We want Gorkhaland'.

'When it is not unfair for a political party to show their political ambitions and contest elections in the democratic set-up, it seemed TMC was in a hurry to eliminate GJM. They had the police, administration and money power. They started luring the voters and some of our leaders with money,' alleges a GJM activist on the condition of anonymity.

---

[9] Zee 24 Ghanta. 'Mamata's Trinamool Congress breaks into GJM bastion, wins Mirik'. YouTube, 18 May 2017. Available at: https://www.youtube.com/watch?v=8helc2-UpK8

Mamata, however, erroneously assumed that the victory in the civic body elections had given her the mandate to overtake the political space Bimal Gurung had created for himself and the mass connect he had. While Gurung was trying hard to retain his control over the hills and revive the Gorkhaland movement, Mamata used all her administrative power to corner him.

The violence that was sparked off by the decision to introduce Bengali compulsorily in schools continued for nearly 105 days; the agitation saw sporadic violence and the killing of several GJM supporters as well as the young police officer Amitava Malik. Mamata used the police force to crack down on GJM leaders and activists. GJM Chief Bimal Gurung, General Secretary Roshan Giri and other top leaders of the outfit had to go into hiding as several cases of murder, arson, rioting and cases under the Unlawful Activities (Prevention) Act, 1967 (UAPA) etc., were slapped against them and the police could arrest them any moment. Bimal Gurung had to resort to 'audio messages' to reach out to his supporters and media persons from his hideout, which he kept changing, according to police reports. Mamata Banerjee took full advantage of the leadership vacuum in the hills. She was gradually gaining administrative control of the area and was trying hard to normalize the life in Darjeeling by restoring law and order. She put a Board of Administrators (BoA) in the GTA as Bimal Gurung and all other administrators had resigned earlier. Without holding any elections, she engineered a division in the GJM and imposed Binay Tamang, once a close associate of Gurung, as chairman of the BoA. Another breakaway GJM leader, Anit Thapa, who was in charge of the Public Works Department during Bimal Gurung's tenure, was made co-chairman. Both had declared themselves president and general secretary of GJM by summoning a central committee meeting that the Gurung faction termed illegal. Binay Tamang came to the hills under tight security. Both he and Anit Thapa had cases against them that included destroying government property and rioting. Moreover, Binay Tamang was one of the accused in the murder of a Gorkha leader Madan Tamang.[10] The Opposition alleged that the state government ignored them as long as they toed the Bengal government's line.[11] Apparently, Mamata Banerjee's aim was to keep Bimal Gurung out of the hills with murder cases lodged against him.

What the chief minister failed to account for was the sentiment of the people of Darjeeling. Mamata Banerjee did not realize that the issue of 'self-identity' or Gorkhaland was still simmering in Darjeeling. The demand for a separate Gorkhaland is nearly a century old with the first demand for a separate administrative region cropping up as early as 1907. Mamata thought that her development pitch would help the residents of Darjeeling forget the issue.

'In this process, Mamata made Bimal a hero in the minds of people of Darjeeling. She could not understand that the issue of self-identity was bigger than development. By dividing the communities through setting up of several development boards, she also hurt the sentiment of self-identity of the people of the hills as a whole. There has always been a divide between hills and the plains,' says Nag. While the people of Darjeeling saw a leader in Bimal Gurung, his replacement, Binay Tamang, lacked Gurung's guts and charisma. Mamata's

---

[10] Das, M. *The Indian Express*. 'In Mamata's armoury, 256 cases against Gurung and team'. 13 August 2013.

[11] PTI. *Hindustan Times*. 'Mamata criticises Rajnath's meet with GJM leader, BJP hits back'. 20 September 2017.

politics of eliminating the Opposition clearly did not work in the hills. The Lok Sabha results proved it.

'Didi has done development in the hills. People liked it. They breathed a sigh of relief after the 105-day strike, which had crippled the economy of the hills, ended with the intervention of the state government. But, Gorkhaland is and always will be the core issue in the hearts of the people for sure,' says Vikram.

Mamata's ambition to eat up the GJM's political space was much clearer before the 2019 Lok Sabha elections. She had asked the GJM MLA Amar Rai Singh to resign and contest the polls with a TMC ticket. She told a rally in Darjeeling,[12] 'See, I have fielded a *bhumiputra* [son of the soil] as your candidate. Their candidate [referring to BJP candidate Raju Bista] is an outsider, from Manipur or somewhere. I have not brought anyone from outside. He is your man, had been your MLA.' What she avoided mentioning was the fact that the man was not contesting on the ticket of a party from the hills.

Bimal Gurung, from his hideout, supported the BJP candidate Raju Bista, who was born in Manipur but had his businesses in Darjeeling. He was involved in various social activities in the hills too. More importantly, he was an RSS man. Gurung was not in a position to campaign for him as arrest warrants were looming large on him. Still, the people of Darjeeling silently voted for Bista, who won by a huge margin of over 4 lakh votes securing over 59 per cent votes polled. 'Yes, people were in a dilemma with the BJP candidate. They failed to understand why an outsider was chosen to contest the Darjeeling seat. I think people finally voted against Binay Tamang who had betrayed Bimal Gurung and had sided with Mamata

[12] AITC Official. 2019. 'Mamata Banerjee addresses a public meeting in Darjeeling'. YouTube, 11 April. Available at: https://www.youtube.com/watch?v=ss_lVXutL1w

Banerjee. They neither trusted Binay nor Mamata. Identity politics is bigger than the issue of development in the hills,' says Suraj Rai, a local resident. In spite of having no organization in the hills, the BJP managed to ride on the tacit support of the people of Darjeeling, aided by the open support of the Bimal Gurung faction of the GJM and GNLF. Mamata's political gamble had failed. Even Mamata's ally, Binay Tamang, who had declared himself as the president of the GJM in Gurung's absence, lost the Darjeeling assembly seat by 46,285 votes to BJP's Niraj Zimba. It was a strong disapproval for the Binay Tamang-faction of GJM and Mamata Banerjee. TMC Secretary-General Partha Chatterjee claims, 'BJP had pumped in money in the hills to buy votes and brought a businessman from outside.' Local resident and a professor of communication Vikram Rai says, 'There was peer pressure, a psychological pressure on the people, to vote against Mamata and vote for BJP who are supposed to get a permanent solution to Gorkhaland issue. We don't yet know what that would be.'

Darjeeling can be used as a case study to understand Mamata's model of development and dole-driven administrative push, and her desire for political absolutism without realizing the ground realities, which ultimately cause huge damage to her. Mamata Banerjee had tried her best to mobilize her administration to deliver the schemes she had announced for the people of the state and the timely implementation of her projects. Still, she failed on several counts as she lacked an organic support base in the hills.

MAMATA'S REALITY SHOW: DOLES AND DEVELOPMENT

Mamata Banerjee enters the auditorium surrounded by her security men. As soon as she comes to the stage, all the IAS and police officers, mainly the departmental secretaries, SP of the district, DG Police, get up to welcome her. In the audience, the public representatives including local MPs, MLAs, councillors of the civic bodies or members of the panchayats, block-level administrative and police officers stand up. At the back, there are batteries of TV cameras and a group of journalists, all set to capture the moments that are going to follow.

While offering customary namaskars, Mamata exchanges pleasantries with the officers and her ministers who join her on the stage. She is smiling and seems to be in a good mood. As she takes the seat at the centre of the stage, the chief secretary takes the mic and then, the show begins—Mamata Banerjee's flagship administrative review meeting in the district. Her smile can either extend or vanish within a moment as she takes account of the progress of the government projects and schemes, listens to the problems and demands of the public representatives as well as the officials. This is the usual scene in many administrative meetings that are aired live on TV channels and streamed across social media platforms. She has hosted more than 100 televised-administrative meetings in the districts with her full team of ministers and bureaucrats.

'She is the headmistress here and both we and the officials are the students who will have to answer her questions on the lessons we have learnt,' mocks an MLA and veteran leader from Hooghly district on the condition of anonymity. 'You may ask her questions, but you don't know if she would be happy to answer or rebuke you,' he adds.

At such meetings, Mamata indeed behaves like a school principal. She quizzes officials and public representatives on the progress of the projects. If satisfied, she heaps lavish praises on them. If unhappy, she rebukes the person openly, be it her own party leader or a cabinet colleague or an administrative official. The whole episode is beamed live on both TV and social media handles.

Yes, Mamata Banerjee has done something that no other chief minister in Bengal, or perhaps even the country, has ever done. She has taken her entire top administration to the remotest corners of the districts to hold such administrative review meetings to take stock of the government projects in the districts. The meetings are not generally restricted to the district headquarters alone; she often chooses the venue in the remote corners of the district, in the block or sub-divisions. 'Jyoti Basu had given a call that the Left Front government won't work from the Writers' Building [the state secretariat] in Kolkata. He essentially meant that the local self-government must work effectively. Siddhartha Shankar Ray took meetings at the district level. But Mamata Banerjee actually took the government to the towns and villages of Bengal,' says Suvashis Maitra, a senior journalist.

This 'reality show' has always attracted high TRPs for news channels and also for Mamata. It is an innovative way of taking stock of the developmental projects, holding the officer or the minister concerned responsible for delay in implementation and a forum for the MLAs, MPs and the civic body chiefs to present their demands and grievances. This also gives the residents of the districts a sense of importance and belonging. As a grassroots leader, Mamata understands the importance of such a move, the importance of reaching out to areas no chief minister has ever bothered to visit.

'These meetings have helped Mamata to make a connection with the people. They also keep the administrative and police officials on tenterhooks, who are more alert because the CM would check on the progress of the schemes,' says Suvashis Maitra.

She has tried to build the image of an effective and strict administrator who shows the public how she is making her administration accountable. She has reaped the benefit of broadcasting the proceedings live on television and social media. A section of the people have definitely liked this idea.

The administrative meeting is generally followed by a public meeting in an open ground where Mamata distributes the benefits under government welfare schemes to the people of the locality and inaugurates or lays the foundation of various new projects. She hands over the *pattas* (land deeds) to the landless farmers, cycles to the beneficiaries of the Sabooj Sathi project, cheques to the girl students who qualified for her flagship Kanyashree scheme or fishing nets to fishermen. The meeting ends with a political speech in the guise of an administrator speaking to the people. Apart from attacking her rivals, she also reads out from a list the number of projects and funds sanctioned for the district since she assumed power. The public meetings are attended by thousands of local villagers who are mobilized by the government officials and local TMC leaders.

Often Mamata gets off her car to meet and greet the people who wait to see her cavalcade pass by. Those who have travelled with Mamata have seen how she asks her driver to stop the car and goes into the crowd of people to exchange pleasantries. In her trademark style, she gets into a tea stall or starts speaking to an old lady, or asks a mother about her child. She did it when she was in the Opposition. She does it as the chief minister.

In early 2019, on a cold winter evening, she even stopped at a village to play a game of badminton on her way back to Kolkata from Birbhum district, where she had gone to attend an administrative review meeting. Mamata, clad in her trademark saree, wrapped in a shawl and in Hawai chappals (made of rubber), played a game and posted the video on her social media account with the caption, 'We love sports, a token game in a village'.

'After Jyoti Basu, we can say, Mamata is the most popular mass leader West Bengal has seen. Neither Buddhadeb Bhattacharjee nor Bidhan Roy was a mass leader like them. Bidhan Roy who was a doctor by profession had other qualities that made him a visionary leader. He was a pioneer in setting up townships like Durgapur, which is now an industrial town, Kalyani, Salt Lake. He had also set up a couple of medical colleges and the first post-graduate medical college in Bengal. He was behind the foundation of Infectious Disease Hospital as well. He promoted free education and free healthcare facilities. But, Mamata's struggle and the quality of reaching out to the poor, and reacting to the political issue of the tortured people have made her a leader through a process. She has not cropped up overnight like many other Opposition leaders,' says Suvashis Maitra.

Mamata Banerjee has always tried to project herself as the 'common man'. From her attire to her abode, all are simple or *gharoa* (homely) in nature. She has wanted to drive home the point that she is for all the poor and downtrodden people. The impact of such a gesture is seen on the ground. She has become the girl next door to most of the people who meet her. 'Mamata is like our mother. Because of her, my daughter is going to school today [referring to the Kanyashree project]. I have seen a chief minister for the first time,' says Radharani Das, a resident of Gangarampur in South Dinajpur district. The residents of the locality are dazzled by the fact that a chief minister had visited their hometown.

'I have travelled in the districts and there is no scope of denying that fact that she has done some work. A lot of villages have got concrete roads, drinking water and power connections. The government hospitals have got fair price medicine shops. People have got benefits from different schemes like Kanyashree. A section of the people got benefits and Mamata still enjoys their support. Despite BJP bagging 18 seats, Mamata's vote percentage is still 40 per cent. But the popularity with which Mamata Banerjee came in power in 2011 has been dented due to people's outrage on various issues,' says Rantidev Sengupta, a veteran journalist and editor of the RSS's Bengali mouthpiece, *Swastika*.

Interestingly, what Mamata Banerjee calls development is mainly restricted to infrastructure projects and doles. She has created schemes that benefit a person from birth until death. She has not left any section of the electorate out of her dole-politics. Mamata's Kanyashree scheme—a conditional cash transfer scheme that aims to improve the status and well-being of the girl child in West Bengal by incentivizing schooling of all teenage girls and delaying their marriages until the age of 18—has been a megahit. There is an annual scholarship of ₹500 for girl students between the ages of 13 and 18 and a one-time grant for those who reach the age of 18. 'This scheme has been a great tool for the empowerment of the girl child in the state. I have personally done research in Murshidabad and there I have seen how the scheme is changing the lives of girls. The amount may be a meagre one, but government recognizing a section of the society gives a sense of pride to the individuals. A cycle in Sabooj Sathi brings speed and more connectivity to the rural population. In Hariharpara, the local ADM has formed a Kanyashree Yoddha Bahini which is working against under-age marriage. Overall this has created a huge impact and it is increasing the number of female students. It is clear from the number of female students in Madhyamik examination,' says Maitra. In 2015, she announced the Sabooj Sathi scheme for the distribution of bicycles to the students of Class IX to XII studying in government or government-aided schools or madrassas. Anyone visiting any village in West Bengal in the morning or in the afternoon can see groups of young boys and girls going to school on cycles. Not only does that paint a beautiful picture, but it also proves how Mamata's schemes are hugely beneficial.

In 2018, Mamata launched another welfare scheme for girls attaining the age of 18. The government, under the Rupashree scheme, gives a one-time assistance of ₹25,000 when the girls get married. This is to cover the expenses of the girl's marriage. The family's annual income should not exceed ₹1.5 lakh.

In 2013, she launched the Yuvashree scheme in which the unemployed youth in the age bracket of 18 to 45 years get ₹1,500 as a monthly allowance to be used for vocational and other kinds of training. He or she must be registered with the 'Employment Bank' portal launched by the West Bengal government. 'Yuvashree is your right and our responsibility. The financial crisis in the state will not stop the government from performing its duty towards our brothers and sisters. Work will not find you; you will have to find your work. Struggle now and you will reap the fruit in future. This is just a small assistance from the government,' said Mamata while launching the scheme.[13]

For the farmers, who are Mamata's core vote bank, her government announced the Krishak Bandhu scheme. Apart from the Fasal Bima Yojana, an allowance of

[13] AITC Official. 2013. 'Launch of Yuvashree Scheme by WB CM Mamata Banerjee at Netaji Indoor Stadium'. YouTube, 3 October. Available at: https://www.youtube.com/watch?v=iPYkRBhs2Z0

₹5,000 per acre of land is given in two instalments by the government. She also promised a life insurance scheme of ₹2 lakh in case of death of any earning member (in the age group of 18–60 years) of the farmer's family.

Her Swasthyasathi scheme to provide health insurance up to ₹1.5 lakh drew much attention. Even at the time of death of any family member, the kin of the deceased can avail a government scheme called Samabyathi—a grant of ₹500—for cremation.

The TMC government's schemes have been ideal for the social welfare of the people of the state. However, critics find them inadequate in addressing the basic issue of uplifting the entire population by generating and providing employment. Prasenjit Bose, an economist and political activist who was a member of the CPIM's research cell and a leader of its students' wing, Student Federation of India (SFI) feels the government is more concerned with the publicity of its schemes through newspaper advertisements, hoardings, public meetings and live telecast of the administrative review meetings and does not care enough to bring a sustainable social change.

'Here you are doing the work of ₹2 and doing publicity and branding in such a way that you have done the work of ₹10. It is all about branding. The populist politics has given up the agenda of a progressive social change. It has a deeper philosophical neo-liberal approach to undermine the role of government. I believe government plays an important role in social change and in India and Bengal, the employment generation is crucial. There is no thought over structural or fundamental issues. The development has been redefined as giving doles. To them, development does not mean employment generation, increase in agricultural income, getting a just price for the crops, setting up manufacturing units, development of education, increasing enrolment in the schools, increasing healthcare facilities. Why should a person need to be taken to a hospital in Kolkata from Murshidabad when he meets with an accident? Why cannot he be treated properly in any hospital in the district? What development is this?' asks Prasenjit Bose.

However, the state finance minister, Amit Mitra, claims that while the unemployment rate in the country is the highest in the last 45 years, it has decreased by 40 per cent in West Bengal. His claim is supported by the statistics revealed by the Period Labour Force Survey 2017–18, which shows that the unemployment rate in Bengal stands at 4.6 per cent. It is a turnaround from 2011–12 situation when the state was in the fifth position in terms of unemployment. In six years, West Bengal is third from the bottom of the list. Amit Mitra can also take solace in the fact that it is below the national average of 6.1 per cent.[14]

'The statistics Amit Mitra gives is quite confusing like the statistics provided by the central government. There is more to it,' says Prasenjit Bose. 'The same statistics by National Statistical Office [NSO] is saying the rate of daily wage workers or contractual labourer in the labour force is 32 per cent which is higher than the national average of 25 per cent. About 59 per cent labourers don't have social security facilities like provident fund or ESI. This shows the poor quality of jobs being created in the

[14] Government of India, Ministry of Statistics and Programme Implementation, National Statistical Office. 'Periodic Labour Force Survey, July 2017-June 2018'. May 2019. Available at: http://www.mospi.gov.in/sites/default/files/publication_reports/Annual%20Report%2C%20PLFS%202017-18_31052019.pdf

state. Moreover, unemployment is quite high among the certificate or diploma holders too [29.2 per cent in West Bengal compared to 19.8 per cent nationally].'

Amit Mitra, in his budget speeches, claims that the Mamata Banerjee government has always stressed on labour-intensive industries like leather, jewellery, petrochemicals, foundry, textiles and apparels among others. He also claims that in 2018–19, the government had disbursed a loan amounting to ₹44,000 crore for small-and medium-scale industries against the target of ₹38,000 crore. The target for 2019–20 was set at ₹50,000 crore.[15]

The Opposition leaders still criticize the Mamata Banerjee government, asking her that if the employment generation is so steady, then why did nearly 2.5 million people apply for 6,000 vacant Group D level posts in May 2017?[16] According to them, after the Tatas abandoned their Nano car manufacturing project and left West Bengal's Singur in 2008 because of Mamata's prolonged Singur agitation, there has not been any big-scale investment in the manufacturing sector (apart from Jindal's steel-plant-turned-cement-factory in West Midnapore's Salboni) that could create quality jobs for the youth. After she rose to power over a series of anti-land acquisition movements, she has been branded as 'anti-land acquisition'. She was against the acquisition of farmland. But, in fertile Bengal, given the huge amount of agricultural land, one has to acquire farmland to set up any big industry. Mamata Banerjee emphasized forming a land bank for industries. However, there were few takers for the land from the land

---

[15] Chowdhury, P. *Anandabazar Patrika*. 'Unemployment rate is much lower in Bengal, says the central report.' 30 June 2019.

[16] Majumdar, A.D. *Livemint*. '2.5 million compete for 6,000 govt jobs in West Bengal'. 23 May 2017.

bank, except a few small- and medium-scale enterprises. Big industries require a large amount of land and there were no proposals for setting up big manufacturing units due to the economic condition.

Nonetheless, for five consecutive years, since 2014, Mamata Banerjee has been hosting the Bengal Global Business Summit. In its last edition in 2019, there were expressions of interest towards investment intentions of ₹2,84,288.33 crore. 'Every year crores of rupees are being wasted in the name of business summit. But the state government has never given a complete report on how many proposals have fructified. Every year, the state government tries to fool everyone in the name of business summits,' says Adhir Ranjan Chowdhury, a Congress MP. 'If the state had managed to fructify even 50 per cent of the proposals there wouldn't have been so much unemployment in the state,' he adds.[17]

Speaking at the 2018 edition of the Bengal Global Business Summit, Mamata Banerjee claimed, 'Nearly 50 per cent of the commitments made in 2017 are underway.' In 2017, investment commitments of ₹2,35,000 crore were made. There was also an ambiguity in providing a detailed break-up of the investment commitment by the industrialists.

Nevertheless, Amit Mitra had said in an interview[18] before the fourth edition of the Bengal Global Business Summit,'Despite demonetization and faulty GST system, we are getting investment and bank lending of significant nature in the country. Number one in small and medium enterprises. Around ₹1,82,000 crore have been lent

[17] *Outlookindia.com*. 'Bengal business summit a waste of public money: WBPCC chief'. 16 January 2018.

[18] Bengal Global Business Summit. 2018. 'Amit Mitra Interview'. YouTube, 15 Jan. Available at: https://www.youtube.com/watch?v=xJbZU5IKRS4

to industry by banks in West Bengal. West Bengal has become the cement hub of India. Every major cement company has invested here. Germany's BASF comes to our industrial park doing what? Construction chemicals. It is a perfect fit with the cement industry. One feeds on the other. The largest fertiliser plant is using coal-belt Mythen with $1.25 billion investment in matics. Two companies in West Bengal are spewing out the cleanest possible gas from the coal-belt.' He also claimed that 12,000 kilometres of road has been constructed during Mamata Banerjee's government and there was an ease of doing business as the government had effectively introduced e-tendering and e-tax payment systems. More importantly, the state focussed on asset creating capital expenditure.

Under Mamata's rule, there has been a boost in infrastructure. Finance Minister Amit Mitra claims planned expenditure in the state has increased six times in the last eight years, while the capital expenditure in the state has increased eleven times.

Unfortunately, the manufacturing projects that Mitra mentioned could not generate massive employment opportunities and all these infrastructure projects and schemes, in a way, have also paved the way for corruption at the grassroots level since the TMC came to power in the Bengal. Local party leaders would either grab the construction contracts or demand a hefty cut from the government enlisted contractors or they would extort money from the beneficiaries of the projects and welfare schemes. This corruption surfaced as the 'cut money' debate only after the ruling party was stung by the 2019 Lok Sabha election results.

What made the matter worse was that though these malpractices were reported time and again, Mamata

Banerjee did not acknowledge these problems in public for the first eight years of her tenure. In a meeting with the TMC councillors of the civic bodies at Nazrul Mancha in Kolkata on 18 June 2019, Mamata Banerjee accepted[19] that there was corruption in her party while extending benefits of government welfare schemes and infrastructural projects. 'In the "House for All" scheme [*Banglar Bari*], you will help them get the benefits and get 25 per cent commission, will the party tolerate this? We will not tolerate... From Samabyathi scheme, should you take ₹200 out of ₹2,000? I know some of you did it,' she said.

However, as stated earlier, despite the reports of these extortions, Mamata Banerjee had not taken any strong, meaningful and long-term action. It was only after the Lok Sabha upset that she asked her party colleagues to return the 'cut money' they had taken from the people. 'If you have taken it, return it. This is people's money for the people and you have no right over the money,' she said.

Mamata Banerjee failed to realize that this disease of 'cut money' could cause her electoral damage until the people taught her party a lesson in the Lok Sabha elections in 2019. 'Her confidence that she would project herself as the candidate in all the seats and win elections did not work this time. It is true there has been a dent in her charisma,' explains Suvashis Maitra.

It was for the first time that the people of West Bengal poured their anger into the EVMs, disgusted with the corruption of the local TMC leaders. The negative votes went to the kitty of the BJP. Mamata was so confident that her development and dole pitch would work as

[19] AITC Official. 2019. 'Mamata Banerjee meets Councillors at Nazrul Mancha'. YouTube, 19 June. Available at: https://www.youtube.com/watch?v=eJu1jrlV2yc

always that she failed to feel the pulse of the people. It was really strange to note that she, being a mass leader, could not read the people's growing outrage.

OVER-DEPENDENCE ON POLICE AND ADMINISTRATION

Mamata's failure to read the voters' minds probably stems from her tendency to depend more on her police and administration than her own party colleagues.

In an administrative meeting in South 24 Parganas district[20] in December 2018, Pratima Mondal, the TMC MP from Joynagar, told Mamata Banerjee, 'There are some problems with the electricity in Kumirmari area in Gosaba.' This area falls in Pratima Mondal's constituency. Mamata asked her officer, 'I think Gosaba's electrification has been completed. Isn't it?' The officer nodded and the chief minister told her MP, '100 per cent electrification has been completed in Gosaba.' The MP said nothing else. She silently went back to her chair. This has been a continued practice in Mamata's administration—rely more on the words of the bureaucrats and the government officials than her own elected representatives.

In the same meeting, Baruipur (Purba) MLA Nirmal Chandra Mondal drew the chief minister's attention[21] at the new police station in his locality. Mamata Banerjee became furious. She told the MLA, 'Only building cannot help. We need police personnel to make it running. You need to understand. I have recruited a lot [in the police force] in the last seven

---

20 AITC Official. 2018. 'Mamata Banerjee addresses an administrative meeting at South 24 Parganas'. *YouTube*. 27 December. Available at: https://youtu.be/31rtfNZbcvo

21 Ibid

years.' When Mondal interrupted the chief minister in a polite voice saying, 'I am just placing my request, Mamata shouted over him, 'No, you cannot place requests all the time. When we will get a chance, we will do it. Why do you keep on asking for more all the time. I haven't heard you say we have got enough. The government is going crazy in formulating schemes after paying a debt of ₹48,000 crore. Centre is not cooperating. We have opened 149 new police stations and six new police commissionerates. Nowhere in the country, it has been done.'

It is not unusual for a party chief or the chief minister to hold their party colleagues accountable for their mistakes or setting unachievable targets. But the way Mamata chides her MLAs and MPs in front of the administrative and police officials, especially on live television, undermines the person and their office in the eyes of the public and also the bureaucrats. This also shows how the administration overrules the party in power and the public representatives who are trying to raise the people's issues. Sometimes Mamata may act as a 'Santa Clause' in such administrative review meetings and approve the demands of the public representatives, but the next moment she may lose her cool. It is difficult to gauge her mood. Like in one such meeting in West Midnapore,[22] when an MLA asked for street lights on a bridge and a cold storage, the chief minister immediately approved it. Moments later, Narayangarh MLA Pradyut Ghosh was lodging a complaint saying, 'Since Public Works Department is not cooperating with us [in construction of a bus

[22] AITC Official. 2018. CM Mamata Banerjee attends Paschim Medinipur edited. *YouTube*, 16 March. Available at: https://www.youtube.com/watch?v=ZsUWTPL8Oho

stand]', Mamata was furious. She shouted at the MLA, 'Do you cooperate with yourself? You tell me, you, Kausar, Mihirbabu and Surya [local TMC leaders]—do four of you cooperate with each other? Then you will blame PWD.' No one had expected that the demand for a bus stand could irk the chief minister so much that she would bring up the party's infighting in the administrative meeting.

While this tactic might be appreciated by many as Mamata apparently 'teaching a lesson to political leaders', but it is also true that she lets the bureaucrats and the police dominate over her party leaders.

During the Left Front rule, this was unimaginable. Under the Left, a zila parishad sabhadhipati (district board chief), who is an elected public representative, was considered to be the ultimate authority in the district. The district magistrate and the superintendent of police followed his orders. This established the supremacy of the political executives or elected public representatives who were accountable to the public.

'It was possible in the Left rule because there was democratic centralism. Almost all the leaders would talk in the same line. Here, I think, Mamata depends more on the administrative officials for the reason that there has been so much of factionalism that she cannot trust her party colleagues. Moreover, she might have tried to use the expertise of the bureaucracy to run an effective government machinery in implementing her dream projects and schemes. She could not rely much on her party colleagues to do the same,' says Suvashis Maitra.

What Mamata does not seem to realize is that the public representatives need to deal with the people directly and more frequently than bureaucrats. Government officials or the police may or may not be accountable to the public, whereas a political leader's stake in public opinion is much higher. Moreover, public servants may shift their loyalties with the change of guard in the government.

Top TMC leaders, however, refuse to believe that this process, in any way, undermines the role of the public representatives. TMC Secretary-General Partha Chatterjee says, 'Yes, we might have suffered 25 per cent in the Lok Sabha election, but the chief minister did not want to follow what the Left did. You must look at the rest 75 per cent, at how Mamata changed the face of Bengal through such review meetings following the administrative calendar.' He also argues, 'BDOs, ICs [Inspectors-in-charge] knew that the chief minister would check the progress of the schemes or measures taken. Public representatives got a chance to lodge their grievances in front of the administrative officials and the chief minister.'

The TMC has a valid defence ready as far as the administrative review meetings are concerned. The accountability of public servants has increased as no one really wants to be rebuked by the chief minister in full public glare. However, like her Left counterpart, it is alleged by the Opposition leaders that Mamata Banerjee uses the police and administration to gain political ground by intimidating the Opposition.

In June 2015, senior TMC minister Subrata Mukherjee, along with his party colleagues, was seen celebrating with green *abir* in West Midnapore's Kharagpur. They were rejoicing the victory in forming the board in Kharagpur Municipality despite not having a majority. Many thought the victory was the handiwork of the then Superintendent of Police of West Midnapore district, Bharati Gosh.

Some time back, the district SP, Bharati Ghosh (now a BJP leader after resigning from the Indian Police Service), was seen standing guard near the municipality building. Some TMC supporters claimed, 'SP Madam [Bharati Ghosh] is the man of the match. The credit for this victory goes to her.'[23] Bharati Ghosh was accompanied by two additional SPs, four DSPs and a large contingent of the police force to ensure there was no violence on the day of the municipal board formation in this IIT town. The TMC and Congress were tied at 11 seats each. When the results of the chairman election were declared, the TMC was seen to have pushed the tally to 19 in the 35-member municipality. Local Congress leader Rabi Shankar Pandey, who contested for the post of chairman, told the journalists of *Times of India*, 'Yes, the district SP Bharati Ghosh is indeed the man of the match for helping Trinamool form the board in Kharagpur... We were framed in a false case. The police, working at Trinamool's behest, wanted to arrest us so that we could not participate in the vote for the chairman.'[24]

There are many such allegations of harassing the Opposition against Bharati Ghosh, who raised many eyebrows when in an open public meeting in Midnapore town in 2011, she addressed Mamata Banerjee as the 'mother of Junglemahal'. She might have effectively handled the Maoist insurgencies in the area, but she was also accused of running both the police force and the TMC organization there on behalf of the top leadership of the party.

---

[23] TNN. *Times of India*. 'Trinamool forms board in Kharagpur'. 5 June 2015.
[24] Ibid.

A local leader from Kharagpur, on condition of anonymity, claims, 'She decided who would run the party in West Midnapore, who would be the block president and who would contest the elections in the civic body. Not only the Opposition, but she also used to support one faction and scare the leaders of the opposing faction in the district. She used to scare the local leaders and threatened to put them in jail if her orders were ignored.' She became so powerful that the chief minister allegedly started depending more on Bharati and did not care about the inputs from her own party leaders. During the 2016 assembly elections, Bharati had to vacate the post of SP of West Midnapore to adhere to ECI rules (the administrative or police officers involved in the election process must not have served in the same post for more than three years prior to the announcement of the election date), but Mamata kept her in the region as the Officer on Special Duty (OSD) of the Left Wing Extremism zone. After Opposition leaders complained and the Election Commission intervened, she was moved to Kolkata as SS, CID.

But when Bharati's relations with Mamata Banerjee soured as she was closer to breakaway TMC leader Mukul Roy (who allegedly looked after the 'police affairs' including their transfers and postings on behalf of the party) she was transferred. It was considered that Bharati Ghosh was picked by Mukul Roy to be posted in this Maoist-affected district. Since Mukul Roy was in charge of the TMC's organization in this region, he too depended on this IPS officer to run the party affairs. However, after she received her transfer orders, an angry Bharati resigned from the service, and the TMC in West Midnapore became directionless.

'The way Bharati Ghosh acted, the party has to take responsibility for that. We cannot deny that. If there is *ghun* [rot] in the bricks, even if you plaster, it will not go. Then you need to take out the brick and place a new brick. Now the infectious disease has been cured, but the damage has been done. The damage was done in the organization. It created mistrust among the workers and it weakened us. A section was made corrupt. But now it is in the past,' says Debasish Chowdhury, a councillor of Kharagpur Municipality.

Later, Bharati was slapped with a case of extortion of a goldsmith. She went into hiding for some time and later, armed with the Supreme Court order, she joined BJP only to contest the Lok Sabha elections from Ghatal, which fell in the same district where she once 'ruled'. She could not win.

Not only Mamata, but other TMC leaders also depend on the police and administration so much that there were rumours that the TMC top leadership had sent a list of candidates for panchayat elections in 2018 to the respective SPs of the districts to combat factionalism within the party. They had decided who would be allowed to file a nomination and who wouldn't. According to some TMC leaders, in a *Big Brother*-like move, the government started tapping the phones of its own leaders. Many leaders and ministers shifted to WhatsApp call facilities to avoid their conversations being recorded.

The overuse of government and administrative machinery has eroded the local TMC leaders' trust in their once beloved 'Didi', the moniker Banerjee claims. A leader from Bankura alleges, 'The leaders from Kolkata would come and instruct the district police about what to do. They would not even listen to the local grassroots leaders. How can you expect that they would know the ground reality? The result is evident in the Lok Sabha elections. Many old party leaders and workers have distanced themselves from the party.'

Her affection towards certain police officers has even surprised the urban voters. Take the case of former DGP Surajit Kar Purakayastha, whom she had given an extension. An able IPS officer, Surajit Kar Purakayastha had served in various positions during the Left rule, including the post of inspector general of police (law and order). He was appointed the commissioner of police of Kolkata by Mamata and later elevated to the post of DGP. He soon became one of Mamata's most trusted police officers. Later, when the law did not permit her to give him further extensions, she made him the chief security advisor of the state in the line of national security advisor, giving him powers almost superseding those of the incumbent DGP.

Another case was that of the chairman of the Human Rights Commission. Former Supreme Court judge Ashok Ganguly, who was the chairman of the Human Rights Commission, was forced to resign in December 2013 under the allegation of molesting an intern; in his place, former DGP Naparajit Mukherjee was appointed as the head of the commission. No other state has probably seen a retired police officer take on the post of the Human Rights Commissioner. If nothing, most of the complaints to the commission are against police inaction or atrocities.

When the CBI closed in on former Kolkata police commissioner Rajiv Kumar in February 2019 and attempted to raid his residence in connection with a chit fund case, Mamata rushed to his rescue. Applying her old tactics, she sat on a dharna. Her decision to almost blindly support the former commissioner of Kolkata did not go down well with a section of the voters. She did not make such a move when her party colleagues were arrested in the chit fund case.

'It definitely had a negative impact. It has been a blunder. It was an impulsive decision. You know people take wrong decisions when they get angry,' says Suvashis Maitra referring to the Rajiv Kumar incident.

Perhaps, Mamata Banerjee believes that the police is an extension of the state power and she is in a commanding position; that it will not indulge in 'factionalism' like her party-men, rather, they will follow her orders in absolute terms. It is easier to tame both her party men and the Opposition by using the police force. Both police and general administration have a structured and organized apparatus that a chief minister can use to rule. However, unlike the CPIM, the TMC is not a cadre-based regimented party. Moreover, there has always been a trust deficit between the supreme leader and her party colleagues. In a single-leader party like the TMC, Mamata has been forced to take the help of the police and administrative officials to run both the government and the party.

Despite her complete faith in administration and police, she could not protect them from being attacked by her own party supporters. In November 2014, in the heart of Kolkata, Alipore, policemen had to take shelter under tables inside the police station when it was attacked by a mob led by TMC goons of the locality for arresting their men over a land dispute. Such attacks have taken place again and again. She has taken action against the culprits in many cases and even got her own party men arrested, but these misbehaviours continue whenever there is a clash of interest between the police and the local leaders or supporters.

ELIMINATING THE OPPOSITION

If one of Mamata Banerjee's vices is over-dependence on police and administration, her other weakness is her resolution to completely decimate all opposition. Mamata came to power in 2011 with the slogan, 'No Revenge, Only Change'. Even though there had been no large- scale violence, as many had feared, after the change of regime in West Bengal, the political rivalry between the Left and the TMC was so potent that the 'revenge' came in some other way. Apart from digging up old cases and slapping new ones against the Left workers and leaders, the TMC began poaching Opposition workers and leaders on a large scale. The Left had other vices, but they did not try to poach the opposition leaders in such a way.

Over ten Congress and Left MLAs have switched over to the TMC camp since 2016. The ruling party takes the help of the assembly Speaker to ensure they do not face action under the anti-defection law, which states that unless two-thirds of the legislators of a political party merge with another party, the members defecting from the party they were elected from can be disqualified on the basis of the petition of any member of the house. The Congress leader of the house lodged a complaint to the Speaker, but the cases are still pending before the Speaker. Several municipalities and panchayats have been taken over by TMC as the elected representatives from the Opposition parties have joined the ruling party. Mamata allegedly uses the police to intimidate many Opposition leaders into crossing over.

On the eve of the 2016 assembly elections, TMC leader Joydeb Jana was murdered in West Midnapore's Sabang. The Congress–Left alliance candidate and then veteran Congress leader Manas Bhunia was named as one of the accused in the FIR along with 22 others. Local TMC leader Amulya Maity even alleged that Jana was beaten to death in the presence of Bhunia. The day an arrest warrant was issued by the Midnapore Court in July 2016, Bhunia had a meeting with Mamata Banerjee in her chamber in the state assembly. Soon after the meeting, on the same day, he was nominated as the chairman of the Public Accounts Committee (PAC) bypassing Bhunia's own party's decision to leave the post to CPIM legislature party leader Sujan Chakraborty. The norm is to appoint the leader of the Opposition or someone nominated by the leader of the Opposition as the chairman, but here, the government did not even consult the Congress. This move came as a surprise when the Speaker announced the name of Bhunia as the chairman of the PAC.

Bhunia had once told me he was happy that he never had to leave the Congress, unlike most of its top leaders, to reach the top post in the state Congress. He, however, had to eventually leave the Congress after a serious tiff with other state party leaders in a disgraceful manner. He joined the TMC and became its Rajya Sabha MP and also contested the Lok Sabha elections on a TMC ticket.

'Yes, our leaders were intimidated, charged with [various] false cases. A murder charge was slapped against Manas Bhunia. They were opportunistic to hit the soft targets. They looked for weak persons and tapped them. Those who have businesses were also threatened with serious damage to their businesses if they did not join TMC. One of our MLAs from North Bengal was threatened that his daughter would be kidnapped if he did not join them,' says Abdul Mannan, the leader of the Opposition from Congress.

During an informal chat with some journalists at her chamber in Kalighat, way back in 2009, Mamata Banerjee, who was then the Opposition leader, had said she would be in a better position when the police and administration would support her after she came to power. They would listen to her and not the communists. She was then upset by the police excesses on the Opposition leaders by the Left Front government.. No one knew she would apply the same tactics once she came to power.

Three months after Bhunia joined the TMC along with his brother Bikash, their names were dropped from the charge sheet of the Joydeb Jana murder case. It was the same Bharati Ghosh who was at the helm of police affairs in West Midnapore at that time.

The deceased TMC leader's wife, Manasi Jana, told a reporter of *Ananda Bazar Patrika,*[25] 'He has left Congress to join TMC. I have tolerated it in the interest of the party because I love my party. But as a wife, will I ever be able to accept my husband's killer?' The slain worker's family has been side-lined in the party and locality. Manas Bhunia's wife was given a TMC ticket for the assembly by-election in Sabang (after Manas became the Rajya Sabha MP, quitting the post of MLA), depriving the local leaders a chance to contest.

During the Left rule, the communists had allowed the Congress, the TMC, and fringe parties like Socialist Unity Centre of India (Communist) (SUCI) to function as

[25] De, Barun. *Ananndabazar Patrika*. 'Sabang's Manasi Jana still thinks that Manas Bhunia is a murderer'. 23 September 2016.

an Opposition party in certain pockets such as Joynagar in South 24 Parganas, Raiganj in North Dinajpur, Malda and Murshidabad for decades. 'We did not win Kolkata's Chowringhee seat or Sealdah assembly seats. Murshidabad, Malda, North Dinajpur had been the bastion of the Congress for long. We did not snatch the zila parishad from them,' says Mohammed Salim, CPIM politburo member. The Left believed in reaping the benefits of a divided Opposition. In the hay days of the Left regime, the Congress and later the TMC ruled some zila parishads in some districts. The Left did not show any intention to topple these by forcing defection. Though the Left has a terrible record of suppressing Opposition workers and supporters, they allowed some local satraps to reign as long as their support base remained intact across the state.

Mamata, however, had other plans. 'TMC wants absolute power in local and district bodies without the presence of any opposition,' says Mannan. This practice has had a long-term impact on the TMC. 'Defection politics' has created a division in the party—'adi TMC' and 'nabya TMC' (old and new TMC, respectively). For many TMC leaders, it's a bitter pill they have to swallow. It is not easy for them to embrace the same Left leaders and welcome them into the party who had once unleashed terror on the TMC cadres.

For example, Rejjak Mollah, a minister in the Left Front government and a prominent Left face in the state, ditched CPIM after developing differences with the leaders and joined the TMC. Rejjak and his men had allegedly terrorized villagers in his constituency in Canning in South 24 Parganas during the Left rule. Later, Rejjak Mollah was also allegedly assaulted by top TMC leaders, Arabul Islam and Kaizer Ahmed, in the area. He had to be hospitalized. When Rejjak joined the TMC, the discomfort was visible. The leaders who had opposed him for long had to work to get Rejjak elected to the assembly. This uneasiness prevailed for a long time as the local TMC leaders were not on talking terms with Rejjak.

A similar situation has cropped up in many parts of the state where TMC leaders have had to work for someone whom they have opposed all their lives. Mamata's annexation politics has not gone down well with the rank and file of her own party. Many leaders and cadres have distanced themselves from the party and sabotaged the elections.

THE MISTAKEN CALCULATIONS

According to many political pundits, Mamata's desire to eliminate the Opposition has been to keep the minority vote bank intact. She did not want this vote bank to be split among the Left, the Congress and the TMC. She knew the minorities in West Bengal would not vote for the BJP, so even with the BJP's growth in the state, the Trinamool's minority vote bank would be intact. This explanation works as long as the TMC's own majority vote bank stays intact. There is around a 30 per cent minority vote in Bengal. The fight was over the remaining 70 per cent majority votes.

'In a polarized situation when the Left and Congress vote percentage was going down and BJP was gaining out of it, mainly with the majority votes, TMC had to suffer. It would have been prudent if Mamata let a divided Opposition to exist and the votes were divided among three Opposition parties,' explains Rantidev Sengupta.

However, the 2019 Lok Sabha election results are proof that Mamata's arithmetic did not work. Despite bagging 3 per cent more votes (43.28 per cent) as compared to the 2014 Lok Sabha elections (and about 3 per cent less compared to the 2016 assembly elections), the TMC lost twelve seats. They won a few seats where the CPIM candidate polled a sizeable number of votes to halt the BJP's gains. The election results prove that the Left and Congress's decline has also not helped her arithmetically. Left vote share dwindled from nearly 30 per cent in the 2014 Lok Sabha elections to mere 7.46 per cent in 2019, while the Congress too lost about 5 per cent votes compared to 2014. The BJP's vote share rose from 17 per cent to 40 per cent in the last five years (about 30 per cent increase compared to 2016 assembly elections). Had the Left wielded more influence and polled more votes in certain seats eating a slice from the BJP's pie, she would have managed to win a few more seats.

Prasenjit Bose says, 'A section of the TMC base has also shifted to the BJP, which accounts for its losses in South Bengal, but another section of the LF and Congress votes have shifted towards TMC, especially in Central and North Bengal, which is why the state-level net vote share loss of TMC has been low. Anti-democratic and irresponsible politics practised by the West Bengal chief minister has certainly played a role in the BJP's rise.'

As the Left crumbled, the BJP came up as the principal Opposition force in the state. Sunil Deodhar, the architect of the BJP's Tripura victory, once said that the party's goal in West Bengal was to be number two first and then give the final punch to the Mamata government to topple it. The local BJP leaders, in a friendly chat with journalists, said they did not want to put much effort in the local body elections but save their energy for the Lok Sabha elections. They rearranged their home front gradually and Mamata's politics of absolutism helped them portray her as a 'totalitarian' leader and also gain electorally.

The BJP is now using Mamata's annexation politics against her in Bengal. They are poaching Trinamool MLAs and elected representatives to gain political control in the state. Prime Minister Narendra Modi, during the Lok Sabha election campaign, had claimed that around 40 MLAs from the TMC were in touch with the BJP, indicating that they were ready to switch sides and make Mamata Banerjee's government a minority stakeholder. It was a pressure tactic used by Modi. So far, eight MLAs from the TMC have joined the BJP camp. The Speaker is in a fix over taking action against them lest he has to do the same against the Congress and Left MLAs also who had joined TMC without resigning.

After witnessing the Lok Sabha debacle, Mamata Banerjee's men are now helping the CPIM open their closed party offices. She is also appealing to the Left and Congress to work together with the TMC to block the BJP's aggression. It might, however, be too late for Mamata Banerjee to resurrect her house of cards.

Mamata's administrative faux pas has also significantly helped the saffron army gain ground in Bengal. Those who suffered because of the TMC's extortion racket and corruption voted for the BJP just to teach Mamata a lesson. The polarization arithmetic has also helped the BJP to do well electorally since the bypolls in the assembly starting from 2014. Though the BJP's vote share had declined in the 2016 Lok Sabha elections, it has otherwise been on the rise.

Mamata's over-dependence on the police and administration cost her dearly when the Election Commission transferred the police commissioners of Kolkata and adjacent Bidhannagar and several SPs of the districts before the Lok Sabha elections. Mamata alleged that the BJP had a tacit understanding with the Election Commission and that is why they had removed the SPs and the CPs. The allegation did ring true when two days later, BJP leader Mukul Roy threatened Cooch Behar SP Abhishek Gupta[26] for his partisan attitude. 'I will see you, Abhishek Gupta. How powerful you are!' Mukul Roy had said. Gupta was thereafter transferred by the Election Commission of India (ECI). The TMC cried foul over the transfer and eventually did not get any 'support' from the police on the day of the polls, such as prompt action at the behest of the ruling party of the state or attending the complaints made by the local TMC leaders among others.

Mukul Roy also wooed rebel TMC MPs and leaders and accommodated them in the BJP's candidate list. Just before the elections, TMC's Bishnupur MP Soumitra Khan and Bolpur MP Anupam Hazra joined the BJP. Bhatpara MLA Arjun Singh jumped ship and joined the BJP after he found his name missing from the TMC candidate list. He subsequently contested as a BJP candidate from Barackpore and won.

Once close to Mamata Banerjee's nephew Abhishek, Cooch Behar's youth TMC leader Nishith Pramanik also joined the BJP to win a Lok Sabha seat. Mamata made a last-ditch attempt by digging up old criminal cases against Soumitra Khan and Nishith Pramanik and slapping new ones. Though Nishith managed to

---

[26] *Anandabazar Patrika*. 'SP transferred after Mukul Roy's threat'. 10 April 2019.

campaign, Soumitra Khan was barred from entering the district. His wife looked after his campaign and he won the Bishnupur seat on a BJP ticket.

The elections were a moment of truth for Mamata. They made her understand what it takes to fight the Opposition without the help of the police and administration. It has been witnessed that the state machinery is always tilted towards the ruling party whenever it comes to election. The rapport that the local leaders build with the police in the districts also helps them during the polls as the police officers may 'overlook' certain malpractices of the ruling party. If the administrative officials are loyal to the political executive, it helps them in conducting the elections according to the whims of the ruling party. This is true about any election in the country and not just about Mamata Banerjee. That's why the ruling parties in the states often restructure the police and administration before every election by posting the loyal officers to strategic positions so that they work in their favour or at least do not disturb the workers of the ruling party if there is any malpractice. However, technically, during the Lok Sabha or assembly elections, the police and administration are controlled by the Election Commission of India. They have the power to transfer any officer if they deem fit. The state government cannot do much about it. This time, when the ECI transferred a few officers Mamata depended on, things went out of her plan.

During the 2019 Lok Sabha elections, Mamata's home secretary Atri Bhattacharya was transferred and Rajiv Kumar, who was shifted out of Kolkata Police to be posted in the Criminal Investigation Department (CID) to adhere to the rules of ECI, was asked to report to the Home Ministry in Delhi during the elections.

Mamata's style of governance, which included eliminating the Opposition, excessive dependence on police and administration bypassing her own party colleagues and being overconfident that her dole-development politics would make her victorious cost her dearly during the elections while the BJP benefited greatly by doing barely anything.

2

The TMC's Political and Organizational Weakness

A resident of AE Block in Kolkata's Salt Lake area had to approach Bangladesh Prime Minister Sheikh Hasina to draw the attention of Bengal Chief Minister Mamata Banerjee against extortion by a local councillor (Ward No. 41) Anindya Chatterjee. Allegedly, Chatterjee had demanded ₹12 lakh from the senior citizen to allow him to construct an extension in his house.[1] When he had refused to pay, building materials were dumped in front of his house, blocking the entry. After media reports suggested that Sheikh Hasina herself took up the issue on a telephonic conversation with the chief minister, it created an uproar. Under pressure, Mamata got Anindya arrested on 3 July 2016.

However, this is hardly an isolated incident– several such cases have been reported in the media. The practice is known as 'Syndicate Raj' and Mamata Banerjee and other TMC leaders blame the CPIM for launching it. The truth is the birth of the concept can indeed be attributed to the Left rule. 'During the construction of the Metro Railways in Tollygunge–Garia route

[1] Ghoshal, A. *Indian Express*. 'After Didi, Sheikh Hasina chat, TMC man Anindya Chattopadhyay lands in jail'. 13 July 2016.

and buildings in Rajarhat, a Left Front minister had conceptualised this system to accommodate the local unemployed youths. Whenever there was eviction in the name of a development project, such as the Metro Rail, there was agitation among the people. They were rehabilitated, but they also wanted economic rehabilitation. It was then that they came up with this model. The local youth were asked to form a group or "syndicate" and invest money to form a fund. They were then asked to supply raw materials for the construction of the project using the fund. The project supervisors were forced to take raw materials from these "syndicates" but not compromise on quality. It opened up an enterprising avenue for the local youth and stopped them from joining anti-social activities. There was no partisan politics in choosing the local youth to form the syndicate,' says a TV journalist who has extensively reported on syndicates in Rajarhat–Newtown.

However, during Mamata Banerjee's government, the idea behind the concept was diluted and distorted. The 'syndicates' turned out to be an avenue to earn money by the local TMC leaders.

It is not that Mamata Banerjee was unaware of this menace. She was well aware of the extortion racket run by her party colleagues. She herself admitted it in June 2019 when the chief minister opened up the 'cut money' debate (mentioned in Chapter 1). Still, she did not take strong action against all the culprits. There had been numerous reports and allegations. The case of Anindya Chatterjee, one of the many, had disturbed Mamata Banerjee so much that just before Anindya's arrest, on 3 July 2016, she had ordered the DGP to launch an action against those involved in running syndicate irrespective of the party. It created a ripple in the state politics, but the result has been unsatisfactory. Such 'syndicates' are still operating across the state. There have been repeated clashes between two factions of the syndicates patronised by two leaders of the ruling party in Rajarhat–Newtown area. Police do take action by arresting the goons, but they cannot completely eradicate the problem.

In July 2018, soon after Prime Minister Narendra Modi's public meeting in West Midnapore where he had raised the TMC 'Syndicate Raj' issue, a video clip went viral. In the clip, TMC MP and the leader of the All India Trinamool Trade Union Congress (AITTUC) Dola Sen was caught on camera telling the party workers in Purulia, 'After 21st of July, I will come and check the audited accounts [of the AITTUC local units]. How much you have raised, how much you have transferred in the bank and how much you have taken back home. You ensure that 75 per cent of the raised money is donated to the party fund and the rest is kept with you.'[2]

The Opposition alleged that there could be no better proof than this video, which was a clear endorsement of the extortion racket. This was an example of the 'cut money' or 'commission' the ruling party leaders sought from the beneficiaries of the government schemes or contractors of government projects. 'The chief minister did not clarify her stand on this instruction given by her party MP,' says CPIM leader Mohammed Salim. Neither did Dola Sen.

The Opposition's claim that the chief minister was in denial cannot be completely brushed aside. The victims of the 'extortion' or 'cut money' racket have mostly been the small- and medium-scale businessmen.

In September 2011, Pankaj Dhanuka, the chief executive officer of Lalbaba Seamless Tubes Pvt. Ltd,

---

[2] *Times Now*. 2018. Twitter, 18 July. Available at: https://twitter.com/timesnow/status/1019791650636230656?lang=en

had gone public with the allegation of extortion by the TMC's labour wing, Indian National Trinamool Trade Union Congress (INTTUC). His company alleged that there was interference in the functioning of the factory in East Midnapore's Haldia. They reportedly got a call from one of its 'employees' for 'payment' to a group having a connection to the Trinamool Congress.[3] There are many such instances in the industrial belt.

This practice has damaged the development of small- and medium-scale industries in the state, where big manufacturing industries are absent and SMEs are crucial for the state's economy. It has also been used to raise money for the party fund. Local leaders are accused of extorting individuals and businessmen in their area.

In November 2014, the then TMC MLA from Purbasthali (Uttar), Tapan Chatterjee, had told me how his own party men were involved in extortion from the local businessman. 'They send blank receipts and empty envelopes with the amount written at the back to the local businessmen. They do it in the name of organizing blood donation camp and for any other party programme,' he said. The video of his speech[4] in a party meeting claiming some people were extorting money in the name of the TMC went public. He had apparently told the top leadership, but that did not yield any action against the accused leaders. There were allegations against some of the top TMC leaders as well.

Take the Saradha chit fund scam, which also pointed to the alleged corruption amongst the top-level TMC

---

[3] Basu, A. *The Telegraph Online*. 'Black sheep' CM can't tame-Haldia industrialists groan under demands for money and interference by satraps claiming ties with Trinamul'. 12 September 2011.

[4] ABP Ananda. 2014. 'Tapan Chatterjee, TMC, MLA alleged that all the leaders in TMC engaged in extortion'. YouTube, 3 November. Available at: https://www.youtube.com/watch?v=1Ml8quR7YSI

leaders. The allegation was that Sudipta Sen, the promoter of the Saradha Group, had raised money from across the state for his microfinance company (in which the middle class and poor people had invested their money in the hope of higher returns than mainstream schemes of the banks) using his political clout. In turn, he had siphoned off this money to various other businesses, including hospitality and media. Several MPs, ministers, and senior leaders, including Sudip Banerjee, Mukul Roy, Shuvendu Adhikari, Srinjoy Bose, Kunal Ghosh, Madan Mitra, were either summoned for questioning or arrested.

'What exactly is the Saradha scam? Look at the model. A businessman was raising money from the people in the name of a Ponzi scheme. Local TMC leaders were supporting it. Some were even directly involved in raising money on behalf of Saradha. Then the Saradha chief, Sudipta Sen, was either acquiring media houses or floating new ones with this money. All the TV channels were turning out to be pro-TMC and the party was getting maximum positive coverage. Sudipta Sen also bought Mamata Banerjee's paintings, an issue now being investigated by the CBI. So, they used Sudipta Sen and his companies to fund TMC's campaign and other projects. It is the same funding model the local TMC leaders followed in the course of time,' alleges Mohammed Salim.

Mamata Banerjee was on the defensive when news about the Ponzi scheme broke out and Sudipta Sen was on the run. The party's Rajya Sabha MP Kunal Ghosh, a journalist-turned-politician who was accused of siphoning off Saradha's money, alleged that he was being made a scapegoat for demanding a CBI probe into the scam. Kunal served as the Group CEO of Saradha Media and had dragged the chief minister Mamata Banerjee into the Saradha controversy.[5] 'She was reluctant to take action against any other leader,' he alleged. Madan Mitra, a minister in Mamata Banerjee's cabinet at the time, was spared until the CBI took over the case and arrested him as well. The party did not protest when Madan was arrested and had already deserted Kunal Ghosh.

The same happened when the Narada sting operation tapes surfaced days before the 2016 assembly elections in the month of March. It was for the first time in Bengal's history that a bunch of political leaders were caught on camera accepting bribe from a journalist, Mathew Samuel, posing as a businessman. The Narada News claimed that their investigation to expose the corrupt elements in the TMC had begun around the time of the 2014 Lok Sabha elections and continued for the next two years.[6]

Shankudeb Panda, a former TMC student wing president and now a BJP leader, was seen in the Narada tapes as well. Ironically, in 2007, Panda had exposed[7] the then CPI MLA from Nandigram, Mohammad Iliyas, of taking a bribe on camera for allowing an NGO for children to run a project in Nandigram. Though Shankudeb was not seen taking a bribe in the Narada tapes, he was one of the mediators heard speaking about Benami investment in the company that he would own. Starting from the then Kolkata mayor, Sovan Chatterjee, to minister Firhad Hakim,

[5] IANS. *Business Standard*. 'Kunal Ghosh arrested in Saradha scam, opposition demands CBI probe'. 23 November 2013.

[6] Narada News. 2016. 'X Files: Narada News sting operation exposes Trinamool Congress'. YouTube, 13 March. Available at: https://www.youtube.com/watch?v=fsWCZ4NNZhg

[7] TNN. *Times of India*. 'Nandigram MLA caught on camera accepting bribe'. 6 December 2007.

several other ministers, MLAs and MPs were named in this sting operation by Matthew Samuel. The leaders were apparently taking hard cash in lieu of helping the business that the disguised journalist was proposing to set up. The then SP of Burdwan district, S.M.H. Mirza, was also caught in the sting operation and was allegedly mediating on behalf of Mukul Roy. This created a shockwave on the eve of the 2016 assembly elections. In March 2017, a year after the alleged video surfaced, the CBI took over the investigation on the order of the Calcutta High Court despite the opposition by the West Bengal government, which wanted the case to be investigated by the Bengal police. Later, some of the leaders like TMC MP Kakoli Ghosh Dastidar admitted that she had taken the money as a 'donation' during 2014 Lok Sabha elections and had declared the same to the ECI while filing the records of expenditure in the election campaign. 'I accept that I had taken donations from Mathew Samuel, I have receipts too. All political parties accept donations to fight elections. I have taken money as a donation for election and I have declared it to the Election Commission,' she said.[8]

However, Mamata Banerjee was silent for weeks after the Narada tapes came into the public domain. Her party branded it as a 'malicious campaign'. Finally, during the election campaign in Kolkata, she reacted to the sting operation in public. 'Had it been earlier [before the announcement of the candidates' list], I would have thought about it. Nothing can be done now after we have released the candidate list for the 2016 assembly election. I cannot change candidates after announcing

[8] DNA Web Team. *DNA*. 'Donation, declared it to EC: TMC MP admits to taking money from Narada CEO'. 28 September 2019.

their names,' she said while addressing a rally at central Kolkata's Bowbazar.[9]

She successfully turned the game around and projected herself as the TMC candidate in all 294 assembly constituencies. 'Vote for me,' she said. She knew that as long as the allegations of corruption did not touch her, people would still vote for the TMC. She was perhaps right. The TMC came back to power in 2016 with a higher margin and more seats in the assembly despite such allegations of corruption. She had proved it in the 2013 panchayat elections after the Saradha scam and again in the 2016 assembly elections. It is probably this confidence that stopped Mamata Banerjee from taking action against those charged with corruption at the grassroots level and complicate organizational equations.

The BJP understood that to hurt Mamata Banerjee, politically the issue of corruption would have to hit Kalighat (Mamata's residence). Things started changing when BJP leader Mukul Roy, who is an accused in the Narada and Saradha scams, was interrogated by the CBI and raised charges of corruption against Mamata Banerjee's nephew Abhishek. At a public meeting at Rani Rasmoni Road in Kolkata in November 2017, Mukul alleged that Abhishek Banerjee's company owned the Biswa Bangla copyright and the right of the logo was with Mamata Banerjee. The Bengal Chief Minister had drawn a logo for the state government with 'Biswa Bangla' (Bengal is the world) as its theme. Mukul Roy alleged that the name 'Biswa Bangla' is a trademark owned by Abhishek's company and the right of the image of the logo is with Mamata Banerjee. If these were 'private properties', how can they be used by the government of West Bengal?

[9] Bhabani, S. *India Today*. 'Didi distances herself from Narada-tainted TMC leaders'. 19 April 2016.

Mukul showed a bunch of papers to prove his point. It created an uproar in political circles. Soon after the rally, the Trinamool government, which generally never replies or reacts to such political allegations, had to defend an MP who was not even a part of their government. The then home secretary Atri Bhattacharya and the medium- and small-scale industry secretary Rajiv Sinha had to hold a long press conference to defend the government's stand and Abhishek Banerjee's stance. They claimed that the government had applied for the trademark rights of the logo and was awaiting the approval (further details in Chapter 4).

In August 2017, a Kolkata-based journalist from a national news channel had to face police interrogation when the channel carried a report suggesting a 'business transaction' between a real estate promoter accused of land grabbing and murder, and the company of a top TMC leader close to Mamata Banerjee. The journalist had to go into hiding for a few months to avoid arrest and the channel did not follow up the story.[10] The TMC leaders in a private conversation alleged that it was a planted story by the BJP.

As early as April 2014, CPIM leader Gautam Deb had held a press conference and accused Mamata Banerjee's brother and sister-in-law of buying properties worth ₹20 crore since she came to power. Questioning the source of the money, Gautam Deb, the former state minister, told a newspaper, 'I have got photocopies of the land deeds and I am ready to face any investigation. The chief minister's family, by using her position, has bought the properties. I do not believe that the CM did

[10] Ray, S.G. *Newslaundry*. 'How clean is Mamata Banerjee's "honest" nephew?'. 2 August 2017.

not know anything. In fact, 70 per cent of Kalighat is now owned by the Banerjee family.'[11]

In March 2019, news claiming that Mamata Banerjee's brothers had multiplied their properties within a short period of time since 2011 surfaced. The CPIM mouthpiece *Ganashakti* published a series of reports showing how Mamata Banerjee's family members owned 35 plots in Harish Chatterjee Street and Kalighat Road.[12] The report alleged that in most of the cases, the properties were bought using 'force'.

Mamata Banerjee has never addressed these issues directly. She and her party leaders have always refuted such charges calling them the 'conspiracy' of the CPIM (and later CPIM–BJP) to malign her. They have always highlighted the simple lifestyle Mamata Banerjee herself has maintained living in a house that does not even have a concrete roof but a *taalir chhad* (tiled roof). Having distanced herself from her brothers after her mother's death, Mamata Banerjee has often claimed in public that she doesn't have a family, that the people of the state are her family.

The question remains why Mamata Banerjee let it happen despite leading a middle-class life. Her plain and simple white sarees with a thin border is her only style statement. Her Hawai chappal (made of rubber) has become a trademark of her down-to-earth image. Despite becoming the chief minister, she has not moved out of her Kalighat house with the *taali* roof. She has made a couple of foreign trips to Singapore, Italy, the Vatican, the Netherlands, the UK, but she cannot do away with her habit of munching *muri* (puffed rice) in the evenings. In several interviews, she has said she did

---

[11] Bandopadhyay, S. *Indian Express*. 'Mamata brothers bought Rs 20-crore property after she became CM: CPM'. 30 April 2014.

[12] Basu, S. *Ganashakti*. 'Kalighate Ek Paribarer Haate 35 plot'. 30 March 2019.

not eat rice for a long time and loves to eat egg curry from the roadside stall near her residence and often orders it. At home, she is like any other *nanad* (sister-in-law) gossiping with her *boudis* and watching Bengali serials on television. She still travels in a small car, which is not bulletproof.

If she can lead such a simple life, why cannot her leaders? She had refused to enter the home of TMC leader Sheikh Sufian in Nandigram during one of her visits as she was apparently taken aback by its palatial appearance.[13] Sufian was one of her comrades during the Nandigram land agitation in 2007–08. He had come up from grassroots politics and later became the deputy chief of the zila parishad. Not only Sufian, but many TMC leaders also have multiplied their properties and lead lavish lifestyles. They have simply lost touch with the people at the grassroots.

'Mamata lost her credibility and authority to take action against her party leaders when it came out in the open that she had meetings with Ponzi scheme chief Sudipta Sen and her paintings were sold at an exorbitant price to him and many others. She has even admitted that she had to paint and write to raise money for the party,' says Mohammed Salim.

'You must have noticed, earlier TMC used to have placards and banners with Mamata's picture and a caption '*sototar protik*' [symbol of honesty]. Where are they now?' asks the leader.

The clean image that Mamata portrayed has indeed been maligned by many of her party leaders, who are neck-deep in corruption and extortion. 'Every political party needs money to run the expenses of elections. The big parties like BJP and Congress take donations. So

---

[13] Ghosh, A. *Ei Samay*. 'Sufiyaner Dalan Dekhe Rege Kain Didi'. 22 December 2015.

does TMC. But the way of raising the fund is different in case of the smaller parties. There are problems with technicalities of raising the fund,' says Suvashis Maitra. It seems Mamata too cannot take care of her party leaders, especially at the grassroots level as it is not as organised as any regimented party. TMC leaders often get exposed while raising funds while parties like Congress or the BJP do take donations to the party fund in a subtle manner.

LOOSE ORGANIZATIONAL STRUCTURE

In a press conference on 29 July 2019, Mamata Banerjee admitted, 'TMC is not an organized party.' The main reason why Mamata has not been able to control her party leaders is the absence of a strong organizational structure in the party. 'This is not a problem with just TMC. Congress has this problem and as an offshoot of Congress, TMC has been carrying this tradition of a loose organization unlike the communists,' says Suvashis Maitra.

There are many local satraps and factions in the party, which are difficult for the state party leadership to control. As a measure to have control over the leaders, Mamata has let factionalism grow in the party. It is like a 'divide-and-rule' policy that she has adopted to keep pressure and counter-pressure among the factions. This has helped the TMC chief to put a check on the leaders from outgrowing each other. If rivalries stayed in the party, no one would gather enough strength to challenge her authority. She also knows that during elections, voters would vote for her name and not these leaders. But, her strategy of keeping the factions alive boomeranged during the Lok Sabha elections and these rivalries damaged the TMC's image in the public eye as the media kept reporting them.

On 1 January 2014, local TMC leaders in South 24 Parganas' Bhangar were seen enjoying a *jalsa* with crass Hindi songs and scantily-clad female dancers as they observed the party's foundation day. The video went viral but when we reached Bhangar to trace the leaders, they were on the run. When I, along with my video journalist, was filming the local panchayat samiti office and the room where the local leader and the chief of the samiti Arabul Islam was supposed to be, we were intercepted by two men. They later identified themselves as local TMC leaders. We were concerned about our safety. To escape their ire, we told them that we were ready to leave.

To our surprise, the two took us to their chamber in the samiti office and offered us tea. Apparently, these two TMC leaders belonged to Arabul Islam's rival group. The rivalry between Arabul and another leader Kaizar Ahmed in the Bhangar area is a well-known fact in state politics. When Arabul Islam had become a headache for the party, Mamata had let Arabul's rival Kaizar Ahmed grow. She even got Arabul arrested on different charges on several occasions and once expelled him from the party. When several interventions by the state TMC leadership and even the expulsion of Arabul Islam from the party could not bring a halt to the fight between these two factions, she let both of them rule in their areas and fight it out among themselves.

The two leaders from Kaizar's camp told us in detail what Arabul and his men were up to, and how they were stifling the voice of the locals and party colleagues. After a long chat, they provided us with the address and directions to the houses of other local leaders, who were present at the *jalsa* that night and even told us about their hideouts. We went ahead with their tips and filed the story. This had only been possible because these two men belonged to the TMC. If they were CPIM cadres, it would have been impossible to extract such sensitive information from them. The CPIM leaders also might have had rivalry among themselves, but they generally wouldn't reveal revealed such internal information to the media.

A senior journalist Biswajit Bhattacharya elaborates, 'During the Nandigram agitation, about 100 families were evicted from the villages for supporting CPIM. They had to take refuge in neighbouring Khejuri. Did you get any stories about their camps in Khejuri? The media was not even allowed to enter the area. But you would get plenty of stories around TMC's factionalism and how they had taken the help from Maoists during the Nandigram movement. This is the difference between CPIM and TMC.'

Mamata Banerjee was mostly in denial whenever such incidents came into light—she seldom took strong action. In January 2018, a nine-year-old student Riyazul Mollah was killed as two Trinamool factions were engrossed in a turf war in Basanti in South 24 Parganas. A few days later, when I visited the village, the bereaved mother, Maroofa, alleged that the Trinamool men had even tried to snatch her son's body as he was hit by a bullet while returning from school. The villagers, after much prodding, revealed that it was a factional feud between Gosaba MLA Jayanta Naskar and Canning MLA Saokat Molla. There was no reason to disbelieve the villagers' allegation. There was hardly any presence of the Opposition in the area. The Left leaders had not dared to visit the victim's family because they did not have any organization in the locality. There was no flag or graffiti by the Opposition except a few saffron-coloured flags atop a few houses. The villagers said the Bajrang Dal was operational in the minority-dominated village but not politically active. Neither the chief minister nor any of the local leaders visited Riyazul's house. Congress leader Adhir Chowdhury was the only politician to visit the family and provide monetary support. A few arrests were made, but there was hardly any effort on the part of the ruling party to rein in the infighting. Jayanta Naskar, who hailed from Basanti, was asked by the TMC chief not to interfere in any organizational affairs of Basanti. 'I was asked to look after my constituency Gosaba and I am doing my duty. I do not poke my nose in Basanti affairs,' said Jayanta. At the same time, he accused Saokat, saying, 'There was no trouble in the area between 2011 and 2016. Trouble began only after Saokat became the youth wing president.'[14]

Saokat Molla had joined the TMC from the CPIM on the eve of 2016 assembly elections and was chosen to lead the youth front in South 24 Parganas under the leadership of TMC youth wing president Abhishek Banerjee. He also won the Canning (East) assembly constituency. Saokat, on the other hand, denied his involvement in the incident. 'I am being blamed without any reason. Check my mobile call list and you can see if I have spoken to anyone in Basanti in the last six months.'[15]

While the slugfest in the TMC was on, at an extended core committee meeting of the party on 31 January 2018 at Alipore's Uttirno, Mamata Banerjee herself raised the Basanti incident. She denied that it was the result of the TMC's infighting. To her, it was a 'fight between two neighbourhoods'. She asked her party colleagues why MLAs should be involved in petty fights between two groups of people from the adjoining neighbourhood. In the same meeting, she

[14] Pal, S. *Ebela*. 'Not tears but blood in the mother's eyes with the body of her child on her lap! The terrible truth behind the tears of Basanti'. 26 January 2018.

[15] Ibid.

warned Canning MLA Saokat Molla, 'I will not tolerate [trouble in] Basanti, Canning, Bhangar anymore. Saokat, there is a complaint against you. I will remove you if there is any further complaint.'[16]

Despite her warning, the infighting didn't stop. Though Mamata has often strategically allowed factions in the party, incidents like Basanti expose how the top leadership feels helpless in the face of ugly fights between factions. This also illustrates the top leadership's lack of control over the party functionaries and workers. 'Mamata has got little control over the party and the local party leaders let themselves go scot-free,' says Biswajit Bhattacharya.

In the TMC, unlike a cadre-based party, the top leadership's grip over its ranks and file has been missing for a long time. Earlier, only the district president and the office-bearers of the district units were chosen by the top leadership. And the district presidents were authorized to appoint the office-bearers at the block level. There was not much control from the top leadership in that regard. In certain areas, there were self-proclaimed block-level leaders, about whom even the state leadership was not aware. It often happened that someone involved in antisocial activities would claim to be an office-bearer of the TMC. Since there was no official record of such appointments, the party would be quick to deny the involvement of its party leaders and disown the accused.

Once, in the West Bengal assembly, a senior TMC leader was carrying an exercise book, which had 'Disciplinary Committee Minutes' written on it. When a senior journalist and I caught a glimpse of the document, we saw several pages at the beginning of the

---

[16] *Ebela*. 'Child's death in firing during factional feud, explosive Mamata Banerjee as she speaks out for the first time'. 31 January 2018.

notebook were blank and one proceeding was recorded in handwritten notes. When asked, the leader smiled and said, 'There are several cases where we have not recorded the proceedings of the disciplinary committee. If needed, we would put them in the blank pages.'

This practice of not recording the proceedings of the party committees is proved by the fact that almost none of the TMC leaders who were suspended received any formal letter from the party. 'I have not got any letter of suspension from the party. I have also paid my subscription to TMC from my bank account, which was used to credit my salary as a TMC MP. No one stopped taking my subscription,' said former TMC Rajya Sabha member Kunal Ghosh, who was suspended after demanding a CBI probe into the Saradha chit fund scam and dragging the chief minister's name into it.[17]

On the occasion of the foundation day rally of TMC Chhatra Parishad, on 28 August 2013, former TMCP chief and deputy speaker of the West Bengal Legislative Assembly Sonali Guha admitted the often-spoken words, 'We are all "lamp posts", there is only one post and her name is Mamata Banerjee.'[18]

In a one-man party, the supreme leader has the last word, and here it is Mamata Banerjee. The whole party is driven by her popularity. This is also a boon for quick decision-making as unlike the Left parties, Mamata does not have to go through a rigorous process of various committees and platforms to get a decision endorsed. It helps in the smooth running of the party and the

[17] *Anandabazar Patrika*. 'Is Kunal back in TMC? Question and embarrassment'. 14 February 2019.

[18] TOI Video. 2013. 'Only "one post" in TMC, rest "lamp posts": Sonali Guha'. *Times of India*, 28 August. Available at: https://timesofindia.indiatimes.com/videos/news/Only-one-post-in-TMC-rest-lamp-posts-Sonali-Guha/videoshow/22112653.cms

administration. On the flipside, the top leadership does not have control over different factions in the party.

THE ABSENCE OF IDEOLOGICAL FOUNDATION

December 2006. Mamata Banerjee is lying on a cot on the dais erected for her hunger strike demanding the return of farmland in Singur, where Tata Motors was supposed to set up their Nano car factory. She is joined by a radical Left trade union leader, Amitava Bhattacharya, from the Mazdoor Kranti Parishad; Sonali Guha, Mamata's long-time associate and TMC MLA; and Bijay Upadhyaya, a local Samajwadi Party leader. All of them are also fasting in solidarity with Mamata. A woman named Dola Sen, another radical Left trade union leader is seen singing, *'Hei samalo dhan re...'*, a song the CPIM and its associates used to sing during the land reforms movement in the 1960s and the 1970s. Mamata is flanked by Pradip Banerjee and Purnendu Basu, former Naxal leaders who were part of the violent movement of the late 1960s. The TMC leader is seen speaking to Samir Putatundu, a breakaway CPIM leader who formed his political outfit, Party for Democratic Socialism, with another prominent comrade Saifuddin Chowdhury, who was expelled from the CPIM for asking the party to ally with the Congress.

This scene depicts how all anti-CPIM forces had joined hands and gave an impetus to Mamata's 'anti-farmland acquisition' movement in Singur and Nandigram. Mamata Banerjee fought for the farmers by forming a broader platform—Krishi Jami Raksha Committee in Singur in 2006. Later, in 2007, she led the Bhumi Uchchhed Pratirodh Committee (BUPC) in Nandigram in East Midnapore. In both places, the then Left Front government had planned to set up industry by acquiring farmland. Leaders and activists from across the political parties or organizations and even individuals opposed to the Left Front government in general and land acquisition policy in particular came together in Mamata's platform. Their only purpose was to dethrone the Left Front government in Bengal. The CPIM would later term it as a 'Rainbow Coalition'.

About a year later, in November 2007, intellectuals considered close to the CPIM or the Left, as a whole, organized a rally in Kolkata against the Left Front government condemning the CPIM's atrocities on farmers in Nandigram. 'Operation Sunrise', on 9 November 2007, was the CPIM's bid to regain their lost turf in this block in East Midnapore district, and several villagers lost their lives in the exchange of fire between CPIM goons and TMC-led BUPC which was allegedly aided by the Maoists. The CPIM leaders, supporters, and workers were forced out of Nandigram in January 2007 after the villagers went violent hearing the government officials had come in the local panchayat office to put up a notice of acquiring 10,000 acres of land to set up a Chemical Hub. The villagers, irrespective of the party affiliations except the Left, had formed the BUPC. Later Mamata Banerjee's TMC took up the leadership of the outfit. Between January and March 2007, not only the CPIM cadres, but the administrative or the police officials were also not allowed to enter Nandigram, which was almost declared a 'Free Zone'. The CPIM had lost control over the area completely after the police fired on the farmers in March that year killing 14 villagers when police tried to enter the villages to establish rule of law. After the November 2007 clash, the likes of film director Aparna Sen, theatre personalities Kousik Sen, Bratya Basu, Shaoli Mitra, Arpita Ghosh, writers and poets Shankha Ghosh and Joy Goswami, painters Shuvaprasanna, Jogen Chowdhury, et al. were seen marching on the streets of Kolkata, supporting Mamata's cause. The city of Kolkata was adorned with banners carrying photos of these Left-leaning intellectuals appealing for *poriborton* (change). Mamata Banerjee had accommodated all of them for the final leg of her struggle against the Left Front government. The Left leaders and intellectuals were upset and tired with the 34-year-rule of the Left and believed that Mamata could lead from the front and end it.

Was Mamata more Left than the Left? The question was asked often. What is her ideology? Many thought Mamata was replacing the Left with an ideology that the Left should have followed. She was fighting for the farmers and the downtrodden, who were being oppressed by the rulers. Wasn't it what the Left, which led the land reforms in Bengal and stood by the farmers and labourers, always should have done? Ironically, the Left was on the receiving end. Mamata was surrounded by those who believed in the core Left ideology. In fact, Samir Putatundu was the architect of Mamata's Singur agitation and he continuously advised her on how to build and keep the pressure on the Buddhadeb Bhattacharjee government. Being an old party whole-timer (he left the party as the South 24 Parganas district secretary), he knew the nuances of the Left Front's operation. It helped Mamata clinch victory in her struggle. Mamata needed the support of Left intellectuals to climb up the ladder and she got almost all of them on her side.

Thirteen years down the line, Dola Sen is TMC's Rajya Sabha MP and Purnendu Basu is a minister in Mamata's cabinet. Pradip Banerjee was made the chairman of an advisory committee on agriculture. None of them carries their Naxal tag any more. They are more of TMC now than ultra-Left leaders. Many from the Left-leaning intellectual brigade contested elections on TMC tickets. Theatre personality Bratya Basu is a cabinet minister. Arpita Ghosh was a TMC MP and headed the South Dinajpur district unit. Shaoli Mitra was the chairperson of the Natya Academy and a part of the Railway Heritage Committee along with painter Suvaprasanna when Mamata was the railway minister. Another renowned painter, Jogen Chowdhury, was a TMC Rajya Sabha MP. A few like actor-director Arindam Sil and poet Subodh Sarkar, who vehemently opposed Mamata Banerjee and the TMC before 2011, switched sides and joined Mamata's camp post the regime change.

However, some of the Left brigade, who also fought for Mamata during the changing of guard in West Bengal, could not absorb the Trinamool's way of functioning. Samir Putatundu is nowhere to be seen, especially after Mamata refused to share any seat with his party, Party of Democratic Socialism (PDS), during the 2014 Lok Sabha elections. Amitava Bhattacharya, too, distanced himself a long time ago and organized labour and other civil rights movements against the TMC. Some others, like theatre personality Kousik Sen and singer Kabir Suman (he served as a TMC MP for five years), could not come to terms with Mamata's way of functioning and distanced themselves. Some ultra-Left activists also accused Mamata of using Maoists and their frontal organizations to gain support during the 2011 assembly elections only to desert them after coming to power. Senior journalist Biswajit Roy writes,[19] 'It's another matter that CPM had harped on TMC-Maoist nexus while Mamata denied it during Nandigram movement but she did not mind having them involved in people's resistance against

[19] Roy, B. *Frontier Weekly*. 'Days of Outrage'. Vol. 44, No. 44, 13-19. May 2012.

proposed land-grab in 2007. Later, she tried her best to keep the Maoists in good humour by feigning friendly concerns about the demands of the Maoist-dominated People's Committee Against Police Atrocities in Lalgarh in 2008–10. She echoed the demand of judicial probe into the "encounter" killing of top CPI (Maoist) leader Azad before the 2011 assembly polls, evidently to ensure Maoist support to her party in Junglemahal.'

When Mamata came to power, she followed the rules like a strict administrator. On one hand, she extended her party's influence in Junglemahal and, on the other, she freed herself from the clutches of Maoist sympathizers. 'Post-regime change, the equations changed drastically. Especially, after the half-hearted peace process between Mamata and the Maoists ended in the killing of [Kishenji], the rebel top gun in eastern India,' writes Biswajit Roy.[20]

The Left, which was busy fighting an 'ideological battle' with the Maoists or Naxals until the Red Army attacked the then chief minister Buddhadeb Bhattacharjee, acted against the armed rebels only in 2009. Unlike them, Mamata had no ideological compulsion to stop fighting the menace of Maoism. While the Left government was unsure of ordering the killing of top Maoist leaders operating in Lalgarh in 2009–11, Mamata did not hesitate to take the administrative decision of eliminating the Maoist cadres from the area and approved strict police action when there was an encounter between Kishenji and the security forces.

In fact, not only has Mamata been a popular leader, but she has also followed populist measures and reacted to situations as demanded. After coming to power, she inducted hordes of actors from the local film and TV industries into

[20] Ibid.

her party. The first Shaheed Divas, the famous 21 July rally, at the Brigade Parade Ground in Kolkata in 2011 turned TMC into a 'Paglu Party' as film star Dev sang his popular number 'Paglu' and other actors joined him to dance. Later, Dev even became a TMC MP. Many raised their eyebrows as 21 July has been observed as Shaheed Divas or Martyr's Day because on this day in 1993, 13 Youth Congress activists were killed in a police firing. Mamata Banerjee was the Youth Congress president at that time. She was leading a march to the state secretariat, Writers' Building, demanding the introduction of voter identity cards. The main allegation was that the Left Front government won elections after elections by allowing irregularities in the voters' list. When the protest march turned violent, police opened fire, killing many people who participated in the march and injuring a lot of others. But, Mamata Banerjee did not hesitate to turn the day of mourning into a day for entertainment with the actors dominating the stage. This is an example of Mamata's style of politicking, that is, adapting to the situation and acting like a popular leader taking populist measures.

Mamata has kept the celebrity quotient alive by nominating more and more actors like Sandhya Roy, Debashri Roy, Shatabdi Roy, Mimi Chakraborty, Nusrat Jahan to the assembly or parliament elections. She, all of a sudden, even nominated veteran actor Mithun Chakraborty to the Rajya Sabha. However, after being accused in the Saradha scam and due to his failing health, Mithun resigned and completely distanced himself from Bengal politics.

From a party supported by Left politicians and intellectuals, the Trinamool has turned out to be a party of Tolly-Telly (Mamata's favourite coinage for Tollywood film industry and Bengali television industry) actors. In between, there has been no ideological grounding of the party. It is neither Left nor Right. It is a mixture of everything. Being an offshoot of the Congress, it's not unnatural. In 1998, when Mamata Banerjee had quit the Congress, she alleged that the then Congress leadership was not keen on fighting the Left in Bengal. So, she launched the TMC only to throw the Left out of power. Long before she formed her own party, Mamata Banerjee had made her anti-CPIM stand clear. On 25 November 1992, she had rung the symbolic *mrityu ghanta* (death bell) of the Left Front government at a Brigade Parade Ground rally as the Youth Congress president. She was not successful then, but she kept the anti-CPIM struggle going until she finally achieved success in 2011.

However, as the old Congress accommodated a broad spectrum of politicians from the extreme Right to the extreme Left, so did the TMC. In the TMC's constitution, it is known as a nationalist party. However, it has been following whatever ideology suits it the best in their present situation. While on one hand, she co-opted the former Naxal leaders, the civil rights activists and Left-leaning intellectuals, on the other, she accommodated former bureaucrats and leaders of the minority groups in her cabinet and the party. During the peak of debate over industrialization in West Bengal under Mamata Banerjee, some industrialists were hopeful that the chief minister would change her position on land acquisition. In July 2011, industrialist K.N. Memani, the chairman of KNM Advisory Pvt. Ltd, told a business daily in Kolkata, 'Investors have confidence in Banerjee, who has no ideological baggage like the Marxists... The question is how the government makes land and labour available to new industries.'[21] The point that Mamata Banerjee did not

[21] Ray, A., K. Parbat and D. Sengupta. *Economic Times*. 'India Inc divided over prospects in West Bengal'. 4 July 2011.

have any dogmatic position on any ideological matters is proved by the fact that she appointed long-time FICCI secretary general Amit Mitra as her finance and industry minister. During the Singur movement, Amit Mitra, on behalf of FICCI, used to regularly issue statements against Mamata Banerjee and her farmland movement, and he even defended the cause of corporate India for a long time.

A party that was formed with a single-point agenda of throwing the Left out of power lost focus when the Left forces dwindled in the state and the BJP became a challenge. She resorted to the two-pronged strategy of bringing back an old agenda—the 'Bengali sentiment' (she had accused the central government of neglecting Bengal and demanded a special package for Bengal as the Opposition leader), and equating the BJP with the CPIM. She often told her supporters, '*Dine* BJP, *rate* CPIM,' (in the daylight they are BJP, at night the same people are CPIM members).

Raising the point of the 'neglected Bengalis' sentiment was not new. Even the Left survived on this agenda of the 'deprivation of Bengal' for long. The main allegation was that the Centre did not help Bengal get investment. Mamata took up the same agenda in a different way. She branded the likes of Narendra Modi and Amit Shah or even Rahul Gandhi as outsiders in the state. She claimed her nativity and tried to evoke the sentiment of the people of the state. She resorted to the same practice during the 2019 Lok Sabha elections when social reformer Vidyasagar's statue was desecrated during Amit Shah's roadshow. She claimed that she was here to protect the 'Bengaliness' of the state and the BJP leaders didn't share this sentiment. She had sent her representatives to Assam when a lot of Bengalis were being driven out by the National Registration of Citizens (NRC). She received a lukewarm response there.

Her rhetoric of equating the CPIM with the BJP worked only till a point. When the BJP came up as the main Opposition in Bengal by invading her bastions with Hindutva and the politics of polarization, her strategy went awry.

The BJP and the RSS have a definite goal and it is based on a specific ideology of building 'Bharat' and triggering a cultural revolution which would take the people of this country to the roots of Indian culture. The Left, too, has a clear ideological standing following the Marxist theory of bringing a classless society through revolution. The other strand of the Marxist ideology is to make a socialist country through class struggle in a democratic way. However outdated the ideology may seem, the Left follows a certain path. Mamata, on the other hand, has none.

'We are an offshoot of Congress and a nationalist party. Our role model is Mamata Banerjee and we follow her principles,' says Partha Chatterjee. Following a personality and having a strong ideological grounding are perhaps two different things. 'If someone believes in and follows the Indian Constitution, it should be good enough to be an ideology. What I personally feel is that Mamata Banerjee lacks the understanding of history and that is the root cause of TMC's problem,' says Suvashis Maitra.

She failed to understand it was not easy to counter the BJP ideologically. When faced with the BJP's Hindutva politics, she failed to counter it and, like many other parties, indulged in soft Hindutva like highlighting her party leaders' visit to the temples, her visit to Kapil Muni Ashram in Sagardweep and attending the celebrations of Loknath Baba among others.

Mamata's economic policies are not based on any particular ideology or long-term plan. She had opposed the farmland acquisition simply because she thought the Left was doing injustice to the farmers and it would get her votes. After assuming power, Mamata announced several sops for farmers since it helped her popularity. Due to the lack of any strong ideological grounding, she failed to take a concrete vocal stand on the Triple Talaq issue as well. It was easy for her to govern the state since she did not adhere to any dogmatic ideology and unlike the Left, she did not have any hesitation to deal with private entities. As long as it served her short-term populist goals, she was fine with any deal. In the political sphere too, she allied with the BJP and the Congress at different points of time only to throw out her main enemy—the Left. In the future, perhaps, she would not hesitate to join hands with the Left to counter the BJP's aggression. However, with such a loose, ad-hoc ideological standing, it seems difficult for her to counter a force like RSS–BJP that have a strong ideological ambition.

THE FALL OF THE TRIO

With a loose organizational structure and lack of ideological foundation, Mamata Banerjee's third problem is the lack of any strong second-rung leaders in the Trinamool because she did not let them grow. The number two in the TMC, Mukul Roy, who looked after the organization, deserted her to join the BJP and the incumbent number two, Abhishek Banerjee, has proved to be a disaster so far.

Apart from Mamata Banerjee, if someone knew the ins and outs of the party organization, it was Mukul Roy. The trusted aide of the TMC chairperson, Mukul was with her from day one and if anyone had full access to her decision-making process, it was him. When Mamata Banerjee became the chief minister and got busy with administrative matters, Mukul Roy took over the organizational issues as the national general secretary of the party. He, like Mamata, knew almost all the block level TMC leaders. The general secretary also worked as a bridge between the leaders and the party chief. He allegedly used to look after the appointments of police officers in the districts following the lines of the Left Front rule. During the Left regime, the party secretary used to handle the administrative appointments. Mukul was the mastermind behind bringing the Opposition MLAs, councillors, panchayat members, and other leaders into the TMC fold. He was also the master of defection.

Mukul Roy is marvellous when it comes to poll calculations. Though he isn't a psephologist, he knows exactly how much swings in the polling percentage in certain areas would ensure a victory for the party nominee. Coupled with his knowledge of the ground realities, as he maintained his connections at the grassroots, his exact calculations of votes helped him formulate strategies for the TMC. When he was the general secretary of the TMC, there was no large-scale violence during the elections, but there were reports of sporadic violence. When journalists asked why there was 'violence' during the polls, his standard answer was, 'There are 78,000 booths in the state and you are talking about violence in just two or three, it's negligible.' He would identify pockets where the TMC was weak and ask his party colleagues at the grassroots level to concentrate on those areas and clinch victory by hook or by crook.

Mukul Roy was also aptly helped by two party colleagues, Subrata Bakshi and Partha Chatterjee. Bakshi was made the state president of the TMC and Partha Chatterjee was accorded a post which has no validation in the TMC constitution, that is, the secretary-general.

Bakshi and Chatterjee still hold their respective posts, though their roles have changed.

Initially, Subrata Bakshi looked after the grassroots organization of the party and had knowledge about the block-level party leaders; he was more like a school principal. Even though many a time his curt replies baffled the party leaders, he was a master in resolving internal disputes. A former bank employee, who had given up his job to join Mamata Banerjee, Bakshi used his excellent managerial skills to handle internal and external dissent. Once, when he was the minister in charge of Public Works and Transport Department in Mamata Banerjee's first cabinet, his managerial skills were tested. He wanted to carve out a branch of the Motor Vehicles Department (MVD) to make it easy for the consumers to avail its services from two different locations in the city. It required some employees of the MVD to be transferred from the old office to the new. But, trade union leaders, who were mostly affiliated to the Left parties, were reluctant to join the new facility. They were trying to block the implementation of Bakshi's plans. Subrata Bakshi called the union leaders to his chamber and told them that he would give the unions a deadline within which they had to submit the names of the employees who could be transferred. He was not in favour of arbitrary transfer if the unions cooperated. He also told them that if they failed to provide the list of names within the deadline, he would be forced to transfer them arbitrarily. Bakshi got the names of the employees who could be transferred to the new facilities within the deadline and he implemented the plan smoothly. His straightforward solutions, like elaborated in the MVD case, impressed Mamata as well.

Subrata Bakshi has probably been one of Mamata's most loyal comrades. He has never faced the media's lens until forced to give a reaction. Even during a soundbite, he will take Mamata Banerjee's name twice in every sentence. He has been a silent worker who knows how to tackle unruly leaders and workers. Mamata Banerjee had nominated him from the Bhabanipur assembly constituency in the 2011 elections. But, everyone knew he would have to vacate the seat for Mamata once the TMC came to power. He did exactly that and Mamata gifted him the South Kolkata parliamentary seat in the by-election, the seat she had held for six terms.

Partha Chatterjee was the leader of the Opposition in the West Bengal assembly during the last two terms of the Left Front government. Then, as the secretary-general of the TMC, he was the face of the TMC legislature party. Mamata would use him wherever there was any trouble. Chatterjee, who worked at a senior position in the human resource department of Andrew Yule, brought his corporate skills to party affairs. He looked after the MLAs and was a bridge between the administration and the party leaders.

During the Left rule and as the deputy leader of the House in the West Bengal assembly after Mamata came to power, Partha Chatterjee was assigned the task of maintaining a liaison with the Opposition leaders. He was part of the mediation process on behalf of the TMC during the Singur Tata Factory impasse. He maintained the track-two dialogue with the then government and was, in a surprising move, exposed by the former chief minister Buddhadeb Bhattacharjee on the floor of the House. Bhattacharjee had said, 'Does your leader know that you came to speak to me?' The then chief minister was criticized for exposing Chatterjee when this kind of off-the-record meetings were a part of political negotiations and Partha Chatterjee was trying to help the Left Front government find solutions to the Singur crisis.

First as the industry minister and later as the education minister, he became the political face of the government. As the second-in-command in the Mamata Banerjee cabinet, he would come to brief the press after every cabinet meeting. He dealt with political issues involving the administration.

So, the TMC had a semblance of an organisational structure even after Mamata became the chief minister. A senior journalist had written in a Bengali tabloid that the Mukul–Bakshi–Partha combine was like the 'Brahma–Vishnu–Maheswar' of the TMC. They had held the party together on behalf of the TMC supremo. On Mamata's instructions, they kept running the organizational affairs from three different positions but had the same authority and good communication among themselves.

It seemed as if Mamata did not want any other leader to rise to the level of the trio. There was potential in Nandigram-famed Suvendu Adhikari, who was elected to the Parliament twice from the Tamluk constituency and was the architect of Mamata's success in the Nandigram movement. Later in 2016, on Mamata's insistence, he contested the Nandigram assembly seat relinquishing his Lok Sabha membership and was made the transport minister of West Bengal. He and his father, Sishir Adhikari, had singlehandedly diminished the powerful CPIM leader Lakshman Seth's supremacy in East Midnapore district. A brilliant speaker with excellent organizational skills, Suvendu was the Trinamool Youth Congress's president and helped the youth wing grow. There were other second-rung leaders like former Kolkata mayor Sovan Chatterjee, ministers Firhad Hakim, Arup Biswas, Madan Mitra, among others, who were with her since the beginning of the TMC. However, she did not elevate them to the level of the trio. Though Firhad Hakim was made a minister and Kolkata's mayor (after Sovan Chatterjee had a tiff with the party), Arup Biswas was taken into the cabinet, and all of them were given organizational responsibilities, she does not seem to trust them as much as she trusted the original trio.

However, this organizational structure fell apart soon after Mamata Banerjee's nephew Abhishek rose up to be the number two in the party. First, a new wing called All India Trinamool Congress Yuva was launched at the unofficial TMC Shaheed Divas rally on 21 July 2011 and he was accorded with the post of its all-India president. At a press conference, Abhishek claimed that this party wing would bridge the gap between the student and the youth wings of the party and nurture future leaders. Though many could not understand the necessity of such a frontal organization when, in the TMC, anyone could graduate from the TMC Chhatra Parishad to Yuva Trinamool Congress organically. 'It was created to launch Mamata Banerjee's nephew into politics,' said a political commentator. Mamata created the launchpad for her nephew. She might have been worried about the introduction of Abhishek, a family member, into politics lest the Opposition accuses her of 'dynastic politics'. So, it was considered to be a soft launch.

Then, Suvendu Adhikari was removed from the post of TMC's youth wing president in 2014 after the Lok Sabha elections. For a brief period, a former Congress MLA from Bishnupur, Soumitra Khan, who had defected from the Congress to join the TMC, became the youth wing president. Abhishek Banerjee, who won his maiden election from Diamond Harbour constituency to go to Lok Sabha, was made one of the general secretaries of the youth wing. His induction as the member of the TMC state committee was the first official post he held in the parent party. However, no one could come up with a logical explanation for having a parallel youth wing called Yuva alongside the original Trinamool Youth Congress. So within three months, Abhishek was made the president of Trinamool Youth Congress on 18 October 2014, and Yuva was merged with the parent youth wing. He was also taken into the committee to run the parliamentary party in Delhi.

While Suvendu Adhikari was side-lined, which many believe was due to his rivalry with Mukul Roy, and brought back to the forefront later by Mamata when he was made a minister in the state, Mukul Roy also developed a tiff with Abhishek. They avoided each other at the Trinamool Bhavan. Abhishek had allegedly complained to Mamata against Mukul taking over the party's rein from her by appointing his loyalists in key party posts. As Mukul Roy realized he was no longer the Number Two in the organization and he had to follow Abhishek's instruction, the organizational equations changed within the party. Subrata Bakshi and Partha Chatterjee were also superior to Abhishek in the party structure and he showed respect to the duo, but gradually the authority in the party shifted to the young leader.

With the rise of Abhishek, endorsed by Mamata Banerjee, the Brahma–Vishnu–Maheswar trio fell apart. In 2014, Mukul Roy was interrogated by the CBI in connection with the Saradha chit fund scam and later he was also caught on camera in the Narada sting operation asking the journalist disguised as a businessman to meet the then Burdwan superintendent of police, SMH Mirza, and apparently hand over the 'bribe' money to facilitate their business. Mirza, in turn, claimed on the Narada tapes that he handled the cash for the TMC party and acted as a conduit for Mukul Roy. As Mamata Banerjee wanted to keep her image clean, she shunned Roy and started maintaining a safe distance from him. Abhishek was happy with these developments and the party leaders understood that it is Abhishek who would now call the shots.

With Mukul Roy's exit from the party and him joining the BJP, the whole organization was in the hands of Abhishek. Senior party leaders like Partha Chatterjee and Subrata Bakshi at a party meeting in Diamond Harbour had to hail Abhishek as the future chief of the TMC. Both Partha and Subrata ceased being as active as they earlier were. A lot of district leaders also fell out with the top leadership.

A new crisis started brewing within the party as the BJP rapidly gains ground in the state. 'Now we have a collective leadership and it works well,' says Partha Chatterjee. But, on condition of anonymity, many senior leaders allege that there is no such thing called a 'collective' leadership. 'You know who the second in command is,' they say.

ABHISHEK'S ORGANIZATIONAL SKILLS IN QUESTION

On a winter afternoon in November 2017, people experienced an unprecedented security cover in a 10-kilometre stretch on the Kolkata–Diamond Harbour Road. At every junction, there was a group of police personnel and traffic movement was being restricted on the two-lane highway. At a place near Falta, in the South 24 Parganas district, loudspeakers were bellowing Trinamool slogans. A cavalcade of cars, mostly SUVs, was lined up near a stage erected at the junction of two roads. There was a jammer atop a car like we see in the prime minister's convoy. Apart from top-ranking police officers, there were around 15 commandos in safari suits or dressed as black cat commandos carrying automatic guns and keeping a close eye on the crowd.

Looking at the security protocol, for a moment, it seemed as if the prime minister was holding a rally. Even though Mamata Banerjee (or any other chief minister) is entitled to this kind of security, she has never flaunted it. A little probe confirmed that it was Mamata Banerjee's nephew Abhishek who had come to attend a party programme. People had lined up on both sides of the road as Abhishek and the national spokesperson of the TMC, Derek O' Brien, both clad in a white kurta and pyjama, along with other local leaders and TMC supporters walked towards the stage. People were seen clicking photos from roadside and Abhishek was offering them customary *namaskars* with folded hands. At the end of the march, Abhishek delivered a fiery speech against the Modi government, the BJP in general and Mukul Roy in specific. He did not take Mukul's name, but told the rally, 'Among us, there were many who thought they had become a big leader. They thought they had touched the sky with the blessings of Mamata Banerjee. The party allowed it and that's why they had developed wings to fly. But Mamata Banerjee is the sun, no one can touch her.' After the meeting, he left the spot like a prince. As the cavalcade sped away, TMC workers shouted slogans, 'Abhishek Banerjee zindabad'.

Mamata Banerjee, even at the peak of her political career, has not used such security cover, but Abhishek, without holding any portfolio either in the government or in the parent body of the TMC, using such a huge security cover raised many eyebrows. However, Mamata Banerjee tried to dispel such speculation, and at a public meeting on 2 February 2018[22] in Howrah's Dumurjola Stadium even claimed that the TMC was

[22] AITC Official. 'Mamata Banerjee addresses party's annual Student-Youth Convention at Dumurjola Stadium in Howrah'. YouTube, 2 February, 2018. Available at: https://www.youtube.com/watch?v=9N_c_toUIzc

run in a collective leadership pattern. She said that she had prepared the second- and third-generation leaders in the party. Mamata named Abhishek Banerjee and Nandigram anti-land-grab-movement-famed Suvendu Adhikari as her second-generation leaders. Even though she might have spoken of a row of second-rung leaders, including Abhishek Banerjee, Suvendu Adhikari, Arup Biswas and Firhad Hakim, the truth remained that after Mamata it would be Abhishek. Even senior leaders like Partha Chatterjee and Subrata Bakshi endorsed Abhishek's elevation. When Abhishek released a booklet *Nishobdo Biplob* (Silent Revolution) detailing his achievements in the four years as the MP of Diamond Harbour constituency, the senior leaders were all praises for him. Party state president Subrata Bakshi said, 'Abhishek is the future leader.' Secretary-General Partha Chatterjee said, 'Mamata Banerjee will not be there forever. We will also not be there. Abhishek's leadership will protect the people of the future generation.'[23]

However, Abhishek was modest enough to tell the crowd at the same rally where he released *Nishobdo Biplob*, 'Mamata Banerjee is everything in the party. Leaving her, there is no number 1, 2, 3 in the party. But whatever responsibility the party will give me, I will discharge it.'

Initially, Abhishek grew under the tutelage of Subrata Bakshi, Partha Chatterjee, Sovan Chatterjee, and Derek O'Brien before he spread his own wings. Abhishek occupied the space vacated by Mukul Roy. He had taken up the task of running the organization as his aunt was busy with the government and the administrative work. On his part, Abhishek tried to organize the party using modern techniques that were absent from the TMC. He

---

[23] *Anandabazar Patrika*. 'Abhishek is the "face", the message of top leadership'. 6 June 2018.

started preparing a database of the booth and block-level leaders, met the party leaders from the districts regularly at the Trinamool Bhavan or his office in Kalighat near Mamata's residence, visited the districts, and addressed rallies with his good oratory skills that moved the crowd. However, he failed to reach out to the common people, the way his aunt could. Mostly, he acted like a prince, living in a palatial building in South Kolkata's Harish Mukherjee Road, seldom meeting the journalists except for one or two close ones, making a public appearance at his will and revealing most of his schedule at the last moment. He lacked the mass connection his aunt possessed. He maintained a distance from the workers and interestingly from the media too.

Moreover, as the heir apparent, his one key decision caused permanent damage to the TMC's organization. He knowingly or unknowingly formed a parallel organization with his trusted men from the Yuva and youth wing of the TMC. Without holding a formal post, he would send out instructions to the district leaders of the parent organization. This irked many old-timers in the party. The district leaders, most of them senior to him and loyal to Mamata Banerjee, refused to bow before Abhishek and were side-lined. Those who showed loyalty survived Abhishek's test. The factionalism that led to violence in certain parts of the state was allowed to continue in the TMC. This divided the party into Yubo TMC (youth TMC led by Abhishek Banerjee) and Mul TMC (main TMC belonging to the main organization).

His organizational skills were also questioned after the TMC suffered a huge setback in the panchayat elections in the districts of Junglemahal where Abhishek was in charge. As mentioned earlier, though the TMC did not lose the majority, the BJP made deep inroads into the panchayat bodies in Jhargram and Purulia.

When the TMC won 34 per cent seats uncontested in three-tiers of panchayat set up across the state, the result in Junglemahal districts was a cause for concern for the TMC leadership. The primary post-mortem of the results revealed the local leaders lacked connection with the people and there were allegations of nepotism and corruption against the local TMC leadership. Though Abhishek visited Purulia at regular intervals and held meetings, both internal and public, he perhaps failed to detect the disease in the party and act in time.

After the results were declared, there were efforts to shield him by blaming the district leaders and removing the local TMC leadership. For Jhargram, it was projected that he was not in charge at all. Other senior leaders had to cover up for him.

Abhishek's style of functioning caused more damage to Mamata than her strategy. Moreover, the Opposition got a chance to attack Abhishek on the issue of disproportionate assets. During the 2019 Lok Sabha elections, his wife was allegedly intercepted by the customs officials for carrying gold beyond the permitted limit. This created a huge controversy for him at the time.

Abhishek also adopted a new culture. Whenever someone attacked him politically and raised questions about his property and propriety, he slapped the person with a legal notice. He even sent a legal notice to the BJP chief, Amit Shah, for implicating him in the syndicate raj in a BJP Yuva Morcha rally in August 2018. He also slapped a defamation case against Mukul Roy in November 2017 for alleging that Abhishek owned the rights of Biswa Bangla logo.

Until the 2019 Lok Sabha elections, Abhishek had failed to come up with a concrete plan for reviving the organization and instead, had alienated a lot of old leaders. While selecting candidates for the Lok Sabha elections, Mamata Banerjee did overwrite a few of Abhishek's choices, but his importance in the party has not dwindled. However, post the 2019 Lok Sabha results, Abhishek has been instrumental in getting poll strategist Prasant Kishor on board to revive the party ahead of the assembly polls in 2021. Only time will tell if his move will lead to success at the ballots.

3

Minority Appeasement Versus Majoritarian Politics

The year is 2017 and two young boys, one clad in printed trousers and a black shirt and another in black pants and grey T-shirt and wearing a cap, are performing *lathikhela* (a performance using sticks) on the streets of a suburban town of Chandannagar, which was a French colony before Independence. The passers-by look at their intense performance. Behind them, a sea of people chanting 'Jai Shri Ram' and waving saffron flags march through the arterial streets. Among them, some are carrying swords and brandishing them openly. Some, dressed as Lord Hanuman, are carrying maces. A group of young women is seen dancing to music booming out of huge sound boxes placed in a Matador. As some are chanting slogans, '*Haar ghar bhagwa chhayega/ram rajya phir aayega* (Saffron will reach every household, Ram's kingdom will be back again)', trucks carrying pictures of Bharat Mata, Swami Vivekananda and even a group of army jawans follow. Behind the huge cut-out of Swami Vivekananda, there is Lord Ram. His idol holding a bow and arrows moves through the crowd. Girls and boys sporting red scarves around their foreheads, holding crude weapons high in the air, chant, '*Bharat ka abhimaan hai Hindu, Matribhumi ka shaan hai Hindu* (Hindus are the pride of Bharat, Hindus are the pride of the motherland).' Some are even dressed as Lord Ram and Goddess Sita and riding a *ghorargari* (horse cart). The air is fraught with tension, one can feel being in a war field as people give a war cry for Lord Ram and a Hindu nation.

That year, West Bengal got a taste of a different kind of Ram Navami (spring Hindu festival that celebrates the birthday of Lord Ram). 'Earlier, the Ram Mandir in Chandannagar used to bring out a procession on Ram Navami. A few Vishwa Hindu Parishad (VHP) activists used to take part in that. They also organized such processions during Janmashtami. Then, there was just one procession,' says Pinakpani Ghosh, a journalist and a resident of Chandannagar. In 2017, however, one man changed the way the festival was celebrated in the area. A man called Dilip Ghosh had mobilized the people of this mofussil town and took the Ram Navami celebrations to the masses. No one knew his name at that time. It was only later that he stepped into the shoes of West Bengal BJP president. 'People came to know about Dilip Ghosh when he became the BJP state president. But, he was instrumental as the chief of Hindu Jagaran Manch to mobilize the temples to bring out multiple processions and then merge them into one during Ram Navami. It all happened after TMC came in power,' Ghosh adds.

Chandannagar was not an isolated case, similar scenes were replicated across Bengal that year. Interestingly, no slogan was raised in favour of the BJP from these Ram Navami rallies. There were slogans against Pakistan, on Kashmir, etc. This was a way to polarize people.

Before 2017, for the average Bengali household, Ram Navami meant a tame celebration limited to mothers fasting for the well-being of their sons. No-fuss, no noise was involved. A few processions were visible, but they didn't hold much significance. Also, no aggressive show of power or faith was involved. Ram is very close to the Bengalis' heart, more than a deity. Unlike north India, he is not a war hero, but more like the benevolent eldest son of a king. Grandmothers would read the Bengali version of Ramayana written by Krittibas Ojha and we learnt the stories of Ram, Lakshman and Sita through them. People of Bengal chanted Ram naam to scare away ghosts. So naturally, the aggressive Ram Navami celebrations that suddenly emerged in Bengal were a shocker for many.

For Bengalis, in whose lives Maa Durga is omnipresent, 2017 signalled a change in the state's mood and a new social churning was visible with the aggressive emergence of the remodelled Lord Ram. The lavish Ram Navami celebrations were the VHP and its associate organizations' answer to Muharram processions in Bengal. The BJP rode on this wave to extract political benefit out of it. The Bengal BJP state president, Dilip Ghosh, had come out in a new avatar. He was seen in saffron pagri holding a sword in one hand and a mace in the other. He gave a war cry from his assembly constituency, 'Here [Bengal] a fight is on between "Ramzada" and "Haramzada". It is a test to decide who is on the side of Ram, and who is not.'[1]

'I looked after the Hindu Jagaran Manch since 2011 and I wanted to give a voice to the Hindus who saw partition and division in Hindu society. They felt insecure about the way Muslims were being appeased. They felt they would be refugees in their own land. No political party talked for the Hindus. If one talked in favour of Hindus, he was branded as communal. Political parties talked for the Muslims to get votes. We caught that point and we needed an issue through which we could unite the Hindu voices. We used Ram

[1] *Ebela*. 'Dilip may be arrested, speculation in Mamata's stern warning'. 6 April 2017.

Navami for that. This was not part of the Bengali tradition. We got a huge response and it worked well for us,' says Dilip Ghosh.

However, Mamata Banerjee cried foul over the BJP's strategy, saying, 'Earlier, Basanti Puja used to be observed in Bengal. On the ninth day, Ram Navami was celebrated. This has no relation with the BJP. Don't run it as BJP's programme. They don't have any work. They are creating communal tension. They are talking of religion in a party meeting, writing "Om" in party flags and doing politics over religious festivals. In UP, they are saying "Sabka Saath, Sabka Vikash" claiming they have got the Muslim votes. Here in Bengal, they are dividing between Hindu and Muslims.'[2]

She was at an administrative meeting in Bankura on the day of Ram Navami in April 2017 and warned that she would take action against those who marched in these armed Ram Navami rallies. Finally, the BJP state president was booked.

But, this call for armed rallies as a show of Hindu might captured the imagination of Bengali Hindus, stoking their inherent communal sentiment, which had finally found a voice. 'If Muslims can brandish swords [during Muharram], why can't we?' asked a young IT professional, an active member of a shakha (local unit) of the RSS in Hooghly. 'If they can do it during their festivals, we have every right to bring out a procession to commemorate the birthday of Lord Ram.' He was arguing for the rights of Hindus to take out processions during Ram Navami. Thousands of youth, without even understanding the historical context of enacting the battle of Karbala and the holy day of mourning on Muharram according to the

---

[2] *Ebela*. 'Allegations of religious tickling. Mamata's 7 words attacking BJP'. 5 April 2018.

Islamic calendar, jumped into the wave of armed Ram Navami celebrations.

Sensing the mood of aggression, the BJP state president took on Mamata Banerjee for initiating legal action against him, stating, 'The whole of India from Gujarat to Guwahati, Kashmir to Kanyakumari will have "Bharat Mata ki Jai" and "Jai Shri Ram" chants. Those who will oppose it will be history. The way we will beat you like thrashing the clothes, you will never forget. That will change the geography of your face.'[3]

As Mamata Banerjee accused the BJP of polarizing Bengal, the VHP had its answers ready. 'Mamata Banerjee has accused us of polarizing Bengal. But may I ask her, why she did not think about it when allowances for imams were announced, when more funds were given to madrassas and when *visarajan* of Durga idol was held due to Muharram? Was it not polarization then? We are proud of this polarization that is in favour of nationalism,' said Surendra Jain, international joint general secretary of VHP.[4]

A new battle line was drawn between Mamata Banerjee's TMC and Narendra Modi–Amit Shah's BJP. This was for the first time that communal polarization took a concrete shape in the political landscape of Bengal through Ram Navami debate and snowballed into a new political ballgame where Mamata Banerjee suffered a huge setback and the BJP gained significantly in electoral terms. This was a new beginning in majoritarian vs minority politics in Bengal.

---

[3] Dilip Ghosh in West Midnapore on 17 April 2017.

[4] ET Bureau. *Economic Times*. 'We are proud of this Polarisation: VHP general secy on Bengal Ram Navami celebration'. 11 April 2017.

INHERENT COMMUNAL SENTIMENT IN BENGAL

There has been a long history of communal hatred in Bengal: the fissures between Hindus and Muslims run deep in the state. No one can deny that communal sentiment has been ubiquitous among Bengalis. This hatred was well nurtured by the British in the pre-Independence era. Some historians argue that the religious faith was not the primary identity of the people of Bengal in the pre-modern stage. Categorizing the communities on religious lines and using them as a 'theoretical base' for policy implementations and finding allies to support the colonial powers, have been a 19th-century phenomenon patronized by the British rulers. Ultimately religious identity and communalism turned into a social reality.

This communal divide took root during the time of Muhammad Ali Jinnah, the leader of the Muslim League, and was fuelled by the colonial rulers, who wanted to split Bengal as early as 1905. They didn't get much success then. But in 1946–47, communal violence in various parts of Bengal, including the Great Calcutta Killings, and the subsequent division of Bengal on religious lines put the final nail in the coffin of so-called 'communal harmony'. While the Muslim League fought for the cause of the Muslims, the Hindu Mahasabha, a Right-wing political outfit, acted as a counter-force. Both the outfits rejected a sovereign Greater Bengal consisting of the undivided province and independent of either India or Pakistan floated by the then Bengal chief minister, H.S. Suhrawardy, and Congress leader Sarat Bose. West Bengal was created for Hindu-majority Bengal while the East Bengal went to Pakistan as East Pakistan in 1947. The partition on religious lines left a permanent scar of religious identity and resultant tension in the Bengali consciousness.

Professor Suranjan Das, vice-chancellor of Jadavpur University and a historian writes, 'Studies on communalism in India tend to fall into one of several competing stereotypes—ranging from the colonial to Muslim, Hindu and secular versions. Many of these works rely on one of the two extreme positions—the pre-colonial golden age of Hindu-Muslim relations or a fundamental Hindu-Muslim rift as a fact of history.'[5] He thinks that it was hoped by both the British and the Indian ruling classes that the creation of Pakistan and dividing the subcontinent along religious lines would restore communal harmony, but it had been badly shaken during the 'prelude to the partition' and there were questions on the secular foundation of India from the experience of subsequent communal riots in independent India. The tension between the two communities has always prevailed and has been visible through sporadic riots. Suranjan Das posits this changing character of communal tensions culminating in a politically charged phenomenon in the 1935 Act where provincial autonomy was provided based on separate Hindu and Muslim demographic calculations. This, Professor Das feels, 'is the turning point in the development of communal politics in Bengal'.

Fear mongering and rumours of aggression by the opposing sides in both the communities resulted in sustaining the communal tension. The rise of the Hindu Mahasabha dreaming of a Hindu Rashtra and the empowerment of the Muslim League added to the communal divide on political lines; both projected themselves of serving the interests of their respective communities. Professor Dwaipayan Sen writes, 'True

---

[5] Das, S. *Social Scientist*. 'Communal Violence in Twentieth Century Colonial Bengal: An Analytical Framework'. 18(6/7),21-37. 1990.

to their obsession with demography, the Mahasabha claimed sole spokesmanship of a supposedly neglected and persecuted Hindu minority, and as the realities of Muslim-majority rule were contemplated during the increasingly charged decade of provincial autonomy, their defence of Hindu interests found ready reception primarily amongst the urban intelligentsia, students and professional classes of the region.'[6]

The communal riots in pre-independent Bengal used to be sparked off by minor incidents, such as 'cow slaughter' in the locality or Hindu processions playing songs in front of the masjids, and they were mostly local. However, after the 1940s, the character of the communal riots changed gradually. If in the 1920s, the communal tensions were class-oriented—between poor Muslim peasants and Hindu zamindars—the rioters in the 1940s were politically patronized. Running a provincial government under the 1935 Act, it was easier for the Muslim League to use its administrative machinery. In this complex politics, the Congress's dominating power in Bengal also reduced to a large extent. Many believe the Congress leaders who were mostly upper-caste Hindu *bhadralok* (a term used for elite, educated, and intellectual Bengalis), had tacitly supported the politics of the Hindu Mahasabha. At the end of the day, nationalism and the anti-British movement largely turned into communalism and a fight among the Hindu and Muslim Bengalis.

After Independence, as the Muslim-majority districts of undivided Bengal went to East Pakistan, the political power of Muslim League diminished in West Bengal. The Congress, which was the main opposition in West Bengal assembly till independence, formed the government under Prafulla Chandra Ghosh. In 1952, after

[6] Sen, D. *The Wire*. 'Memories of 1946 great calcutta killings can help us understand violence in today's bengal'. 2 October 2018.

the general elections held under the new Constitution of India, the Indian National Congress came to power in West Bengal with 150 seats out of 219. They polled 38.93 per cent votes. Hindu outfits such as the All Indian Bhartiya Jan Sangh won nine seats with 5.8 per cent votes and the Akhil Bhartiya Hindu Mahasabha won four seats with 2.37 per cent vote share. In Lok Sabha, Bhartiya Jan Sangh won two seats. One of the winners was Shyama Prasad Mookerjee, its founder, and the other was Durga Charan Bandopadhyay. From Hooghly constituency, N.C. Chatterjee was elected on the Hindu Mahasabha ticket. However, the electoral power of the Hindutva forces in West Bengal diminished over the years. The Bhartiya Jana Sangh could not win any seat to the Lok Sabha from Bengal thereafter. Their vote percentage also declined over the years and hovered around 1.4 per cent. In the assembly, they won only one seat in 1967 and 1971. They drew a blank in the rest of the elections. A question that is often asked is how in the land of Shyama Prasad Mookerjee, former president of the Akhil Bhartiya Hindu Mahasabha and founder of the Bhartiya Jana Sangh (the root of the BJP), Hindutva politics could not flourish for so long since Independence. The answer perhaps lies in the development of the Left movement in Bengal and the revival of radical sentiment prevalent among a section of the Bengalis during the Independence movement. Revolutionist freedom fighters like Khudiram Bose, Masterda Surya Sen and Netaji Subhas Chandra Bose represented this section.. However, there are other reasons as well. Shyama Prasad had joined the Jawaharlal Nehru Cabinet in 1947. He advised the Hindu Mahasabha leadership to abstain from political activities and concentrate more on socio-cultural programmes. On 15 February 1948, the Mahasabha had adopted the resolution to transform itself into a socio-cultural organization, thereby, its political activities had been curtailed. This impacted their organization in West Bengal. However, in 1949, the Mahasabha had decided to re-enter politics. Shyama Prasad Mookerjee was opposed to this idea and resigned from the post of its executive president. He formed the Bhartiya Jana Sangh in 1951 before the first general elections in the country. Though the Jana Sangh had its presence in Bengal and fought elections, in 1953, after Shyama Prasad's demise, it remained more of a North Indian, upper-caste Hindu party which could not align with the east Indian or, for that matter, south Indian, Hindu ethos. By that time, the partition of Bengal and the exodus of the refugees from East Pakistan had rattled the state politics. The RSS had its presence in Bengal and the Hindu outfits worked with the refugees immediately after Independence. Still, the ban on the RSS after the assassination of Mahatma Gandhi in 1948 restricted their activities for a few years. The overall situation prevented the Hindu organizations to expand their base in Bengal. By then, the Left had filled the vacuum in the Opposition in West Bengal.

The Bangladeshi Hindu refugees who had faced the wrath of the Muslims in East Pakistan and migrated to West Bengal could have been the most vulnerable force in communal politics. However, the Left trade union movements, the Food Movement (1952) or the mass movements against the tram fare hike, among others might have directed their political goals towards class struggle. The emergence of Bengali *bhadralok* culture in which a man is considered *bhadralok* if he is educated and secular, at least in appearance, must have added to limiting the communal tensions in the state. Even Shyama Prasad Mookerjee had rued that the Hindu Mahasabha could not penetrate the heart of the Bengal province.

Post 1950s, communal harmony prevailed in a large part of the state, keeping in tune with the philosophy of the great sons of Bengal like Rabindranath Tagore, Kazi Nazrul Islam and Netaji Subhas Chandra Bose. It was considered to be the real character of this Eastern Indian state.

Suranjan Das, however, cautioned as early as the 1990s that 'it would be wrong to deny the existence of communal tensions in Bengal. Potential of communal violence is not totally absent. Religious identities remain strong. People voting the Left Front remain astute Hindus and Muslims, continuous infiltration across the borders is providing fertile ground to VHP, despite strong Leftist and democratic traditions, the dangers of communal solidarities haunt secular forces'.

Despite efforts by Bengali intellectuals and moderates, the communal divide hardened through a broader national narrative of Muslim fundamentalism that has been witnessed especially since the 1990s.

Both the Left and the Right have always charged Bengal's chief minister Mamata Banerjee of 'Muslim appeasement' and blamed her for turning Bengal into a fertile ground for communal politics since 2011. The rhetoric grew louder in the run-up to the 2019 general elections. 'Mamata Banerjee has imported communal politics in Bengal. First, she allied with BJP soon after the formation of Trinamool Congress in 1998 and let them grow in Bengal. Second, after coming to power, her blatant Muslim appeasement and joining hands with the hardliners [referring to Barkati, the then Shahi Imam of Kolkata's Tipu Sultan Masjid, and Jamiat Ulema-e-Hind leader Siddikullah Chowdhury, and others who were considered to have taken tough stance when it came to the rights of the Muslims] helped BJP to get a strong foothold in the state,' says CPIM Politburo member Mohammad Salim.

After losing the assembly elections in 2001 and the Lok Sabha elections in 2004, Mamata realized that she needed to sever ties with the BJP to capture the 25 per cent (then) minority votes that mostly remained with the Congress and the Left.

'I won't say Mamata Banerjee is communal, but she lacks the understanding of history. A popular perception was created that through various doles to the Muslim clerics and sharing the stage with the imams, she was appeasing the Muslims. But if you look at the statistics, the percentage of minority undertrials is more than the percentage of Muslims in government jobs in West Bengal,' says Suvashis Maitra.

There is another view that the polarization has always been there in West Bengal politics and the Left had nurtured it subtly. It is true that former chief minister of West Bengal Jyoti Basu had not allowed veteran BJP leader Lal Krishna Advani's Ram Rath to enter the state in the 1990s and had called the first NDA government 'a barbaric government by uncivilized people'. At the same time, the Left Front could not come entirely out of the communal calculations in the state. 'When the Left regime was at its peak, they also did not dare to put up a Hindu candidate in a Muslim dominated area. They have always favoured a minority candidate there. So the communal undercurrent has always been there in Bengal,' says Rantidev Sengupta, the editor of the RSS's Bengali mouthpiece *Swastika*.

However, despite having a separate Minority Development Financial Corporation and the minority development department in the West Bengal government, there have not been many efforts to uplift the community as a whole. The top leadership of the CPIM in Bengal was devoid of any Muslim face in the three decades they ruled the state until Md Salim, the former minister and MP, was elevated in the state secretariat and later in the politburo.

The minorities had also gradually started shifting their allegiance from the Left when in 2001, the then chief minister, Buddhadeb Bhattacharjee, from the corridors of the state secretariat, said that some madrassas in the state were turning out to be hotbeds of Muslim fundamentalism. Though he was not completely wrong (as was proved much later when the Khagragarh blast took place in 2014), he could not crack down on such unaffiliated madrassas. Moreover, the state's minority leaders did not appreciate the way Buddhadeb Bhattacharjee was hobnobbing with the then union home minister, L.K. Advani, during the first NDA government.

The 2006 Sachar Committee report was another evidence of the poor condition of Muslims in Bengal. The report on the social, economic and educational status of Muslims in the country placed Bengal in the category of the worst performing states.

Around the same time, the Left Front government suffered another setback which caused further damage to their support base among the minority community. A Muslim youth, Rizwanur Rahman, committed suicide after marrying a Hindu Marwari girl on 21 September 2007. Apparently, her industrialist father had taken the help of the top brass of the Kolkata Police to allegedly abet Rizwanur's suicide. A large section of the Muslim community turned hostile towards the Left Front government.

The Left's hypocrisy was also exposed in 2008 when they forced the exiled Bangladeshi author Taslima Nasrin to leave Kolkata under pressure after an alleged 'planned and coordinated' riot (as the then Chief of Police of Kolkata Gautam Mohan Chakraborty told the journalists) happened in the heart of Kolkata. 'That was a grave mistake by the Left. They had bowed down to the pressure of some Muslim fundamentalists and forced Taslima to leave Bengal. This was nothing but Muslim appeasement,' says journalist Biswajit Bhattacharya.

Rejjak Mollah, a former minister in the Left Front government, had informed[7] the party leadership that the Muslim and Scheduled Caste population comprised most of the peasants and landless labourers in the state. Still, they were not taken into confidence while launching the industrialization process by large-scale land acquisition. This policy decision by the Left Front government angered the section of the population that had participated in the resistance movements in large numbers. The land acquisition efforts in the minority-dominated Nandigram for a chemical hub and the infrastructure projects in Bhangar, Amdanga and some other parts of North 24 Parganas district alienated the Muslims from the Left.

Later, there were many deliberations over the issues of minorities within the CPIM and the Left Front as they were desperate to win back the faith of the minorities, but they could not recover lost ground.

It was at this juncture that Mamata Banerjee cemented her position among the minorities, leading the anti-land acquisition movements. She could feel the tides turning. During her dharna in Singur, I had to wait for over half an hour for an interview she had promised because she had gone to offer namaz and attend iftar. She would wear a hijab to perform the rituals. The symbolic gesture of wearing the hijab was unnecessary but politically expedient.

In 2011, the minorities of Bengal, like a large section of the electorate, voted for Mamata. She wanted to project that she was the messiah of the minorities and she knew holding on to this vote bank would give her electoral dividends in the future. On the occasion of Independence Day celebrations in 2011, people were

[7] Roy, R. *Business Standard*. 'Change in Muslim stand towards CPI(M) in Bengal'. 20 January 2013.

aghast to see Mamata Banerjee covered from her head to the shoulders in a white cloth as she stepped out of her car in front of the Writers' Building. She was probably trying to send a message to the minority community. Mamata made it mandatory for herself to be present at the central morning namaz on Eid at Red Road in Kolkata. So, it's safe to derive that symbolism was present even before she became the chief minister and continued with the agenda after. Mamata was always confident of having the backing of minorities.

'After Mamata came to power, she launched her Muslim appeasement politics in a naked way. This was the mistake she committed. When she was voted to power in 2011, she got the votes of both majority and minority communities in a big way. So it was unnecessary,' says Rantidev.

The first move that put a seal on the allegations of Muslim appeasement against Mamata was the decision to provide an allowance of ₹2,500 to the imams and ₹1,500 to the muezzins of masjids across the state. Her decision to give imam *bhata* (an allowance to Muslim priests) was challenged in court. The court questioned how she could spend money from the government exchequer on such schemes and declared it unconstitutional. She was adamant and went on with her plan by allocating about ₹500 crore to pay the allowance to imams and muezzins through the Wakf Board. This decision irked many in the state. With this allowance, she wanted to influence those Muslim leaders who had the power to mobilize a large section of the community. Imams are clerics who sermonize during Friday prayers. She happily accommodated this section in her scheme of things to woo minorities. This is the reason why Mamata preferred the hardliners in the community over progressive Bengali Muslim intellectuals.

It explains why people like Syed Mohammad Noor ur Rahman Barkati, the then Shahi Imam of Kolkata's Tipu Sultan Masjid, got to share the dais with Mamata, and Siddikullah Chowdhury, president of the Jamiat Ulema-e-Hind's Bengal branch, who openly refused to accept the Supreme Court order on Triple Talaq, got a place in Mamata's cabinet in 2016. Hard-line Muslim leaders surrounded the chief minister and blinded by the minority vote bank, she allowed them to get powerful.

'Posters showing Mamata wearing a hijab, the government providing imam *bhata*, hobnobbing with the Muslim clerics, created a wave in the state; this Mamata Banerjee's government is for the Muslims and does not work for the Hindus. She would not protect the Hindu interest. This gave leverage to the BJP,' explains Rantidev.

The fertile ground of communal politics was once again revived by Bengal Chief Minister Mamata Banerjee and the BJP, which was not pro-active before. However, the BJP got a golden opportunity to assert their presence and mobilize the people creating the same fear of Muslim domination over the majority Hindus that had created much tension in this part of the country during the 1940s.

KHAGRAGARH: A LANDMARK IN MINORITY APPEASEMENT

The BJP's pitch against Mamata's minority appeasement got further momentum when Bangladeshi terrorists were found hiding in the heart of Burdwan, a district town. Just a few kilometres away from the Burdwan station, a moram (red soil) lane off the G.T. Road takes you to a quiet neighbourhood called Khagragarh. About 200 metres down the lane, a two-storied building at the corner of the lane taking a slight left turn, witnessed an explosion on 2 October 2014. The local people panicked and immediately called the police. Smoke was billowing out of the first floor of the building where two couples had been staying for the last few months on rent. The gate that led to the stairs to the first floor was locked. When police and the fire brigade officials reached the spot to rescue the residents of the building, two women, who had survived the blast, refused to open the door. They even threatened to shoot the officers. By that time, the residents spotted blood coming out of the pipe connecting the first floor and the drain. After much pressure, the door was opened.

The police recovered two dead bodies, one injured man and two women with a baby. The two dead men were identified as Shovan Mandal and Shakil Ahmed, also known as Ghazi. The injured man was identified as Abdul Halim, also known as a Hasan Saheb. The two women who were later arrested were Ahmed's wife, Rumi Bibi, and Halim's wife, Amina Bibi.

This explosion on the eve of Durga Puja in Bengal was almost waved off as just another crude bomb blast, common in politically volatile West Bengal. No one noticed the fact that, initially, the women had refused to open the door and had even threatened to shoot the policemen. No one bothered to find out what they were doing for so long before they gave fire brigade and the police access to their rooms. The building which housed a TMC party office on the ground floor did not raise any suspicion about what these men were up to in the minds of the workers of the ruling party. The landlord, a local TMC leader, Nurul Hasan Chowdhury, who had rented out the first floor of the building to the couple on the recommendation of the cleric of the local masjid, did not know who used to visit the couple and what they carried in the big bags that used to be ferried on motorbike every other day.

The gruesome details of the incident got drowned in the buzz of Durga Puja celebrations. After the Puja was over and the National Intelligence Agency (NIA) took over the case from the West Bengal Police, chilling details started coming out. It was found that the men in that building were making improvised bombs to be supplied to the Jamaat-ul-Mujahideen Bangladesh (JMB) terrorists across the border. A huge network of JMB terrorists who were opposed to the Sheikh Hasina government in Bangladesh was in operation in at least four districts of Bengal. Immediately after the blast, the two women were trying to clean the blood and burn the fundamentalist literature and pamphlets calling for Jihad. The user manual for making improvised bombs and a DVD supporting Al Qaeda and Chechen rebels were also recovered.

The Khagragarh blast is a glaring example of how the TMC party apparatus and the police as well as the administration underplayed suspicious activities on the fringes of a prominent town in Bengal. No one had any clue that such a huge network was in operation for so long. About 20 kilometres from the blast site, in a madrassa in Shimulia in Burdwan district, a training camp was being run by the JMB. It was using Bengal as their sanctuary and a recruitment field. By the time police activated a serious investigation, all the madrassas were used by the JMB terrorists were vacated and there was almost no trace of the network. Almost ten days after the blast, just a kilometre away from the blast site, another rented, under-construction accommodation of one of the terrorists was found stacked with explosives and live bombs.

NIA's bomb disposal squad helped the West Bengal Police disarm the bombs. There too the residents were clueless about the activities of their neighbours. In West Bengal, where every inch of the state has been politicized, it was shocking to see such apathy on the part of the people and the political leaders to gather information about each other. Moreover, the police, if serious, should have suspected something bigger was at play on the basis of the intelligence inputs.

This incident put a question mark on the seriousness of the Mamata Banerjee government in tackling fundamentalist activities in the state. The BJP soon took up the issue, alleging that the Mamata Banerjee government was soft on terrorism and was letting the state be used by foreign nationals working against the government in the neighbouring country of Bangladesh.

Mamata was unhappy with the way she had to hand over the case to the NIA against her will. She expressed her displeasure to National Security Advisor Ajit Doval who met her in Kolkata after visiting the Khagragarh blast site.

Many reports at the time also claimed that the ruling party had a tacit understanding with the fundamentalist elements across the border in Bangladesh. The role of one of her MPs, Ahmed Hassan Imran, was also questioned. He was a student leader of the banned minority students' organization—Students' Islamic Movement of India (SIMI). He told me during an interview that he had nothing to do with any banned organization and that he had been a SIMI leader before the outfit was banned. The Opposition claimed that he had helped the Jamat in Bangladesh by siphoning off money. Nothing could be proved, but it raised several questions about Mamata Banerjee's functioning. Mamata had nominated Imran to the Rajya Sabha when he was the editor of a Bengali daily for the minority community, *Kalam*, which later got the patronage of Saradha chit fund boss Sudipta

Sen. The Opposition, however, found a bigger stratagem behind this nomination.

On 30 November 2014, in his first major public meeting in Kolkata after Narendra Modi came to power at the Centre, Amit Shah said, 'Bengal needs a patriotic government, which doesn't save the culprits of the Burdwan blast, which does not indulge in corruption. Our mission is to make Bengal a TMC-free state, and looking at the huge gathering, I am sure that the countdown for the Mamata-led TMC government has begun.'[8]

In the same rally, Amit Shah drew a connection between the TMC–Saradha chit fund money and the JMB terrorists, directly accusing the TMC of being involved in the Khagragarh blast. 'Saradha chit fund money was used in the Burdwan blast. The NIA is not being allowed to probe the blast properly. Hurdles are being created. It is being done in order to save TMC leaders who are involved in the blast' he said.[9]

Though the then MoS, PMO, Jitendra Singh, told the Parliament that the NIA probe had not found any link between the TMC–Saradha chit fund money and the JMB terrorist network yet, a narrative was getting stronger that Mamata Banerjee and her party were 'anti-national' (not patriotic) and shielding the terrorists (culprits of the Burdwan blast) who belonged to the minority community. This was good enough to gradually consolidate the majority votes against Mamata.

As Mamata once refused to give a reaction to Amit Shah's comments saying, 'Who is Amit Shah?', the BJP national president from the public meeting on

---

[8] Ali, A. *Indian Express*. 'Begal needs a patriotic govt that doesn't save the Burdwan blast culprits: Amit Shah'. 30 November 2014.

[9] Ibid.

30 November 2014 replied to Mamata's jibe, 'I am Amit Shah, a BJP worker. I have come to Bengal to uproot TMC.' It was clear that with the end of the Vajpayee–Advani era, the political game plan of the BJP was changing fast. The Amit Shah–Narendra Modi duo was not going to spare Mamata Banerjee any more. Her Muslim appeasement policies along with corruption were going to be the main weapons of the saffron camp.

POLITICS OF RIOTS

Mamata's inaction against the culprits who belonged to the minority community and her attitude of denial were again exposed during an incident of rioting in Malda's Kaliachak in 2016. The villagers protesting against a self-proclaimed Hindu Mahasabha leader Kamalesh Tiwari's alleged comments against Prophet Muhammad ransacked the police station and destroyed documents, and computers, and nearly two dozen police vehicles, including one belonging to the Border Security Force, were set ablaze. The violent protestors also ransacked the office of the BDO-Kaliachak I. They also put up a *rail roko* at nearby Khaltipur railway station. When the police tried to remove the agitators, a clash between the mob and the police broke out injuring several policemen. The police could not prevent the backlash by the villagers of this minority-dominated border district. They did arrest some offenders, but the chief minister did not condemn the incident vigorously.

Some reports suggested that there was cross-border infiltration and miscreants from across the border had joined hands with the local criminals to target the police station. Here, we must note that the government agencies have time and again accepted that Kaliachak, a small region in the Malda district of West Bengal sharing a border with Bangladesh, has been the hub of a fake currency racket. Way back in 2012, the then additional director general (East) of the Border Security Force (BSF) had told media persons that Kaliachak had become the nerve centre of the fake currency trade.[10] The racket in Malda operated along with its counterpart in Bangladesh from where the fake currency notes were supplied to this part of the border and then were distributed across the country. This provided more ammunition to BJP's polarization agenda.

Swapan Dasgupta, a BJP MP, writes, 'It would seem that the area has increasingly become a no-go area for the local police because the criminal groups have taken full advantage of the West Bengal government's known reluctance to do anything that could be interpreted as offending minority sentiments. This is the same logic that explains the ease with which criminal networks thrive in some Muslim ghettos in Kolkata and neighbouring South 24 Parganas.'[11]

Though it was not exactly a riot in the proper sense of the term and the government preferred to call it violence, but Kaliachak incident was the beginning of regular sporadic riot-like situations in Bengal under Mamata Banerjee's rule, with the growing clout of the BJP in certain pockets.

'It was seen that police hesitated to take action against perpetrators of communal tension in different pockets in the state simply because they belonged to the ruling

[10] Express News Service. *Indian Express*. 'Malda's Kaliachak is hub of fake note smuggling: BSF'. 1 October 2012.

[11] Dasgupta, S. *The Asian Age*. 'Why the "nation" fell silent on Kaliachak'. 7 January 2016.

party. It emboldened the rogue communal elements,' says Suvashis Maitra.

In such a volatile atmosphere where police were getting intimidated and a few criminal-minority links were emerging, insecurity of the Hindus in the Muslim-dominated districts was getting endorsements by incidents like Kaliachak. What also grabbed attention was the brazenness of the Muslim youths in various minority-dominated areas.

When I visited Sankrail in Howrah, about 15 kilometres from Kolkata, after an incident of communal violence, a local Hindu shopkeeper told me, 'The Muslim youths are aggressive these days. They are getting hard cash from the tailoring business, dominated by their community, and bringing a different culture to our locality. They speed away on their bikes and tease girls and hit cycles or people. If anyone raises their voice, it leads to a fight in which two communities get divided.' Another local, a Muslim man who runs a chicken shop, lamented, 'The Muslims and Hindus were good friends. Now, things are changing drastically.'

Either because of social insecurity or empowered by the ruling party's patronage, the Muslim community was asserting themselves like never before, something that did not go down well with the Hindus. Similar incidents were observed in other Muslim-dominated pockets such as Park Circus, Raja Bazar, Metiabruz and Khidderpore in Kolkata.

The balance of power between the two communities was changing, and some fringe Hindu groups such as Hindu Sanhati, Bajrang Dal and VHP were gaining ground. A number of riots between the two communities in Dhulagarh in Howrah, Bhatpara and Basirhat in North 24 Parganas and Asansol town in Asansol district were reported following the Kaliachak incident.

There were often allegations that the local TMC leaders supported the Muslims during the violence and the Hindus had no option but to seek protection under the BJP umbrella or that of the fringe Hindu organizations. A police officer, on the condition of anonymity, said, 'My hands were tied during Dhulagarh riot. I knew I had to be strict to maintain law and order. But there was no instruction from the top administration. We had to hold ourselves back.'

It may seem unrelated, but it is important to note here the incidents revolving the killing of Tapas Chowdhury, a special-branch police officer on duty during a college students' union election in Garden Reach on 12 February 2013. Soon after the incident in this minority-dominated locality in Kolkata, Urban Development Minister Firhad Hakim claimed that the associates of local Congress leader Mukhtar were behind this killing.[12] Much to the minister's embarrassment, camera footage caught during the incident by a young video journalist of a local channel showed the assailant while shooting the police officer and it was clear that TMC leader Mohammed Iqbal alias Munna was behind the killing. He was seen attempting to assault a police officer, instigating the mob and, most importantly, the assailant was seen next to Munna when he was addressing the media.[13] Later, a local TV channel broadcast a conversation Munna had with someone over the phone where he was heard saying, 'I am silent. Should I go underground for some time? You find out...ask Firhad Hakim saab to find out if I am telling anything to anyone...you ask Firhad Hakim

---

[12] ABP Ananda. 2013. 'Bobby Hakim on college clash'. *YouTube*, 11 February. Available at: https://youtu.be/TA9wwISl_jw

[13] ABP Ananda. 2013. 'Gardenrich college clash: TMC councillor Iqbal still not arrested'. *YouTube*, 13 February. Available at: https://www.youtube.com/watch?v=NbUrChFCoAI&feature=youtu.be

saab what should I do? Go away from here?'[14] As soon as the then Kolkata Police Commissioner Ranjit Kumar Pachnanda reached the local Garden Reach police station, he was gheraoed by the officers of his force. He sat in the office of the OC and asked his men to go out and get the killer. He told them that he would wait till they brought the killer to the police station. He had no other option to boost the morale of his force. He defied every attempt by the powerful ministers in Mamata Banerjee's government to alter the FIR and make the local TMC leader look innocent. Pachnanda stood his ground and within two hours, the shooter Suvan was arrested from a local TMC party office by the Anti Rowdy Squad of Kolkata Police.[15] However, Pachnanda lost his job a day after taking action against Munna. Pachnanda's dismissal enforced the notion that Muslim leaders, under the patronage of the ruling establishment, could get away with any crime. Any action against them would mean punishment for the officers on duty.

Visits to riot-hit areas also revealed that moderates in the Muslim community were slowly disappearing. Mohammed Salim says, 'During the Left rule, wherever there was any communal tension, local leaders from both the communities used to intervene and defuse the situation. Unfortunately, during Mamata's regime, the moderate leaders have no space in such a situation.' The community leaders believe in a show of strength. It's why when Maulana Imdadul Rashidi, an imam of an Asansol mosque, who lost his son to communal

---

[14] ABP Ananda. 2013. 'Senior minister asked Iqbal to go underground'. *YouTube*, 14 February. Available at: https://www.youtube.com/watch?v=Gso0pSI_kj8&feature=youtu.be

[15] TNN *Times of India*. 'Pachnanda sacked for doing his jobs, says cops', 16 February. 2013.

violence in April 2018, refused to name the suspects and appealed for calm, the news report was dubbed as 'fake' by Right-wing supporters. His own community leaders ignored the appeal as well.

A mobilization among both, the minorities as well as the Hindus, was going on to show their strength or find shelter in the time of communal tension. The growing number of Bajrangbali or Shiv temples in almost every neighbourhood was a reflection of the communal assertion by the Hindus while Muslims opened up mosques in those areas of Kolkata that until recently had not heard any azaan. 'This is what we call competitive communalism being practised by BJP and TMC. The Hindus were getting the patronage of the BJP while minorities came under Mamata's umbrella,' says Md Salim.

The mainstream media seldom report incidents of communal violence in great detail. Following classic rules of journalism, editors generally do not highlight such incidents, lest it fans more violence in parts of the state which are not directly affected by the situation. However, social media has changed this situation. Propaganda, fake news and incidents of communal violence have started surfacing through citizen journalism. The government, too, could not deny it for long. During the Baduria riots in July 2017, the chief minister, for the first time, had to step up and condemn the attitude of the minority community leaders. The riots started after a boy forwarded a meme on the Prophet. Even after Mamata's government took action against the boy, the rioting continued. There was instigation by the fringe Hindu groups in this case. But, Mamata could not handle the pressure from the Governor, who had asked for reports on the situation. Without naming anyone, she stated in a press conference on 4 July 2018,

'I am sorry to say, [but] because of your [rioters] deeds, my head was bowed before the Governor.'

THE BJP CAPITALIZING ON THE ISSUES OF MINORITY APPEASEMENT

Even in such a communally charged atmosphere, one didn't notice the BJP taking charge. It was the fringe Hindu organizations which took the lead and did the groundwork. Lesser-known organizations like the Hindu Sanhati, under the leadership of the late Tapan Ghosh (who was once a part of the RSS) were at the forefront of mobilizing Hindus against the Muslims in the state. They reached wherever and whenever Hindus were attacked. They were in constant touch with the mainstream media to highlight the issues of atrocities against Hindus by the minorities. Hindu Sanhati, which was an offshoot of the RSS, also worked relentlessly against Love Jihad.

The central BJP leadership was still sceptical of how communalization would work in Bengal and restrained itself from openly supporting the efforts of the likes of Hindu Sanhati at the ground level. The Bajrang Dal too was involved in mobilizing Hindus in minority-dominated areas. They would help Hindus build temples or raise saffron flags on top of buildings in the locality to assert their position. The VHP organized 'conversion' programmes in various parts of the state. The converted Christians and Muslims were reconverted to Hinduism in those camps. The RSS with its numerous shakhas in the state helped in the process. Though the BJP gained from the activities of these aggressive fringe Hindu organizations, the leadership of the party did not directly engage themselves with these activists.

As the fringe Hindu groups worked at the grassroots level, the BJP took up the issue in the mainstream. They repeatedly attacked Mamata's appeasement politics, ultimately leading to a societal change. In the fertile ground of politics of polarization, the BJP went step by step to build a narrative against Mamata.

There were many strands in the BJP's strategy against Mamata's appeasement politics. Social media was flooded with memes of Mamata wearing a hijab and she was branded 'Begum Mamata' by Right-wing activists. Portraying Mamata as pro-Muslim was the first step. Rather than going for provocative communal speeches, the BJP leaders improvised their Hindutva agenda for Bengal quite subtly to counter Mamata. Encouraging Bangladeshi (Muslim) infiltration, not allowing Durga and Saraswati Puja in schools and compromising national security were few of the allegations that the BJP levied against her.

Bangladeshi infiltration had been a key issue for long in Bengal. The BJP state unit had time and again published leaflets, booklets and white papers on it. It was an issue that the BJP often highlighted and they even associated Mamata's appeasement politics with Bangladeshi infiltration. 'It looks so interesting that the leader [Mamata Banerjee] who threw papers on the face of Lok Sabha Speaker Somnath Chatterjee for central and state government's inaction to stop Bangladeshi infiltration is now going all out to protect the illegal infiltrators for the political gains,' wonders BJP leader and former MLA Samik Bhattacharya.

The infiltrators who were mostly Bangladeshi Muslims were no doubt changing the demography of the border district. In some districts like Murshidabad and Malda, the Hindus turned out to be the minority.

Mamata, however, blamed the central government, saying, 'Who looks after the border? BSF. And they are under the Centre. They have to stop infiltration at the border.' It is imperative to note here that security experts have often pointed out that unchecked infiltration has been responsible for growing terrorist and antisocial activities in Bengal and India. They claim that terrorists are using Bengal and Kolkata as a safe passage for going in and out of the country.

Recently, some TMC leaders, in the guise of NGOs, also gave shelter to the Rohingyas in South 24 Parganas on humanitarian grounds. When the Narendra Modi government was vouching for deporting the Rohingya refugees who had taken shelter in India, here in West Bengal, under the banner of Desh Bachao Samajik Committee, a local TMC leader Hossain Gazi set up a camp for over 100 Rohingya refugees in Hardaha village in South 24 Parganas district. The state government allegedly did not follow the central government directives on Rohingya refugees and took no action against such a camp.

The BJP turned Mamata's soft corner for refugees and Bangladeshi migrants as a poll issue. They successfully projected that Mamata's attitude was causing law and order problems in the state and creating a serious threat to the country's security. Mamata, however, stuck to her stand and attributed her attitude to taking a humanitarian approach. In a press conference in state secretariat Nabanna, Mamata said, 'It is not the right decision by the central government to deport them [Rohingya Muslims], as not everyone is a terrorist...we have to think about several children among the Rohingya refugees. My party's view is that every community has good people and bad people. There is a difference between commoners and terrorists, and that terrorist should be firmly dealt with but commoners should not suffer.'[16]

[16] Nath, S. *News18*. 'Centre Should Not Deport Rohingya Refugees, Says Mamata Banerjee'. 18 September 2017.

During the Lok Sabha campaign, Narendra Modi and Amit Shah raised the issue of infiltration and said that they would extend the NRC to Bengal and enact the Citizenship Bill to single out infiltrators and throw them out of the country. The veiled attack was naturally aimed at the minority Muslims who migrated from Bangladesh. Mamata Banerjee opposed the move vehemently. The Assam experiment with the NRC was not a good experience and implementing it in Bengal would be difficult, as hordes of people had migrated to West Bengal from East Bengal during and after the Partition. Their relatives also kept visiting on this side of the border with some of them staying back in India permanently. So there has been a continuous flow of migrants through a porous Indo-Bangla border.

In 2014, Narendra Modi had made a mistake. He had told an election rally in Serampore that all the Bangladeshi (immigrants) living in Bengal would be sent back to Bangladesh. This did not go down well with the *Odeshi* population, people who came from Bangladesh as refugees during Partition. The remark intended towards Bangladeshi infiltrators angered this section of voters, who decided to vote against the BJP. In 2019, the BJP did not repeat the mistake. With the proposed Citizenship Bill, they categorized the refugees under Hindus and other minorities. Anyone other than Muslims, who had come to India from Bangladesh, Pakistan or Afghanistan, would be accorded Indian citizenship by the Modi government.

The idea that Narendra Modi would drive out Muslim infiltrators, who had once forced them into leaving Bangladesh, resonated with the Hindu refugees in Bengal. This proposition was well received by the Hindu refugees who had migrated to West Bengal in 1947 and 1971 or after that. Refugee colonies (no longer typical colonies of the past) which had supported the Left for a long time transferred their support to the BJP.

The same promise to the Matuas (namashudra Bangladeshi refugees following a cult formed by Hari Chand Thakur) about citizenship rights also worked in the BJP's favour. They shifted their allegiance from the TMC to the BJP. Political commentator Prasenjit Bose claims, 'Narendra Modi–Amit Shah's provocative campaign over NRC and Citizenship Amendment Bill polarized the East Bengal's Hindu refugees who had taken shelter in West Bengal. Trinamool failed to counter this. The Left and Congress are silent anyway.' He cites the recent Lok Sabha election results to show that compared to the 2016 Vidhan Sabha elections, the TMC's vote share has declined in 55 assembly constituencies out of which are reserved for Schedule Castes (it includes Matuas and a large section of Bangladeshi refugees mainly in the North Bengal) and Schedule Tribes. 'BJP ate up TMC's votes in bordering districts of Nadia and North 24 Parganas along with the North Bengal districts,' he adds.

The BJP also wanted to prove that Mamata was not just pro-Muslim but also anti-Hindu. A narrative was built around a few administrative decisions taken by her government with an anti-Hindu stance. Or at least that was what the BJP wanted us to believe. The narrative proclaimed that the Mamata Banerjee government does not allow Durga Puja and Saraswati Puja in the state and bans immersion of Durga idols to please Muslims. Also, they never failed to mention that Muharram processions get priority over Durga Puja immersions.

Two incidents helped the BJP create this narrative. A local dispute arose between the two communities in Birbhum district's Kanglapahari village. For a few years, the Hindu community in the village had raised objections to Eid celebrations as the Muslim community sacrificed goats and cows in the open during the festival. The Muslims then objected to Durga Puja celebrations. The dispute reached the administration and the officials asked both the communities to settle the issue amicably. Since they failed to resolve the issue, the administration declared that no festival could be celebrated in the village. However, the Right-wing only highlighted one part and left out the other. The BJP used this incident to project that the Mamata Banerjee government does not allow Durga Puja.

Another incident in Howrah district helped the BJP build the narrative that Mamata Banerjee does not allow Saraswati Puja in Bengal. In Tehatta High School in Uluberia, a communal tension erupted when some students wanted to observe Nabi Dibas (the day many Muslims in India observe Milad un-Nabi, which commemorates Prophet Muhammad's birthday) on the school premises. Despite the denial of permission by the school authority, some students allegedly observed it. When it came to Saraswati Puja, due to communal tension, the school authority for the first time in 65 years refused permission to this Hindu festival of worshipping the Goddess of Learning, which is performed in almost all the educational institutions in the state. The school was shut down for an indefinite period. When the students, demanding to reopen the school, blocked the National Highway, a clash broke out between the students and the police. The BJP and fringe Hindu organizations took the opportunity to attack the Mamata government on this issue as well.

Another administrative decision backfired for Mamata. In 2017, in an already volatile communal Bengal, Mamata Banerjee's government decided not to allow Durga Puja immersion and Muharram processions to take place at the same time. Since Durga Puja immersions can take place over a few days (it has become a norm in Bengal to stretch the four-day Durga Puja festival to seven or more days), the government ordered the immersion to be stopped on certain days to make way for Muharram processions, which is date-specific. It was purely an administrative decision. But, the BJP and other Hindu organizations moved the Calcutta High Court against the government order.

It is in this background that the Ram Navami narrative (described earlier) gathered force. Hindu organizations wanted to have armed Ram Navami rallies across the state. The Mamata Banerjee government banned such armed processions and the BJP cried foul. They accused Mamata Banerjee of being anti-Hindu. As mentioned earlier, they argued, 'If the Muslims can brandish crude weapons during Muharram, why can't the Hindus do the same?'

Another incident in North Dinajpur district's Islampur also helped the BJP mobilize Hindus. On 20 September 2018, a young boy allegedly died in police firing when students, provoked by some fringe Rightist organizations, became violent over the appointment of an Urdu teacher in Darivit High School. The students demanded a Bengali teacher instead of an Urdu teacher. The incident soon took a communal hue and the villagers did not allow the school to reopen for a long time. The BJP capitalized on the issue without highlighting the fact that some schools do need Urdu teachers. Moreover, Urdu was equated with the language of the Muslims and Bengali with the Hindus. There were administrative failures in tackling such situations. TMC's internal conflict in the school management committee was also responsible for the confusion over the requirement for a language teacher in the school.

It is in this communally charged Bengal that the BJP's Hindu majoritarian politics worked well, especially in Muslim-dominated areas like Malda and North Dinajpur, where the demography is heavily tilted towards the minorities. The BJP's Hindutva appeal struck a chord with the majority Hindus in the state. The Hindus who felt they were being side-lined by the minorities found shelter, at least psychologically, in the saffron camp. In some cases, the Hindus have asserted themselves under the patronage of the Right-wing organizations.

By highlighting such sporadic communal incidents, the BJP successfully spun the tale that the Hindus were being oppressed in Bengal by the excesses of the minority community, which had direct patronage from the government. They reinforced the idea that the BJP's Hindutva politics had given the Hindus a voice against such oppression. 'They [Muslims] must be taught a lesson', was a general feeling that helped BJP gain electorally.

A senior BJP leader told me, off the record, that he believed if the Muslims were under pressure from the Hindus and the Hindus dominated the community, Muslims wouldn't be able to raise their voices and show aggression. Thus, there will be fewer riots.

In this process of Hindutva empowerment, the BJP did not exclude the lower-caste Hindus or the Adivasis. This is the reason why saffron flags could be seen in Junglemahal; that the 'Jai Shri Ram' slogan is popular among the SC- and ST-dominated areas; and, why a large section of Adivasis did not care about the BJP's stance and treatment of tribals and Dalits in other parts of the country and flocked to the BJP. The result was that the BJP won most of the tribal-dominated seats in the northern and western parts of the state.

MAMATA'S WEAK RESPONSE

The Bengal chief minister is not the only politician who got trapped in the BJP's Hindutva narrative. Almost all non-BJP leaders in Indian politics got trapped in the majoritarian politics unleashed aggressively by the saffron camp, especially after Narendra Modi came to power in 2014. Mamata was not an exception. She lost her way in countering the BJP's politics of communal polarization. Instead of trying to establish a secular political narrative, she got trapped in trying to prove that she was a proud Hindu and pro-Hindu. This failure was due to the lack of a strong ideological standpoint. Like most Opposition parties, Mamata too never practised truly secular politics. Her tilt towards the minorities was exposed by the saffron camp.

When BJP state president Dilip Ghosh was chanting 'Jai Shri Ram' with a sword in one hand and a mace in the other, Mamata Banerjee was clueless and grasped at an appropriate response. She cried foul, arguing that this was not a tradition to celebrate Ram Navami in Bengal and that the BJP was importing an aggressive, distorted version of Hinduism. In several rallies, her speeches invoked Ramakrishna and Vivekananda's ideals of respecting all religions. However, she could not hold on to this narrative for a long. In the first year, when the BJP went all out to turn Ram Navami rallies into major events, the TMC decided to counter it with Hanuman Jayanti. Unofficially, the TMC leaders across the state got involved in organizing Hanuman Jayanti celebrations. The next year the TMC leaders, too, officially organized Ram Navami rallies. This created tension in various pockets of the state. It also proved a bankruptcy of ideas on the part of the Trinamool to counter the BJP's 'Ram' narrative.

Instead of countering the BJP's aggressive Hindutva pitch, Mamata started a temple run to prove her Hindutva credentials. She rushed to the Kapilmuni Ashram in Gangasagar in South 24 Parganas in 2018 for the first time since becoming the chief minister and announced a bouquet of development projects around the temple. The Bengal chief minister even attended programmes commemorating a religious cult figure, Loknath Baba, apparently to boost her pro-Hindu image. Mamata, who unfailingly visited Durga Puja pandals even as an Opposition leader, had to publicize her visits to pandals and display her knowledge of Chandi by reciting couplets. At every rally, she chanted the Gayatri Mantra, Kali Mantra, Durga Naam just to prove that she was a devout Hindu. Mamata Banerjee, who has been worshipping Goddess Kali at home since she was a teenager, started narrating at every gathering how her family performed the Kali Puja at home to showcase her Hindu credentials.

Criticizing the Hindutva ideology being propagated by the BJP, she told rallies, 'I am a born Hindu. But I am not part of the Hindutva that divides society.' Referring to the BJP's objection to eating beef, she said, 'Why should a political party dictate what one should eat or wear?'

She used to hold the Sanhati Divas rally every year on 6 December, the day Babri Masjid was demolished. In 2017, Mamata addressed the rally and said, 'There are 31 per cent Muslim brothers and sisters. It is my duty to protect them. If you call it appeasement, I don't care.' The next year, her party did not organize the rally. She stopped uttering the words 'Inshallah' as many times as she used to during her speeches. Clerics like Barkati were no longer seen on stage with Mamata. In 2015, at her flagship 21 July Shahid Divas rally, Mamata Banerjee had been heard blowing her own trumpet for introducing the imam *bhata*, but in 2017, she did not utter a word about the same. Instead, her government planned to introduce an allowance for Hindu priests (ultimately implemented it in September 2020). The Birbhum district TMC president Anubrata Mondal, organized a Purohit sammelan (Hindu priests' conference) and distributed the Bhagvad Gita and other materials to Hindu priests. Mondal, who has a larger-than-life image, bowed before Hindu priests and stressing on the importance of priests in society, he said, 'You are required at every occasion, be it birth, death, wedding or rice ceremony. God cannot be worshipped without you. The society cannot run without you. Please forgive me if I have said anything wrong.' He even told the conference that he had asked Animal Husbandry Minister Swapan Debnath to provide 5,000 cows, which he intended to distribute among the poor in his locality.

Mamata and her party men had to transform themselves under pressure from the Hindutva brigade. For the first time, during the 2017 Baduria riots, while coming down heavily on both community leaders involved in communal violence, Mamata Banerjee told a news conference at the state secretariat, Nabanna, 'Police had immediately arrested the boy. It should have been controlled soon after the arrest was made. An incident took place. Police took action according to the complaint. What did we see? Another group had gone and created the communal flare-up. We could not sleep last night. Two groups, of Hindus and Muslims, are rioting over a Facebook post. How many Facebook accounts will you block? How many Twitter accounts will you block? It is sad for the country if you indulge in riots because of a Facebook post.'

But Mamata Banerjee could not escape the narrative that the TMC was for the Muslims and the BJP was for the Hindus. She was neither into soft-Hindutva nor hard-Hindutva campaigns. Unlike many other Opposition leaders in the country, she also failed to understand and formulate a counter-strategy, even after realizing that the BJP and RSS aim to create a Hindu nationalist majoritarian country, undermining the constitutional nationalism followed by India since Independence. Instead of the Nehruvian ideology highly influenced by Western thinkers and models, the BJP–RSS wants to follow an ideology based on the Hindu concept of Bharat. Thus, instead of visiting temples and trying to adopt the soft-Hindutva narrative, leaders such as Mamata Banerjee should think of an alternative narrative based on constitutional nationalism and secularism. In his speech at the RSS headquarters in Nagpur, former President of India Pranab Mukherjee, had reminded the country, 'The soul of India resides in pluralism and tolerance.'[17] Referring to the history of Indian civilisation in his speech, Mukherjee had detailed the essence of constitutional nationalism as opposed to Hindu nationalism, 'The Indian Constitution, consisting of 395 articles and 12 schedules, is not merely a legal document but a Magna Carta of socio-economic transformation of the country. It represents the hopes and aspirations of the billion plus Indians. From our constitution flows our nationalism. The construct of Indian nationalism is "Constitutional Patriotism", which consists of an appreciation of our inherited and shared diversity; a readiness to enact one's citizenship at different levels; the ability to self-correct and learn from others.' The idea that Mukherjee could outline this in

[17] *Livemint*. 'Full text of Pranab Mukherjee's RSS speech in Nagpur'. 7 January 2018.

front of the top brass of the RSS in their own den perhaps could not be picked up by those political leaders who wanted to counter the Modi brigade. Opposition leaders have neither understood the fact nor tried to carry the message to the masses that secularism does not mean being soft on a particular religion and its followers. That is why it has been easy for the Modi–Shah camp to equate secularism with Muslim appeasement because of the policies followed by most of the Opposition leaders.

The BJP, in turn, has turned it into a victory for themselves by forcing Mamata to toe the 'Hindutva' line. She was forced to use the Hindutva card much more than the saffron leaders. Since Mamata Banerjee failed to come up with a strong counter-narrative, she should have concentrated on her development pitch. However, since 2017, Bengal has been so communally polarized that no other agenda seems to be working in Mamata's favour, at least till the 2019 Lok Sabha elections.

4

BJP's Organization and RSS's Groundwork

'I have to stick to the wicket,' said Trinamool's Mr Fixit Mukul Roy, as he took a drag of his cigarette while informally chatting with the journalists in his chamber at Kolkata's Nizam Palace. The year was 2017. Once a confidant of Mamata Banerjee, Mukul Roy now found himself isolated and unwanted as the CBI closed in on him in connection with the Saradha chit fund scam. The jailed TMC MP, Kunal Ghosh, had accused top TMC leaders, including Mukul Roy, of siphoning off money from Saradha's account to the TMC's coffers. Sensing trouble, Mamata had distanced herself from Mukul Roy as his arrest seemed imminent. A distressed Mukul Roy was desperate for shelter. He ran around Delhi, trying to meet the BJP's Bengal observer Kailash Vijayvargiya and the then Bengal Congress chief, Adhir Chowdhury. But, since journalists were trying to trace his movements in the capital, he simply kept driving around and returned to his flat without meeting anyone.

Joining the BJP had seemed like a long shot then. For one, on 30 November 2014, the former BJP central observer of Bengal, Siddharth Nath Singh, had said at a public rally in Kolkata's Dharmatala, '*Bhaag* Mukul *bhaag*' (run Mukul run) in the same breath as '*Bhaag*

Mamata *bhaag*' ('run Mamata run'). Siddharth Nath Singh later elaborated, 'Neither am I an astrologer nor do I have control over CBI. But what can I do? The acts of your [Mamata Banerjee's] party leaders are such that they have to go to jail. It was your party MP Kunal Ghosh who spilt the beans. In 2015, it will be *Bhaag* Mukul *Bhaag*. In 2016, it will be *Bhaag* Mamata *Bhaag*.'[1] He essentially meant that Mukul Roy and Mamata Banerjee would get arrested in connection with the Saradha chit fund scam. After such a public stance, it was difficult for the BJP central leadership to co-opt Mukul Roy into the party fold. The state BJP president, Dilip Ghosh, too was not in favour of taking him on board. Mukul Roy, in turn, completely ignored the BJP state leadership while lobbying for his entry into the saffron fold. On the eve of Durga Puja in 2017, Dilip Ghosh said, 'He [Roy] is a big leader. I am not aware whether he will join the BJP. But he is in touch with our leaders in New Delhi.'

A few days later, in October 2017, on the side-lines of a party meeting in North Bengal's Jalpaiguri district, Dilip Ghosh said, 'We want the curiosity over Mukul Roy to survive for a few more days. What Mukul Roy will do depends on him. He did not say that he would join the BJP. But the media wants him to join BJP. If he thinks BJP is a fit for him, then let him come. We will also see if he is fit for us.'[2] In a private conversation, a central BJP leader who was working in Bengal had said, quite confidently, 'Mark my words, we are not going to take him.'

---

[1] PTI. *Financial Express*. 'It will be Bhag Mamata Bhag in 2016: Siddharth Nath Singh'. 23 December 2014.

[2] *Anandabazar Patrika*. 'Mukul also deserves justice, said Dilip'. 27 October 2017.

THE ROY FACTOR

Mukul Roy ultimately had the last laugh. After constant lobbying with the help of the BJP's central observer and national general secretary, Kailash Vijayvargiya, he was finally inducted into the party in Delhi on 3 November 2017. Union Law Minister Ravi Shankar Prasad and Vijayvargiya were present at the event. The BJP national president, Amit Shah, was present at the party office and met Mukul after the induction, but neither did he attend the induction press conference nor hand over the party flag to him, thereby, clearly indicating that Mukul Roy had to prove himself useful to share the same dais with the party president. Ravi Shankar Prasad told the media gathering, 'We welcome him. He has been an MP for 12 years and has served as the shipping and railway minister [of state]. He toiled for expansion of Trinamool and [for] 30 years, he fought against the atrocities and excesses of CPM in an effective manner. BJP will expand and benefit in Bengal from his experience.'[3]

Mukul Roy's induction in the BJP was in line with the policy Amit Shah and Narendra Modi had adopted to expand the party. To some extent, they also undermined the state leadership in paving way for Mukul Roy's entry into the saffron fold.

In other states too Modi and Shah followed a similar strategy and poached leaders from their Opposition camp. In Assam, the then finance minister in the Congress' Tarun Gogoi government, Himanta Biswa Sarma, was inducted on the eve of Assam assembly elections in 2016. Like Mukul Roy, Himanta too had been interrogated by the CBI in connection with Saradha chit fund scam. In July 2015, BJP leadership had brought out a booklet

[3] ET Bureau. *Economic Times*. 'Mukul Roy joins BJP, says law will take own course in Saradha chit fund scam'. 3 November 2017.

in Delhi accusing Himanta of his involvement in the Guwahati Water Supply Scam of 2010.[4] Many believed that the booklet was proof that the BJP had shut its doors on Sarma. However, there were rumours that the one-time trusted lieutenant of Tarun Gogoi was in touch with the BJP. A few months later, Sarma emerged as a key player in the BJP's victory in Assam and its political expansion in other North-Eastern states. He, along with the then BJP General Secretary Ram Madhav, worked hard to capture power in Manipur, Mizoram and Tripura. Though he was a strong contender for the Assam CM's post, the BJP denied him that chance. Himanta had to settle for the finance department.

In BJP's successful Tripura experiment of building its organization from scratch, mobilizing its cadres, allying with the tribal outfit—Indigenous People's Front of Tripura (IPFT)—and defeating the 25-year-old Left Front government, poaching the Opposition leaders was an important part. Congress-turned-Trinamool leader Sudip Roy Burman had a significant role to play in the BJP's political game plan and, thus, he was wholeheartedly welcomed by BJP President Amit Shah. In other states too, the BJP had applied the same policy time and again. Like in Gujarat, a stronghold of the BJP, they kept on poaching Opposition leaders. In 2012, they inducted the Congress's Narahari Amin and in 2014, the BJP welcomed former Congress MLA and MP Vitthalbhai Hansrajbhai Radadiya (who died in July 2018).

So, inducting Mukul was part of a similar plan for the BJP top brass. Modi–Shah's one-point agenda was to weaken Mamata Banerjee in Bengal. Inducting Mukul also meant a big blow to the Trinamool as he looked

---

[4] *Assam Tribune*. 'Himanta key suspect in water supply scam: BJP'. 22 July 2015.

after its organizational set-up. They knew that even though the BJP vote share had gone up to 17 per cent in the 2014 Lok Sabha elections, they were in no position to face the TMC. They needed to weaken the TMC organizationally with the help of Mukul Roy while strengthening their own party.

Mukul Roy's entry into the two-storied BJP party office in central Kolkata's Muralidhar Sen Lane brought a drastic change. The reception he was given after landing at the Kolkata airport after his induction into the BJP made the state leadership nervous. Thousands of supporters, mostly Mukul's men, welcomed him. The small party office was full of 'his men'. The BJP old-timers took a backseat as Mukul was in the limelight. Once, Mukul Roy even had to plead with the media persons to attend Dilip Ghosh's press conference on the ground floor as everyone was busy asking him questions.

This was indeed a paradigm shift in the state BJP. Many leaders had defected earlier, but this was the first time someone without an RSS background or without going through the BJP's ideological training had risen to the top level instantly. The state BJP leaders couldn't do much as Mukul Roy was the central leadership's recruit and they knew very well that ideological dilution was not new to the top leadership. It was simply a political strategy keeping in mind the long-term goal of overthrowing the ruling TMC.

A seasoned politician, Mukul Roy knew what he had jumped into. In the press conference that followed his entry into the BJP state headquarters, Mukul Roy tried to ease the tension by declaring, 'I am overwhelmed with the kind of reception I have got from the BJP supporters. At the centre, my captain is Amit Shah and in Bengal, my captain is Dilip Ghosh. I will work in Bengal under the leadership of Dilip Ghosh.'[5] He hugged the state BJP president as the media watched. But Dilip Ghosh's body language said otherwise. It was clear he had to swallow a bitter pill.

Ghosh had already rubbed the former state BJP president, Rahul Sinha, the wrong way. After he had taken over as the BJP state president in December 2015, he had formed his own team ahead of the West Bengal assembly elections in 2016, removing almost all state office-bearers Rahul Sinha had chosen. His bet was a success as he won three assembly seats and secured his own victory from the Kharagpur (Sadar) assembly constituency. Rahul Sinha, who was promoted as the national secretary and posted in Delhi, refused to leave the state and continued to work in Bengal.

After Mukul Roy joined, there was speculation that Roy might replace Dilip Ghosh as state president. This, however, did not happen. Dilip Ghosh being a former RSS pracharak, who had worked in many states, including Andaman and Nicobar, retained the post. Rather, Mukul Roy was not given any party post; he was made the convener of the party's election committee ahead of the 2018 panchayat elections and taken into the national executive of the BJP. Later, he was made the convenor of the 2019 Lok Sabha elections committee in Bengal (and in September 2020 he was inducted in the team of national office bearers as one of the vice presidents of the BJP). Both Ghosh and Roy tried to maintain 'peace' in public, but with Mukul Roy inducting or taking the help of grassroots TMC workers to formulate his strategies for the BJP in Bengal tensions were high.

Many old BJP members were also annoyed with the entry of Mukul Roy. One reason for their irritation

[5] ABP Ananda. 'Dilip Ghosh Is my Captain in Bengal, Says Mukul Roy after returns to Kolkata'. YouTube, 6 November2017. Available at: https://www.youtube.com/watch?v=VBKpXBh2zeA

was that the central leadership had undermined their capabilities to run the party organization. They felt that Mukul would flood the party with his supporters and second, they thought it weakened their fight against Mamata. 'How can we shout against Mamata's corruption and Saradha chit fund scam or Narada sting operation when one of the main accused is in our party?' asked a former office-bearer of the Bengal BJP. At that time, he even predicted the BJP was not in a position to win any seat from Bengal. In the next two years, however, things changed on a large scale, both in state politics as well as in the BJP's organization.

Thus, Mukul had his work cut out for him; he had to prove his worth to the BJP. At a public meeting in Rani Rasmoni Road on 10 November 2017, Mukul Roy launched his first attack on Mamata Banerjee and her nephew Abhishek Banerjee. He was visibly nervous as he shared the stage with top BJP state leadership but was hailed by his mentor in the BJP, Kailash Vijayvargiya. He began his speech saying, 'I have been given 20 minutes to talk.' In the next 21 minutes, Mukul levelled allegations against the chief minister and her nephew, flashing a bunch of documents. 'What TMC had promised to the people, they could not fulfil and there is suffocation in the internal political set-up of TMC,' he said. This was a clear indication to Abhishek Banerjee's rise in the party. Soon, he alleged that Biswa Bangla, which Mamata Banerjee promoted as the brand of West Bengal government (as mentioned earlier, she had sketched the logo of Biswa Bangla, which was being used in every government communication), was not associated with the state government and was owned by Abhishek Banerjee. 'Biswa Bangla is not a government institution; it is a company. The owner of the company is Abhishek Banerjee,' he told the gathering, drawing huge applause from the crowd for exposing Mamata

Banerjee's 'corruption'. Dilip Ghosh along with other top leaders was seen clapping. 'TMC claims that *Jago Bangla* is their mouthpiece. But this too is a company and its owner's name is Abhishek Banerjee [...] Even the owner of the party logo which is to be used for any printed materials like posters, pamphlet, leaflet, handbills, is Abhishek Banerjee. Address 30B Harish Chatterjee Street.'[6]

These allegations that Abhishek Banerjee's company had staked a claim for the same logo with the patent body rattled the ruling party in Bengal. The then home secretary Atri Bhattacharya, and the medium- and small-scale industry department secretary Rajiv Sinha, were rushed to the press corner at the state secretariat, Nabanna. They had a tough time defending the government and said the West Bengal government had already applied for the registry of the trademark of the Biswa Bangla logo and Chief Minister Mamata Banerjee had already handed over the logo to the government unconditionally. 'If anyone claims that it [Biswa Bangla] is a private company, it is wrong. It is a 100 per cent government company,' said Rajiv Sinha. 'She is the creator and we are the user of the logo. Any department of the state government can use it.' Still, there was no answer why Abhishek Banerjee's company had staked a claim on a logo being used by the government when his aunt had already handed over the rights of the logo to the West Bengal government. Sinha only told the media persons that before the West Bengal government applied for the registration of the trademark at the Registry of Trademark, there were two more applicants and Abhishek was one of them. 'Subsequently [before the controversy erupted in public] Abhishek Banerjee had withdrawn his application and the registration

[6] Bharat Darshan. 2017. 'Mukul Roy Speech at Kolkata BJP Meeting'. YouTube, 10 November. Available at: https://www.youtube.com/watch?v=7Q5UF-hUDHQ

authority had accepted it,' he claimed.[7] Soon Abhishek moved court, filed a defamation case and managed to get a prohibitory order against Mukul Roy. The Alipurduar Court ordered that Mukul Roy could not comment on Biswa Bangla or *Jago Bangla* involving Abhishek Banerjee. Later, Abhishek filed a defamation suit in Kolkata's Bankshal Court as well and claimed, 'If he [Roy] can prove that I have done anything wrong, I will leave politics.'

Still, Mukul Roy kept harping on the issue of propriety against the chief minister and other TMC leaders by raising similar allegations of corruption against them at several rallies. However, his discomfort with the BJP's state party leadership was evident when the leadership did not show any interest in launching a sustained campaign against Mamata on these issues. For example, Mukul had threatened to expose Birbhum district TMC president, Anubrata Mondal, for his alleged financial irregularities, but apparently, his words did not carry much steam within the state BJP leadership. The BJP insiders say the state leadership, unlike the central, was not confident enough to go all out against Abhishek Banerjee, or anyone else for that matter, on the basis of Mukul Roy's allegations. Moreover, they were also apprehensive if Mukul Roy's 'Saradha–Narada' scam connection would come back to them if they went ahead with those allegations against the top ruling party leaders. 'I think the state BJP leadership did not get much support from the central leadership on those allegations levelled by Mukul Roy. They also could not assess how Mamata Banerjee would counter those allegations and take on the BJP. At that time, BJP also did not enjoy the mass support the way they visibly enjoyed after the Lok Sabha elections,' says senior journalist Pinakpani Ghosh.

---

[7] *The Hindu*. 'Biswa Bangla not a private entity, it is 100% govt. owned'. 11 November 2017.

Anyway, as mentioned earlier, the state leadership was as it is not very fond of Mukul Roy joining the saffron camp. At one point, it seemed like a solo battle for Roy. So, he concentrated on doing what he did best—setting tactical strategies for elections.

Mukul Roy has never been a mass leader or a great orator or a crowd puller. Rather, he is the backroom guy, someone who is comfortable with numbers, organization and strategies. He knows where and what percentage of votes exist and for which party. He also knows when to knock the door of the ECI to keep the party in the limelight. In the TMC, he would find out weak spots in areas where the organizational thrust was needed. He is also an expert at candidate selection. After he joined the BJP, the central leadership wanted him to use the TMC's weaknesses and poach their leaders and workers to strengthen the BJP in Bengal. Amit Shah wanted to use Mukul Roy to poach more MLAs and MPs from Mamata's camp—the same ploy they had applied in other states. However, those who were considered close to Mukul in the TMC, like MLA Shiuli Saha or Shilbhadra Dutta or Sabyasachi Dutta, did not leave the party along with him.[8] Even his son, Shubranshu Roy, refused to toe his father's line. When his father had just joined the BJP, Subhranshu had said in an interview to me, 'I am not comfortable with the ideology of BJP; I came to politics looking at Mamata Banerjee and on her insistence, I contested the elections. So, I will continue to work under her.'[9]

Interestingly, Mukul's charisma did not work for the BJP in a couple of by-elections in December 2017, a month after he joined the BJP. For example, in West Midnapore's Sabang, there were plenty of opportunities to woo the TMC's disgruntled local

[8] Sabyasachi Dutta later joined BJP in October 2019.

[9] Subhranshu also joined the BJP soon after the 2019 Lok Sabha elections.

leaders. The election was warranted there as the sitting Congress MLA, Manas Bhunia, had joined the TMC and was elected to the Rajya Sabha, but ignoring the local TMC leaders, Mamata Banerjee had nominated Bhunia's wife, Gita, from the seat. However, despite Mukul Roy's meeting with the local BJP workers and the public meetings in Sabang, BJP candidate Antara Bhattacharya came a distant third in the by-election. Mukul not only failed to bring the unhappy TMC leaders on board, but he also could not use the fissures in the local TMC to the advantage of the BJP. Many had thought that Mukul would be able to exploit his connections with the grassroots TMC leaders, but he failed to yield results.

Similarly, in the Noapara by-election in January 2018, Mukul Roy wanted to put up former TMC MLA Manju Basu as the BJP candidate. Manju's husband, Bikash Basu, an active TMC leader, had allegedly been murdered by the opposing faction in the party in 2000. Manju had won the seat twice, in 2001 and 2011 on a TMC ticket, but lost to Congress–Left alliance candidate Madhusudan Ghosh in 2016. When many thought Manju Basu would get the TMC nomination in the by-election after Madhusudan's death, the local TMC heavyweight leader Arjun Singh (who would later join BJP) wanted to nominate his relative and Garulia municipality chairman, TMC leader Sunil Singh from this seat. Mamata obliged. Mukul wanted to take advantage of the situation. He wanted to use the sympathy towards Manju and her husband's victimization. Bikash Basu's killers had not been traced for 18 years and a former MLA who deserved the party ticket was denied nomination—these were the two points Mukul Roy wanted to bank on. He met Manju and arranged a meeting between her and Kailash Vijayvargiya at the airport. After the meeting, the BJP was ready to nominate her as their candidate in the Noapara by-election and were just waiting for Manju's formal consent. Even after the meeting with Mukul and Kailash, Manju said, 'I have not taken any final decision.'[10] In a hurried decision, the BJP announced her name as the candidate for the Noapara by-election. But the TMC launched 'Operation Manju'[11] overnight. The state president, Subrata Bakshi, called Manju. The district TMC observer, Nirmal Ghosh, and MLA Partha Bhowmik visited her house. District President Jyotipriyo Mullick called to remind her how the TMC had protected her after her husband's death. A soft-hearted Manju Basu could not take the pressure and within hours of her name being announced as a BJP candidate, she told a news conference that she would stay back in the TMC.

This put Mukul on the back foot and exposed the organizational bankruptcy of the BJP. It was clear that the BJP did not have enough power to protect their own in an hour of crisis. A BJP insider said, 'State president Dilip Ghosh wanted to send just one name as BJP candidate from Noapara and that was of our organizational secretary of that area. But he had to succumb to pressure from Mukul Roy and Kailash Vijayvargiya. So Manju Basu's name had to be sent.' Mukul alleged that the TMC blackmailed Manju. Still, there was no answer why they could not bring Manju on board even after announcing her as their candidate. Questions were raised that if they could not protect their nominated candidate, how could

[10] Pal, S. *Ebela*. 'BJP waiting for missed call, Monju in dilemma. Drama with Noapara candidate'. 5 January 2018.

[11] Chatterjee, J. *Anandabazar Patrika*. 'Mukul is marking the booths won by Trinamool in red'. 17 September 2017.

they protect their supporters on the face of the ruling party's 'terror'? This incident—a national party like BJP announcing the name of a 'TMC member' as their candidate without her even formally joining the party—exposed the lack of coordination among the state leaders. This was how disorganized the BJP was just two years before the 2019 Lok Sabha elections.

As Mukul had claimed that he had to be 'on the crease to get more runs', he decided to stick to the wicket. Noapara is close to Mukul's native place Kanchrapara and the then local TMC MLA Arjun Singh was opposed to Mukul's rise in the powergraph. Arjun could not show his power when Mukul was second-in-command in the TMC. But, this time Arjun had his way as there was no opposition to him in his fiefdom and Mamata chose him as the best bet to teach a lesson to her former confidant. (Ironically, Arjun Singh later joined the BJP ahead of the 2019 Lok Sabha elections and won the Barrackpore constituency to become an MP.)

Many thought Mukul lacked authority in the BJP and that was why he could not show his 'magic'. Leaving behind the humiliation over the the Noapara by-election, Mukul started his homework for the panchayat elections. Despite his poor performance in the first couple of months, the BJP nominated him as the convener of the panchayat election committee in February 2018 along with former BJP MLA Samik Bhattacharya. Mukul was expected to use the 'inactive' TMC workers and leaders to hit at the TMC bastion. In fact, he had started this work well before joining the BJP. During the period he was growing distant from the TMC, he had used his makeshift office near Khanna Cinema in Kolkata to chalk out his plans for the panchayat elections. He had started by marking the booths where the TMC had won and where they had come second or lost. He had also started preparing a list of booth-level disgruntled TMC workers and leaders who could be used against the TMC. In September 2017, he had told a daily, 'I am preparing a list of workers who are in power and those who are inactive in panchayats. It might come handy in future.'[12] He was, however, told by Dilip Ghosh that old BJP workers would get priority while getting nominations in the panchayat election. An office-bearer of the state BJP said, 'Anyway, we did not want to waste our energy in panchayat elections; kept it to be used in Lok Sabha election.'

THE BJP'S ORGANIZATIONAL REALITIES

The tussle between Mukul Roy and Dilip Ghosh continued till the Lok Sabha elections and even afterwards. 'Initial tension is always there. Soon party workers realized we need more and more new people to make our party bigger and win elections,' says Dilip Ghosh. Many in the BJP, however, were sceptical about the so-called 'Mukul Magic'—they believed that the BJP already had its presence in the grassroots that would help them win a larger share in the 2019 Lok Sabha elections.

'You must have seen that BJP had about 4 per cent vote in West Bengal when it did not have any significant political presence in the state and Mamata was in the limelight,' says a senior BJP leader. 'BJP was more of a rural party than an urban party in Bengal.'

As mentioned earlier, Bengal is where Shyama Prasad Mookerjee, the founder of Bhartiya Jana Sangh and the president of Akhil Bhartiya Hindu Mahasabha, was born. The Hindu Mahasabha and the Jana Sangh

[12] Chatterjee, J. *Anandabazar Patrika*. 'Mukul is marking the booths won by Trinamool in red'. 17 September 2017.

together won 13 seats in the first assembly elections in 1952.[13] However, neither the Jana Sangh nor the BJP could extend its base in Bengal after Shyama Prasad's demise in 1953. The BJP first made its presence felt in Bengal in the late 1980s and early 1990s with the Ram Janmabhumi Andolon. Thousands of BJP supporters and workers from Bengal joined the Shila Pujan in Ayodhya during that period. Fringe organizations like the VHP and the RSS had mobilized the people in the state. 'Around that time, I have seen how VHP workers who participated in Shila Pujan were considered to be representatives of Lord Ram. People used to touch their feet. VHP was formed around that time and Tapan Sikdar who was going to be the state BJP president later, through his oratory skills, utilized the social churning in BJP's favour,' says Prasenjit Bakshi.

Since then the fringe organizations of the Sangh had been working on the ground mobilizing people at the local level, in small towns or villages, but the BJP as a political force could not assert itself. The reason behind this was partly because the BJP, as it was known to be a 'north India party', had not given much importance to Bengal as well as on eastern India. Rather, the BJP leadership rode the Mamata Banerjee wave to oust the Left from the state. In 1998, when the TMC came into existence, the Vajpayee–Advani duo tied their fortunes to Mamata as she was the driving force behind the 'anti-CPIM' movement. While Mamata emerged as the main face in the Opposition, the BJP supported her in every possible way. Allying with Mamata, BJP bagged one Lok Sabha seat in 1998. Tapan Sikdar won the Dumdum seat and in 1999, the BJP won two seats—Tapan Sikdar, who got re-elected from Dumdum, and

[13] Election Commission of India. Report on the first general elections in India 1951–52.

veteran advocate Satyabrata Mukherjee, who emerged as the winner in Krishnanagar.

'You need to understand that BJP's main enemy at that time was not Mamata Banerjee. Ideologically, BJP was opposed to both Congress and the Left. If we had someone who was fighting against both the parties, why would we not support that political force,' says a senior BJP leader.

Around that time, a section of the state BJP leadership was opposed to supporting Mamata at the cost of the BJP's own growth in the state. But the central leadership was not ready to listen. 'I remember, once Shahnawaz Hussain was supposed to do a joint rally with Mamata Banerjee in Bengal. They were supposed to travel in the same chopper. They flew together in the same chopper but he was dropped at one venue and Mamata left to address other venues. Shahnawazji was offered a car to return to Kolkata or he had to wait for Mamata to finish her rallies and pick him up,' says Amal Chatterjee, the former general secretary (organization) of the state BJP. 'There are many such instances where Mamata insulted our leaders or ignored our presence,' he adds.

In fact, there are also instances when Mamata Banerjee kept putting pressure on the then Prime Minister Atal Bihari Vajpayee on various issues—be it for invoking Article 356 (President's Rule) in West Bengal or threatening to quit over the fuel price hike. Central BJP leadership apparently bowed down to Mamata's pressure on many occasions to keep the pressure on the Left Front government in Bengal. The TMC chief's insistence on the imposition of President's Rule in the state was such that at one point, in 2000, after a violent by-election in East Midnapore's Panskura, the then NDA convenor George Fernandes released a resolution of the alliance requesting the government 'to take whatever steps it deems necessary to prevent the destruction of democratic institutions in West Bengal'.[14] The central government followed suit and sent letters to the Jyoti Basu government in Bengal asking for explanations regarding the political violence which was on the rise. This was a direct fight between the Left and the BJP-led NDA coalition, with Mamata being the catalyst. An NDA delegation was sent to the state when it was found that the imposition of President's Rule would be political hara-kiri and Jyoti Basu would make himself a 'martyr' out of it.

Though Mamata had an alliance with the BJP in the 1999 Lok Sabha elections, just before the 2001 assembly elections in the state, she dumped the BJP to join hands with the Congress. There were many reasons for such a move by Mamata. In the 1998 panchayat election, which the TMC fought with the BJP, the alliance did fare well. Mamata was confident of her own strength that the TMC (though in alliance with the BJP) could wrest the Kolkata Municipal Corporation (KMC) election in 2000. Moreover, and perhaps this was the most important reason, she realized that she was losing the support of the minorities due to her alliance with the BJP. She did not want to lose the minority vote bank in the state. Allying with Congress, she thought, would give her better dividends as the BJP was still to grow its strength at the grassroots level. So, she left the NDA and resigned from the Vajpayee government on the pretext of the Tehelka Scam and demanding the resignation of George Fernandes, the defence minister.

Much hype was created over the 2001 assembly elections. The media saw it as a fight between the weakened Left and the strong Opposition under Mamata

---

[14] Bhattacharyya, D. *Economic and Political Weekly*. 'Making and Unmaking of Trinamul Congress', 39(14/15), 1529–37. 2004.

Banerjee. There were also some reasons to believe in the anti-establishment narrative. The Left had been defeated in the recently concluded KMC elections. Mamata was pulling a huge crowd to her public rallies. Sensing the stagnation in the administration, the Left Front government changed its guard. A younger Buddhadeb Bhattacharjee replaced veteran and ailing Jyoti Basu to bring fresh blood into the administration. The industries were languishing under the Left, there were problems of unemployment and, there was an apparent 'anti-establishment' wave in Bengal. However, the results were too disappointing for the Mamata–Congress alliance which had raised the slogan '*Hoy ebar, noy Never* (either this time or never)', stating that the Left Front government could be toppled. The alliance could bag only 96 seats (TMC 60 and Congress 26), which was slightly better than what the undivided Congress had managed (81 seats) in the previous assembly elections in 1996.

As her gamble with the Congress failed miserably in 2001 assembly elections, she again went back to the BJP and joined the NDA government to become the coal minister for a brief period just before the 2004 Lok Sabha elections, which she fought in alliance with the BJP. However, she was the only candidate from the TMC to be elected while the BJP drew a zero. Former union minister Tapan Sikdar had encouraged severing ties with Mamata and strengthening BJP organization at the grassroots level. When in 2003, the BJP was in talks with the TMC for an alliance in the panchayat polls, Tapan Sikdar had vehemently opposed the central BJP leadership's move. 'At her insistence, we let Trinamool contest in many seats where we could have won easily. So, the grassroots BJP workers are now opposed to any alliance,' said Sikdar. 'She called for Gujarat Chief

Minister Narendra Modi's resignation. She agitated against Nitish Kumar after the division of the Eastern Railway. She even cursed Lal Krishna Advani indirectly.'[15]

Despite criticizing the Vajpayee government, Mamata was serving the BJP's purpose. She was fighting against the Left. At that time, Bangladeshi infiltration and how the CPIM was using the infiltrators as its vote bank was on Mamata's agenda. Despite Tapan Sikdar's opposition to any alliance with Mamata, the then state president, Tathagata Roy, kept negotiating with the TMC chief. While Tathagata kept toeing the central leadership's line, Sikdar started growing distant from the BJP. He tried to run a parallel organization disobeying the state leadership and was later expelled from the party in 2005 (though he rejoined it in 2009 in the presence of BJP's PM candidate L.K. Advani). The infighting in the state BJP continued for several years and this was the one reason why the party could not grow the way they should have in the state.

The alliance with the TMC proved disastrous in the 2006 assembly elections in which the TMC bagged 30 seats and the BJP drew nil. But, the BJP leadership were still open to allying with Mamata for the 2009 Lok Sabha elections. However, by that time Mamata had got her mojo back. She could smell the power with her prolonged agitation against the Left Front government's farmland acquisition policy for industrialization for the last three years. She had already breached a good portion of Left bastions in rural Bengal during the 2008 panchayat polls. Moreover, she was tilting towards the Congress as the Lok Sabha elections came closer. The BJP still did not lose hope. The then state BJP president, Satyabrata Mukherjee, told the media, 'We want an

[15] *The Telegraph Online*. 'Sikdar blast at Mamata'. 23 March 2003.

alliance with her. We have kept our doors open. But it is for Banerjee to decide.'[16] In December 2006, senior BJP leader L.K. Advani called on Mamata at her dharna manch in Dharmatala, where she was agitating against the Left Front government's decision to acquire farmland for Tata's car factory in Singur. The then BJP chief, Rajnath Singh, also met Mamata over the issue. L.K. Advani also visited Nandigram after the police firing killed 14 farmers in March 2007.

'Around that time, a central leader who also acted as the national spokesperson of the party came to Kolkata and requested the state leaders to take him to Singur. He wanted to visit Singur without the media glare. When asked [why] he said we need to understand the ground realities and when we are being able to corner the Left at the national level, we should not leave the issue. Let Mamata oppose CPIM here, we will take up the issue nationally,' says a BJP insider.

Despite their intention to take on the Left, the BJP could not benefit during the exodus from the Left camp between 2006 and 2011. Rather, the limelight was on Mamata. 'During the 2011 elections, many of our workers and leaders worked for TMC. It was a landslide election and all the Opposition forces joined Mamata. I personally know a Sangh leader in the Salt Lake area and a BJP Yuva Morcha office-bearer openly worked for TMC at that time. The idea was to throw out the Left,' says the same BJP insider.

Not much changed after the TMC came to power. Between 2011 and 2014, when Mamata was in alliance with the Congress, the BJP central leadership did not show much interest in disturbing Mamata. The state BJP leaders organized sporadic movements, but could

---

[16] IANS. *Hindustan Times*. 'Our doors are still open for Mamata: BJP'. 11 February 2009.

not organize their cadre base in the rural areas. 'I would say the top state leaders did not have a positive attitude. They did not believe that they could win. Naturally, they could not impart any confidence among the workers,' says Amal Chatterjee, former general secretary (organization) of the state BJP. The TMC was also aggressive in demolishing the Opposition around that time to establish its position as the principal, and perhaps, the only Opposition party pitted against the Left. The central leaders were busy capturing power in other states. It is believed that the BJP also needed strategic support of regional parties like the TMC to sail through any vote in the Rajya Sabha. The NDA was still a minority in the upper house and simple abstention from any voting would help the ruling alliance to pass a bill or a resolution in the Rajya Sabha. So, they did not want to challenge the TMC in a big way. It also did not help that infighting within the BJP was so bad that former state BJP president Tathagata Roy was shunted to Raj Bhavan in Tripura and Rahul Sinha was made the state party chief.

Back in the state, 'the BJP lacked two things. One there was an absence of a credible face to take on Mamata Banerjee and two, they were not able to organize sustained movements against Mamata Banerjee's failures as the chief minister,' says Prasenjit Bakshi. BJP insiders blamed former party chief Rahul Sinha for being reluctant to go all out against the TMC. 'I have seen Rahul never wanted other leaders to grow and come at par with him at the state level,' says Amal Chatterjee.

Since the 1990s, Mamata Banerjee has strategically built an anti-CPIM brand around herself. She has been a streetfighter and a mass leader. No other Opposition leader in Bengal could match her stature. Her stance as the Opposition leader gained popularity and credibility among a large section of the population in the state. Even though many were sceptical of her maverick, 'not-so-*bhadralok*' image as opposed to the previous chief ministers like Jyoti Basu or Buddhadeb Bhattacharjee, but her connection with the masses was unparalleled. The state BJP might have *bhadralok* leaders, but they lacked someone who could run around as a streetfighter like Mamata, connecting with the sentiment of the people at the grassroots level to lead a fight against the CPIM or the Left as a whole. No one was as brave as Mamata, who could take on the assault, both political and physical, of the Left on herself and the party workers.

CHANGE IN THE BJP'S STANCE

Things started changing when Narendra Modi came to power in 2014 and Amit Shah was elevated to the position of the BJP national president. By then, Mamata had completed three years as the chief minister of West Bengal. Soon after the Lok Sabha elections in 2014, the BJP knew they had to 'look east'. To retain the majority they got in the 2014 Lok Sabha elections, they had to increase their tally in the eastern part of the country. If Varanasi was the focus in 2014, it was Bengal in 2019. While the RSS-pracharak-turned-BJP-general-secretary Ram Madhav, and Congress leader-turned-BJP-minister in Assam, Himanta Biswa Sarma, were assigned to look after the BJP's political growth in the north-eastern states, an outright RSS organizer from Maharashtra, Sunil Deodhar, was given the charge of Tripura. In Bengal, while they made General Secretary Kailash Vijayvargiya the prabhari, General Secretary (organization) Ram Lal personally started taking care of the state perfectly aided by his junior, joint general secretary (organization), Shiv Prakash.

National President Amit Shah blew the first bugle from the Utthwan Divas (Rising Day) rally on 30 November 2014 in front of the CESC building in Dharmatala, the spot where Mamata Banerjee holds her annual Shaheed Divas rally every year on 21 July. For the last six years, the BJP had been organizing this annual event on Rani Rasmoni Road, half a kilometre away from the new spot they had chosen. This was a political stance to challenge Mamata Banerjee on her home turf. Since Amit Shah was to address the rally, the state leaders were enthusiastic in showing their worth to the top brass.

The state government opposed the BJP's move to hold the rally in front of the CESC building citing a possible law and order situation and put a curb on holding rallies on that spot. The Kolkata Police, Corporation, Fire Brigade, all were reluctant to grant permission for the rally. However, the BJP knocked on the door of the court. After a fierce legal battle, the Calcutta High Court ordered the authorities to grant permission to the BJP leaders to hold the rally at their chosen venue. With the Calcutta High Court's order, BJP leaders got the relevant permissions, but they were asked to erect a smaller stage than they had originally planned. 'Amit Shahji was not ready to come to Kolkata and address the rally without proper permission. So we had to take whatever the court ordered. We had to do this rally and it turned out to be a big day for BJP in Bengal,' says a former BJP state office-bearer.

On 30 November 2014, Amit Shah started his speech with 'Bharat mata ki jai' and asked the supporters to shout so that the noise reached the state secretariat,

Nabanna where Mamata Banerjee sits. Before the rally, Mamata Banerjee had questioned the existence of Amit Shah. During an interview with senior journalist Rajdeep Sardesai, when she was asked to comment on Amit Shah's remarks on her party protecting the Muslim fundamentalists in Bengal, she retorted, 'Who is this man? I don't know him. Haven't seen him.'[17] At the rally, the BJP national president replied, '*Main Amit Shah hoon.* I am a *chhota sa karyakarta* [a small worker] of the BJP. And I have come to uproot Trinamool from Bengal. *Yeh rally dikha rahi hai ki Mamata didi aap ki sarkar ki ulti geenti shuru ho gayi hai.*'

His speech was full of allegations against the Mamata Banerjee–led government and TMC—how she allowed the Saradha chit fund scam to go on, how she allowed terror outfits to use Bengal (like in Khagragarh) and how she allowed Bangladeshi infiltrators to settle in Bengal. He gave the call, 'For development in Bengal, you should vote for BJP. We have given a call for Congress-mukt Bharat, we are also giving a call for Mamata-mukt Bangal.'

While the BJP was satisfied that Mamata had overthrown the BJP's ideological enemy, the Left, they also wanted to elevate themselves to be the main Opposition in Bengal. As the Left got cornered and the TMC launched attacks on Left workers, it was easier for the BJP to fill the gap in the state. However, the BJP lacked a strong organizational presence to counter the TMC.

Even in 2015, the state BJP leadership was not confident to take on Mamata. It was more of rhetoric than any real power on the ground. Amit Shah too knew the ground realities. Despite the Modi wave that

---

[17] *IndiaToday.in*. 'Exclusive interview with Mamata Banerjee: Modi is media, media Modi'. 18 November 2014.

swept across the country in 2014, Bengal could send only two MPs to the Lok Sabha—singer Babul Supriyo won the Asansol seat in the BJP's own strength while S.S. Ahluwalia won the Darjeeling seat with the help of Gorkha Jana Mukti Morcha. The BJP could not fare well in the Kolkata Municipal Corporation elections in early 2015 as well. So, Amit Shah took multiple decisions to boost the party organization in Bengal. First, there was an overhaul of the state party leadership. A former RSS pracharak, Dilip Ghosh (who had left his home at the age of 20 to become a pracharak of the RSS), was made the BJP general secretary and then elevated to the position of party president on 11 December 2015 replacing Rahul Sinha. 'Dilip was first inducted as the general secretary of the state unit. He was looking after Hindu Jagaran Manch. One day, we got a call from Ram Lalji. He asked me to meet him along with Dilip. We met him and it was provisionally decided that he would be made the next state unit chief. RSS wanted this change. We waited for a few days and there was no decision. We were in a dilemma. We also thought should we make this change with someone completely unknown to the political arena just before the assembly elections in 2016. But Dilip knew the state very well due to his activities in the Sangh. Within a few days, Amitji took the decision and we were informed. We had to go ahead with Dilip's elevation. We did,' says Amal Chatterjee.

The BJP leadership wanted to rejuvenate the party with fresh faces before the 2016 assembly elections. The old leadership had been tested and had failed. Some state BJP leaders in private off-the-record conversations would sulk that the central leadership did not support them enough to carry on an all-out attack against Mamata due to the compulsion of national politics. As mentioned earlier, the BJP indeed needed the support of some of the regional parties in order to pass any legislation in the Rajya Sabha as the NDA did not enjoy the majority in the upper house. In an interview to the author, the former general secretary of the state BJP Amal Chatterjee also talked about the lack of positivity among the state and central BJP leaders. Still, when the old guard could not help the BJP grow in the state, especially at the grassroots level, the BJP central leadership wanted an 'organization' man and a new face who could take on TMC.

'The advantages Dilip Ghosh had was his training in Sangh and Hindu Jagaran Manch. So he knew how to build the organization. He hailed from Junglemahal's Gopiballavpur and had rawness in his speech. He has a clear mind. He has no family attachment. Most importantly, he was aggressive,' says Chatterjee. Moreover, Dilip Ghosh was brought into the fold of state BJP around the 2014 Lok Sabha elections. He was assisting the general secretary (organization) at that time and developed an understanding of the party's apparatus within the next year.

Ghosh formed a new team, mostly replacing the old faces, some of whom had a strong Sangh connection. RSS wanted to hold the leash of the BJP in the state. However, the process of rehauling the Bengal BJP had started a few months prior to Dilip Ghosh's appointment as the state unit chief. Already in July 2015, the national secretary in charge of Bengal Siddharth Nath Singh was replaced by Madhya Pradesh BJP leader and national general secretary Kailash Vijayvargiya. The BJP also launched a 'membership drive' through which anyone could become a member simply by giving a missed call on an advertised number. 'I was privy to a meeting where Amit Shah set a target to the state BJP leaders with concrete numbers they needed to achieve. There were rewards like "tea with Amit Shah" or "tea with Narendra Modi" for those who could get the targeted number of new members,' says Pinakpani Ghosh.

The party not only hit the pedal on getting new members, but the central and state leaders also decided to build a strong organizational network from the booth level. The BJP launched the Vistarak Programme, which was not a visible activity of the party before 2015. As part of the Vistarak Programme, a party leader would go to an area far from his or her hometown and spend about a fortnight there. The idea was to gather exact information about the party organization in that area and also give a boost to the local party. 'We have emphasized on vistarak programme for the last three years and it has helped us in mobilizing our workers,' says BJP state chief.

There was also an attempt by the BJP to mobilize the intellectuals of Bengal. The leadership knew that in Bengal, they needed the support of intellectuals to earn the confidence of the common people. They utilized the RSS and other fringe organizations' machineries to gather support for Rightist forces. The new leadership concentrated on reviving the social media team in the state and reach out to young voters in the state, launching an attack on Mamata and the TMC and promoting Narendra Modi and the BJP.

Long-time Bengal general secretary (organization) Amal Chatterjee was replaced by his deputy Subrata Chatterjee. State President Dilip Ghosh, who contested the assembly elections for the first time in his life, won the Kharagpur (Sadar) constituency in 2016. He defeated veteran Congress leader and nine-time MLA, Gyan Singh Sohanpal. The entire RSS organization in the district had worked for Ghosh and mobilized the voters.

Moreover, Prime Minister Narendra Modi kickstarted his 2016 assembly election election campaign in Bengal from Kharagpur, a cosmopolitan town dominated by a railway colony, which gave a boost to the BJP Bengal chief's campaign. The Left-backed Congress candidate Gyan Singh Sohanpal, who had been the longest-serving MLA from the constituency, did not enjoy the support of the voters mainly because of his ailing health at the age of 92. The TMC, due to its organizational feud in Kharagpur, could not fill the vacuum that Sohanpal left behind. There were too many heads with the aspiration to lead the party there. During the civic elections in Kharagpur, the TMC's internal feud could be doused with the help of the then SP of West Midnapore, Bharati Ghosh. She used to call the shots even in the TMC's organizational matters in the district. This time she was absent from the field as the ECI transferred her out of the district. All these factors helped Dilip Ghosh clinch the Kharagpur seat.

His victory along with two other BJP MLAs in the 2016 Bengal assembly elections strengthened Dilip Ghosh's position in the party. Despite the poor organizational position in most parts of the state, Dilip Ghosh did not get glued to the state headquarters in Kolkata. He travelled across the state to boost the party's organization. 'I tried to lead the party from the front. I went to the district regularly which was not the case earlier,' says Dilip.

But Dilip Ghosh's use of language was questionable on several occasions. When the Jadavpur University (JU) students staged a demonstration and allegedly raised anti-India slogans in solidarity with their counterparts in JNU, New Delhi, over the Azadi slogan controversy, Dilip Ghosh had threatened to drag the JU students and teachers by their collars. 'If BJP were in power in the state, then we would have arrested the anti-nationals, irrespective of students and teachers, and would have pulled them by the collar,'[18] he said. He alleged that the vice-chancellor of the university, Suranjan Das, was acting with political agenda and that is why he did not take any action against the students who raised slogans in support of JNU students. In a Left-liberal dominated state like West Bengal, with JU being the hub of progressive Left students, Ghosh's comments created a huge controversy.

The newly elected state BJP chief also did not hesitate to say that the BJP would take 'revenge' against TMC. Next, he set his sights on the controversial TMC Birbhum district president, Anubrata Mondal, who was infamous for his aggressive comments against the Opposition and had always been blamed for instigating and orchestrating political violence in the district. Targeting him, Ghosh said, 'For a long time, he [Anubrata Mondal] has played. Now we will play. He will have to watch our game sitting outside the stadium. There will not be only resistance, but also revenge. He will remember it for a lifetime.'

There have been many more such instances which show that Dilip Ghosh wouldn't act in a soft manner in West Bengal politics and would try to build an image of a bold leader ready to take on the TMC. He dared Mamata, saying, 'We have seen red eyes [the Left]. We can now see "white and blue" eyes [TMC]. Don't show us your angry face. We are not afraid of you.'

'In fact, as the general secretary (organization), I got calls from Ram Lalji on many occasions and I was asked to tame Dilip Ghosh. Ram Lalji told me Amitji was upset

---

[18] Ghoshal, A. *Indian Express*. '"Anti-India" slogans at JU: Would have arrested anti-nationals, pulled them by the collar, says state BJP chief'. 21 February 2016.

with the report of Dilip using abusive language. He used to get regular reports. I told Dilip to control himself. He assured me that he would, but he would violate it again,' says Amal Chatterjee.

The BJP state president has an answer ready in his defence. 'The use of language was strategic. People thought there was no one to talk against Mamata. I used the language to encourage my workers and give them confidence.' He has projected himself as a straight forward leader who does not mind using strong rhetoric to take on the mighty ruling party in the state. However, he was not always successful with his rhetoric. He was assaulted in Darjeeling in October 2017 when he tried to visit the hills. As described earlier (in Chapter One), Darjeeling was simmering after a long-drawn protest and violence over the introduction of Bengali as a compulsory language. Allegedly, Gorkha Janamukti Morcha supporters belonging to the Binay Tamang faction, who were ruling the hills with the support of the TMC and Mamata Banerjee, had also manhandled him. He had no option but to leave the hills. The BJP organized a protest in Kolkata on the same evening, but they could not lead a sustained campaign against the lawlessness. 'Imagine, if Mamata was the Opposition leader and she would have been assaulted, how she would have capitalized the situation. [Due] to organizational weakness and lack of aggressive strategy, we could not use the situation against the government,' says a BJP leader. But Dilip Ghosh says, 'See, I did not back down. People thought there was none to take Mamata head-on. I did. It gave confidence to the workers and the voters too. I did not want to make the attack on me just an issue of the BJP. I wanted people to come up and voice their protest and empathize with us. Because they are also facing the same attack from TMC.'

Dilip Ghosh was again assaulted a year later in December 2018 in Cooch Behar's Mathabhanga when he tried to visit Thakur Panchanan Barma's house to pay his tribute to the social reformer who had passed away decades ago in 1936 but was still revered among the people in the Rajbanshi community in North Bengal. As the BJP's Ratha Yatra programme from Cooch Behar in North Bengal had to be cancelled due to legal fight between the saffron camp and the state government, Dilip Ghosh thought of visiting Barma's house, mainly to woo the Rajbanshi voters. TMC workers blocked his road and he had to return without meeting the family. Again, the BJP could not launch a sustained attack on the ruling party. The TMC claimed the 'attack' was a fallout of the BJP's internal fight, but the reality was that the saffron camp was not ready to take on the TMC.

Let alone not utilizing the nine attacks on the state BJP president (as claimed by him) after Mamata Banerjee came into power for the second time, the BJP was not able to launch an aggressive campaign against the government even when there were plenty of issues to capitalize on. The central leadership was aware of the situation. Be it the May 2018 panchayat elections or the proposed Ratha Yatra in December 2018, the BJP leadership was busier fighting the TMC government in courts rather than on the streets of Bengal. On both occasions, the BJP went to court to get an order against the state government. During the panchayat elections, there were allegations of mass-scale violence against the ruling party. When the BJP planned five Ratha Yatras across the state in December 2018 culminating in Prime Minister Narendra Modi's rally in January 2019 in Kolkata's Brigade Parade Ground, the TMC government refused permission citing a law and order issue and possible communal tension based on an intelligence report. The BJP did not aggressively campaign against the Mamata Banerjee government and instead, took the matter to court. Many such incidents had exposed the BJP's lack of organizational capabilities to act as an aggressive Opposition. This was a cause for concern for the national leadership.

So, after revamping the state leadership, Amit Shah stressed on applying the Gujarat model of organization in Bengal. Narendra Modi and Amit Shah's success was based on the strong grassroots organization they had built in Gujarat and then, to some extent, replicated in Uttar Pradesh. Gujarat BJP leader Indra Vijay Sinh Jadeja once told me, 'We have one mantra. Win the booths, win the assembly.' Amit Shah's mantra for the organization has always been to build strong booth committees that would form a strong base of the party's organizational framework. Jadeja explained the same in detail.

The base of the organizational structure begins with 'panna pramukh', who is in charge of a single page of the voters' list. His job is to take care of 40–50 voters in his area. There are generally 25 to 30 panna pramukhs in a single booth. They may not be the active workers of the party, but their job is to be in touch with the voters and ensure that all voters go to the polling booth on the day of the poll.

Above them, there is a booth committee for every booth in the state. This committee generally consists of 15 to 25 people, including women and representatives of the SC and ST communities. Their assignment is to keep in touch with the voters of their booth over the years through various programmes like celebrating different festivals, birth anniversaries of their leaders, taking care of the requirements of the voters and recruiting new members to the party.

With a few booth committees, the BJP leadership forms the 'shakti kendra', which is generally constituted in every ward in the municipalities (in urban areas) and every tehsil (in case of rural areas). The shakti kendras keep in touch with the booth committees and get reports from the grassroots to be delivered to the 'assembly campaign committee'. Among the members of the shakti kendra, there is one person in-charge of all matters and an individual to look after the social media. They communicate with each other through WhatsApp groups. There is also a 'call centre' in every shakti kendra and its job is to prepare a database of the voters with their mobile or landline numbers. The BJP workers in the call centre would call the voters to check if they have voter ID cards or Aadhaar cards and if they are facing any problem in the area. If any voter goes against the party and the BJP workers at the grassroots level can sense their unhappiness by talking to them or through any other activities at the local level, the shakti kendra workers will alert the party leadership. Every voter generally gets four to five calls from the BJP workers, especially before the elections. This is a psychological game every cadre-based political party engages in. They carefully observe the activities, attitude and public interaction of each voter at the booth level and estimate if the person is going to vote for or against the party. They maintain a list of 'favourable', 'anti' or 'fence-sitter' voters at the grassroots level and act accordingly.

On getting reports from the shakti kendra, the assembly-wise campaign committees point out the weaknesses in their organization as well as in the deliverance of government schemes. They immediately rectify those areas of concern and set the tone for campaigning.

However, the watchdogs in organizational matters are the 'booth vistaraks'. They are the BJP leaders and workers who visit around three booths outside their home turf and get a neutral report on the organization at the grassroots level. They also give necessary inputs to the booth-level workers to strengthen the organization, like how to pacify the disgruntled voters or party workers, how to resolve a political crisis at the grassroots, which are the areas they need to work on to gain the support of the voters, etc. The vistaraks also report to the leaders high up the organization about the ground realities in the area they are assigned to visit. This leaves little scope to mislead the top leadership. Apart from this well-knit organizational structure, the BJP leadership also encourages the party workers to be at the steering wheel of social and cultural organizations, cooperative banks, etc., in their areas to establish proper control over the voters.

This is a direct offshoot of the RSS's organizational strategy. In the Sangh, the young members sometimes work as vistaraks. They are not same as pracharaks, who leave their home to work for the Sangh as whole-timers. These vistaraks reach their destination on their own expense and stay with local RSS activists or sympathizers.

It was, however, difficult for the Bengal BJP to replicate the same model in the state. After the BJP won the Uttar Pradesh assembly elections in March 2017, Amit Shah shifted his focus to Bengal. Following the RSS model of vistaraks, Shah himself adopted the role of a vistarak on 25 April 2017. He landed in North Bengal's Bagdogra airport and with a huge convoy, accompanied by local BJP MP S.S. Ahluwalia and the state president. Dilip Ghosh, reached a tribal village in Naxalbari, the breeding ground of Left-wing extremism known as the Naxal movement in the late 1960s. He spoke to the locals and enquired about their problems and asked if they had Aadhaar cards, if they could open Jan Dhan accounts and whether they received benefits under central government schemes. He then visited Raju and Gita Mahali, a tribal couple, and had lunch with them. Though people in Bengal were used to seeing Mamata Banerjee interact with the public and share a cup of tea and *muri* with them at roadside stalls or homes, in recent past no one in Bengal had seen a national leader visiting a village and having lunch sitting on the floor. Raju and Gita, who were chosen by the local BJP leadership, served roti, rice, daal, sabzi and papad. They offered the food to Amit Shah on a banana leaf. The BJP national president even asked for a second helping.

Shah might have decided to launch this programme across the state and lead it from the front. However, the state BJP leadership's organizational bankruptcy was exposed when the next day, Raju and Gita Mahali went missing only to resurface with State Minister Gautam Deb. In a press conference, the Mahalis said they had 'unconditionally' joined the TMC. Dilip Ghosh alleged that the TMC had forcefully inducted the tribal couple.

Later, in Kolkata, Amit Shah visited a slum-dweller's house in Mamata Banerjee's constituency, Bhabanipur. The family was not forced to join the TMC, but after Amit Shah left, BJP leaders could not make much impact in the area. In September 2017, when Shah came back to the state to take stock of the situation, he was surprised to see that nothing much had changed. The ground was set, but the state BJP leaders were not ready to take charge.

Despite the setbacks, Amit Shah set a target and said each worker must visit at least four to five houses in every booth. The idea was to spread out to 78,000-odd booths in the state and form a strong organizational net. A BJP source said there were applications of 88 workers to be the vistaraks in Bengal. Out of them, only 50 were chosen and trained at the party headquarters and they were asked to work on the ground for at least a year. Over the next one year, the BJP recruited about 200 vistaraks for West Bengal. Amit Shah might have hoped to create a ripple in Bengal politics by exposing the Mamata Banerjee government's failure.

However, his plan didn't get much success. The vistarak programme, which included not only trained workers but also state BJP leaders, faced resistance from the TMC workers on the ground. The BJP leaders were allegedly attacked in various parts of the state by TMC workers. In Purba Burdwan's Kalna, the BJP MP (nominated) George Becker was attacked when he visited the locality to attend a booth vistarak programme on 24 June 2017. He alleged that TMC workers blocked his car, ransacked it and then physically assaulted him with wickets in front of the local party office. The TMC, on the other hand, alleged that it was a fallout of the internal factionalism within the BJP.

This was not an isolated incident. The kind of resistance the BJP faced and the lack of organizational capabilities they had were exposed when a series of such incidents took place across the state and the BJP failed to capitalize on them to garner sympathy votes or new workers. The women leaders were also not spared. Not only George Becker, but also leaders like the BJP Mahila Morcha President Locket Chatterjee were attacked in Birbhum district. The state leadership had drawn flak from the central leaders for not being able to organize any movement when the BJP Yuva Morcha president, Debjit Sarkar, was arrested during a bandh called by the party against the killing of a school student in Islampur in North Dinajpur. The students and local villagers were protesting in Islampur against the appointment of an Urdu teacher when they needed teachers in other subjects. The BJP and the villagers alleged that the student was killed as police opened fire on the agitating crowd.

The state BJP leadership also faced problems with the membership drive. Although it was easy for anyone to give a missed call and become a member, the problem was in getting serious callers. 'The national leadership sent us a database of new members who called the given mobile number, but when we divided them assembly constituency-wise and tried to call them, we found that most of them were disinterested in working for the party. In some cases, someone's friends or relatives had played a prank by giving a missed call to the number from that individual's phone. So the "missed-call-membership" drive was not helpful in getting serious workers and activists,' says a Kolkata-based BJP leader who has contested many elections.

THE BACKROOM BOYS

The BJP central leadership, of course, did not depend only on the so-called membership drive or inducting leaders like Mukul Roy. Amit Shah put his trusted and tested men to work in Bengal. In 2018, while General Secretary (Organization) Ram Lal and his deputy Shiv Prakash were looking at boosting the organizational set-up in the state, Amit Shah brought in Arvind Menon as the deputy to Kailash Vijayvargiya, who was working as the minder of the Bengal BJP.

Shiv Prakash was the khetra pracharak of the RSS in western Uttar Pradesh and Uttarakhand in 2014. He is credited as the brain behind Narendra Modi's success in this area. A great orator with a thorough knowledge of the Sangh's ideology, Shiv Prakash also possesses excellent human resource skills. 'If anyone goes to him with any grievances, he is bound to come out with a solution. Shivji has a capacity of calming down an agitated mind and at the same time, he can be strict with sweet words. I have not seen any such person in the Sangh with such a sharp political IQ. His job was to build up the organization in the booth level and budget was no constraint for him.' says BJP state vice president, Ritesh Tiwari.

Arvind Menon had served nearly ten years in the Madhya Pradesh state unit as the general secretary (organization), which is one of the most crucial posts in terms of the BJP's organizational matters and is generally given to an RSS pracharak. He was believed to be close to the then chief minister, Shivraj Singh Chouhan. Amit Shah had shifted him to Delhi from Bhopal in April 2016 and asked him to look after the UP organization before the assembly elections there. Then, he was appointed co-in-charge of the Bengal BJP on 3 October 2018. Soon after taking charge of the Bengal unit, Arvind, a Malayali, rented a house in Kolkata's EM Bypass. He had spent his youth in Varanasi and had picked up Bengali there while interacting with the Bengalis living in UP. His job was to help Bengal BJP leaders mobilize the grassroots workers and leaders to form booth committees, the sole goal of the national president. He had accompanied Amit Shah during his vistarak programme in April 2017. In 2018, he was moving around in North Bengal to give the necessary boost to the party organization, mix with the villagers and common people to understand their minds, and formulate area-specific campaign strategies. This gave confidence to the grassroots BJP workers. Those unhappy with the TMC local leaders followed the BJP cadres and found shelter in the saffron camp.

The BJP leadership also divided the state into five zones for organizational purposes—Uttarbanga with eight Lok Sabha seats in North Bengal districts; Nabadwip with nine seats in districts bordering Bangladesh; Rarhbanga with eight seats in Burdwan, Birbhum and Junglemahal; Hooghly–Midnapore zone with ten Lok Sabha constituencies; and Kolkata with seven seats in the city and its adjoining areas in North and South 24 Parganas. While each zone had a state leader in charge, it also had *prabharis*, or supervisors, from outside the state, so that there was no complacency or misleading the state or central leadership. Each zone had a dedicated team of around 20 workers from outside the state and they looked after the grassroots level organization to carry out surveys and assist the booth-level leaders and workers. The supervisors and their teams reported directly to the central leadership. The BJP mandal presidents were under pressure to work at strengthening the party. Every Lok Sabha constituency also got a palak, or caretaker, to look after it.

The central leaders, including the party president, Amit Shah, came to the state from time to time to take stock of the situation. While he showed confidence in the organization at public meetings and while interacting with the media, he continuously monitored and pulled up the state leaders whenever he sensed a lack of motivation among them. There was also a tussle among the state leaders about the strength of the grassroots organization. In a meeting with the vistaraks in June 2018 at the Indian Museum's Ashutosh Centenary Hall in Kolkata, Shah's first question to them was, 'Do you want to change the Mamata Banerjee government from the state or do you want to let it go as it is going?' He gave the participants one minute to think about the question before answering. After getting a positive answer from the vistaraks, he began his speech. He reminded them that the party workers would have to overcome the fear of death and fight the TMC.

In a meeting in October 2018 at Mukul Roy's Elgin Road residence in Kolkata, the TMC-turned-BJP leader told the present central leaders that the BJP was ready with its organization in no more than 20 per cent areas in the state. Dilip Ghosh vehemently opposed Roy and said, 'You are demoralizing the party workers. We are ready in 60 per cent areas.' The journalists too questioned Amit Shah about the party's organization in the state and expressed surprise over the claim that BJP's organization had been built in 60 per cent areas. The then BJP national president stood by the state party leaders and reiterated that the BJP was ready to take on Mamata Banerjee.

In the panchayat elections in 2018, the BJP's electoral success in the Junglemahal districts, especially in Jhargram and Purulia, had shown the impact of organizational boost. In Jhargram, the BJP got majority seats in 24 gram panchayats and 10 were hung as no party got a majority. Though the TMC bagged 13 seats in the zila parishad, the BJP bagged three. In the Purulia, the BJP got 10 zila parishad seats while the TMC got 25. In panchayat samiti, the BJP was victorious in 142 seats and in gram panchayats, they won 644 seats. The statistics showed the inroads the BJP was making in parts of Bengal where elections were held. Here, Mukul Roy can perhaps claim some credit for the spectacular result of the saffron camp. In the initial months after joining the BJP, he could not do much in the by-elections of various assembly constituencies. However, as the convener of the panchayat election committee, he used his old sources in the TMC to bring out unhappy TMC workers to vote or work for the BJP. Though they trailed the TMC in electoral numbers, the saffron camp came up to a credible second position in the state politics pushing the Left and the Congress to a distant third and fourth place respectively. For example, in the 2018 panchayat elections, the BJP won 5,779 gram panchayat seats, whereas the Left won only 1,713 and Congress was victorious in 1,066 seats in the state. At the panchayat samiti level, the BJP won 769 seats, the Left won 139 seats and the Congress 133.

'In other states, it is the duty of the polling officers to conduct free and fair polls, but in Bengal, the responsibility lies with the political agents. So, putting polling agents in every booth and fighting the TMC workers is a big challenge for the Opposition parties,' said Rantidev Sengupta, editor of *Swastika*, the RSS Bengali mouthpiece. Since it was important to have a presence of the party agents in the polling booth, Mukul Roy helped in fielding BJP polling agents in most of the seats where the BJP fared well in panchayat elections. However, it did not seem that they were ready to take on the TMC across the state. After all, the TMC had the backing of the government and their presence at the booth level was better than any Opposition. Moreover, they were allegedly not above spreading terror to get their point across.

In May 2018, two BJP workers were found dead in Purulia in close succession. One of them was 18-year-old Trilochon Mahato, whose body was found hanging from a tree in Supurdih village in Purulia's Balarampur block. On his T-shirt, the following lines were written in Bengali, 'This is for doing BJP politics from age 18. Been trying to kill you since the vote. Failed. Today you are dead [sic].' In the police complaint, Trilochan's family named six TMC workers. The murder of two BJP workers in a district where the BJP fared well during the panchayat polls of 2018 highlighted two things—the balance of power in the area was changing with the BJP gaining ground and that the BJP was unable to protect its workers and supporters from such political violence.

Another instance showed how the BJP was unable to protect its supporters from the onslaught of political aggression of the TMC. Amit Shah held a rally in the district a few weeks after the murders. The BJP national president met two tribal families near the helipad during his visit as part of the Jan Sampark Karyakram; apparently, the families showed allegiance to the saffron camp. The next day, however, the families were whisked away to Kolkata by the ruling party leaders and senior TMC leaders, Madan Mitra and Shantanu Sen, claimed that the families had joined the TMC. It seemed as if the BJP leadership, be it at the local level or in the state capital, had no clue how to tackle such a situation. Earlier, the Left had failed to protect its supporters and they could not build up any movement or resistance in the face of the TMC's aggression. The BJP seemed to be following the same path.

However, the central BJP leadership knew that an anti-TMC sentiment was simmering at the grassroots level and they needed to cash in on it for the Lok Sabha elections of 2019. They did not want to lose this chance and, thus, kept working subtly to expand their support base with the help of experienced organizers from the Sangh or the BJP fold. As Shiv Prakash and Arvind Menon were put to work, after their victory in Tripura, Amit Shah also tried to boost the organization with new vigour. He brought the architect of the Tripura victory, RSS pracharak Sunil Deodhar, for a brief period to Bengal to assist Shiv Prakash, Arvind Menon and Kailash Vijayvargiya. The backroom boys' main job was to lead the vistaraks who had come from other states (Sunil Deodhar came with an army of 80 Bengali-speaking vistaraks from Assam and Tripura), organize the campaign at the booth level, look after the candidates, and prepare campaign materials and social media communications. So, they toured the state, having conversations with renowned people state from different localities to understand their sentiments.

The work of these behind-the-scene managers resulted in extending the party's organization in a large number of villages and towns before the Lok Sabha elections in 2019. From 452 mandal committees in 2015, the BJP reached 1,280 in 2019. They had set up 12,407 shakti kendras and had appointed 10,266 full-time shakti kendra pramukhs. Many BJP district units got new party offices and there was much enthusiasm among the grassroots workers.

Another part of the organization that gave the BJP leaders, workers as well as supporters the necessary boost was the IT cell. Shiv Prakash brought in Ujjwal Pareek, a Kolkata boy, to head the BJP's social media team in Bengal. Pareek, an IT professional, had worked with the BJP's social media team in 2014 after which he had gone back to his professional life only to be brought back in 2018. He worked with his team of around 10,000 workers to send out both offensive and defensive messages pertaining to the party to netizens.

The IT cell's job was to operate the 'BJP4Bengal' Facebook page as well as its Twitter handle apart from 50,000-odd WhatsApp groups. 'In 2014, we had used Twitter, but this time the focus was on one-to-one communication. WhatsApp came handy in this and we could reach out to maximum people even in the rural areas,' says a member of the BJP's IT cell. There were multiple workshops to train cyber cell members to maximize the use of social media to draw the attention of young voters. Whenever there were attacks on the BJP by the TMC, messages would be circulated on social media. If the opponent camp faltered at any point, there would be memes and graphics around the issue. During the last leg of campaigning when Mamata Banerjee reacted sharply to the 'Jai Shri Ram' chant in West Midnapore's Chandrakona, the BJP cyber cell did not waste any time in putting together a viral video, which asked the question, 'Is it a crime to chant the name of Ram in Bengal?' This attracted huge traffic and half of the battle was won on social media in rousing people's religious sentiment.

The cyber team also helped the party and the candidates with data analytics to show which issues were popular with netizens and which were going against them. The task of swaying and winning over voters through social media sentiment was an important task that Pareek and his team smoothly handled from a flat near Beleghata.

'Money was never a constraint in running the backroom activities in Bengal by bringing vistaraks from outside the state, running the social media team or meeting the expenses of building new party offices,' says a BJP insider.

RSS GROUNDWORK

The RSS never admits that it takes part in any political activities. 'Some activists may join BJP, but those who support the Sangh are indeed likely to support BJP as its ideological standpoint is the same as the Sangh. We engage in social activities whereas the BJP is into politics,' says the RSS mouthpiece editor, Rantidev Sengupta.

The backroom boys might have helped the BJP strengthen its strategy, but it's the RSS's groundwork in Bengal that evened the playing field for the BJP, especially in North Bengal. The RSS, through its shakhas and other social organizations, could influence people at the grassroots. 'We are more acceptable to people as we don't talk of politics. We have an ideology and we discuss that at our shakhas,' says an RSS activist from Hooghly district. 'But there have been open invitations from the local BJP leadership to campaign for the candidate during the Lok Sabha or other polls,' he adds. And, thus, many young RSS activists joined the BJP in large numbers during Modi's campaign in 2014.

'RSS activists always don't work directly for the candidates. But in every election, they campaign on various issues that align with the RSS–BJP ideology. They form different organizations in different areas. Like in Hooghly this time, they formed an outfit called Hooghly Zila Janakalyan Samiti. This outfit's job is to distribute leaflets and do door-to-door campaign on the issues rather than the candidate. The activists will probably not say whom to vote for, but they will talk about BJP's issues,' says Pinakpani Ghosh.

Till a few years ago, the RSS had about 700 shakhas in South Bengal and about 300 shakhas in North Bengal, but the figure in South Bengal had gone up to 1,200 and 400 in the North by 2018. A large number of people have shown interest in the RSS and its ideology. 'RSS has loosened up its process of extending the organization. Now people can apply online. They don't need to attend shakhas in khaki half pants and white shirt. Instead, there are *ghoroa baithaks* (indoor meetings) where they hoist the flag, worship Bharat Mata, discuss the Sangh ideology, sing a few songs and that's it,' says Pinakpani. 'Sangh periodically organize *parichiti varga* or sessions to introduce the aspirants to the Sangh ideology. Some would stay back while some would not come back. But those who do not come back still grow a sense of attachment with the Sangh culture.'

The Sangh does not hold street meetings, but they have penetration in every social as well as religious organization in the state. The Sangh imparts its ideological commandants to the people they interact with or to who attend the shakhas and then lets them go in to their field of work where they can further spread their ideology.

To understand the Sangh's penetration in a community, one may look at how the RSS worked really hard to capture the Matua vote bank before the 2019 Lok Sabha elections. Mamata was trying desperately to capture the same vote bank for the last several years and donated funds to build infrastructure for their headquarters in Thakurnagar. But, the RSS had some other plans for them. For the last couple of years, they were working with the Matua community. 'Every fortnight Matuas have a programme called the "*mochchab*" where the members of the community meet and greet each other and have a meal together. The RSS activists regularly attended these *mochchabs* and talked about the NRC and Citizenship Bill to gain the confidence of the community in favour of the saffron camp. It worked. The [Lok Sabha election] result is a testimony to it,' says Pinakpani.

Similarly, in some religious organizations, they hold an evening meeting on 'election and Hindutva' to preach their political message. This door-to-door silent campaign was possible in the TMC regime as the TMC did not have a strong ideology-based, well-knit organization. Communists would not have allowed it as their cadres had a strong presence in every sphere of the society through ideology-driven frontal organizations among the teachers, artists, students, women, farmers, unorganized labourers and, most importantly, in the civil society. Nagarik Committee was the one which used to look apolitical in nature, but it also had a strong presence of Left leaders. So, they could monitor every movement of the Opposition in their locality and resist them if required.

Another strategy employed by the RSS is to target the kitchen. They first meet one potential activist at his residence. Then, the pracharak visits his house for a cup of tea. Within weeks, he extracts a lunch invitation with the family, gets familiarized with the members of the family and gradually absorbs the whole family into the fold of the Sangh, at least psychologically.

Throughout the year, they keep on publishing booklets in Bengali on various current issues for publicity. Most importantly, they keep a clean image. If there is a single allegation against any RSS leader, he is shifted out of the core organization to some fringe outfit.

Though the Jan a Sangh or later the BJP could not make much inroads into the electoral politics of Bengal, the RSS kept working across the state with frontal organizations like the Vanavasi Kalyan Ashram (VKA), which mainly works among tribals, running hostels and involving people in social activities. The VKA came into existence in the 1980s and since then, they have formed eight branches in North Bengal districts. Five hostels in this area for the students of class V to X accommodate around 30 students, mostly from the economically backward sections. In South Bengal, they have 10 hostels with about 400 students. They also run Ekal Vidyalaya, as well as night schools and have about 200 such centres in North Bengal and 533 in South Bengal. Their job is to train the economically backward in vocations that can help them earn their bread and butter.

The VKA has also been arranging mass marriages for the last 15 years. Their continuous campaign against religious conversions has helped the Rightist forces fight against Christian missionaries working in tribal areas. Though VKA does not take a direct part in the BJP's politics, their social influence has helped the saffron camp gain popularity and credibility among the tribal and economically backward population in North Bengal. For example, in Darjeeling hills, where the BJP does not have any strong presence, the VKA's activities have helped them make inroads into the minds of the voters. Other organizations like Sree Hari Satsang Samiti, which organizes religious functions among the tribal population, has kept their focus on a kind of social engineering that goes without much publicity and behind the politicking of the BJP. Their idea has been to instil the core of 'Indian culture' in the minds of the most neglected sections of the society. These affiliate organizations do not talk about politics, but when the election comes, the voters of these areas know whom to vote for to keep their social identity alive.

Like the BJP, its parent organization RSS also could not spread its wings aggressively due to the lack of strong leadership. Though it had a presence in a large part of the state through shakhas and affiliate organizations, it could not assert itself under pressure from the Left movement and politics. However, as the Left went out of power, the RSS leaders took initiative to extend their base in Bengal. The turning point in the attitude of the RSS leadership was the Akhil Bhartiya Pratinidhi Sabha, the highest policy-formulation- and decision-making body of the Sangh, in Coimbatore in Tamil Nadu in 2017. In an unprecedented move, the Pratinidhi Sabha took a special and separate resolution on West Bengal. On behalf of the West Bengal unit, Dakshin Banga Prant pracharak Bidyut Mukhopadhyay and karyavaha

Jishnu Basu floated a resolution on the 'growing Jihadi environment' in Bengal. It criticized the West Bengal chief minister for inducting 'fundamentalist' elements in her cabinet and how Mamata was encouraging religious fundamentalism in the state. They cited examples of the Kaliachak riots of 2016 (where communal tension erupted due to a remark by a fringe Hindu outfit leader Kamlesh Tiwari) and the situation in bordering areas and Kolkata's minority-dominated areas. While it appealed to the state government to do away with 'vote bank politics', it also requested the central government to protect the state from such 'Jihadi activities'. In the recent history of RSS, no such separate resolution had been ever taken for any particular state. This point of departure meant RSS was taking a special interest in Bengal, putting pressure on Mamata Banerjee government and boosting the morale of their activists in the state to fight against the TMC's 'pro-minority' stance. 'It also boosted the RSS–BJP organizational mechanism in West Bengal. RSS put their full strength behind the state BJP. Its *pracharaks* were put into service for BJP's vistarak programme. In many cases, the *bibhag pracharaks* [a bibhag in RSS generally consists of two districts] acted almost like political advisors to the BJP leaders in the area,' says Pinakpani Ghosh. In RSS organization, a resolution ratified by the top leadership means a command that is to be obeyed with full faith and strength. This exactly happened in this case.

The change of leadership and regular visits by the sarsanghchalak Mohan Bhagwat to various parts of the state also encouraged the RSS activists to spread their ideology of establishing a 'Hindu Rashtra'. Its activities, like conducting training camps, which had been going on for a long time in the state, came under media glare. 'Arms training' of young RSS members in the training camps, '*shashtra pujan*' (worshipping the crude weapons) on Durga Vijayadasami day, which was hitherto unknown to the common people of Bengal, came into limelight. At the same time, the RSS-affiliated organizations carried on with their functions of reaching out to the intellectuals of the state and bringing them on board. They too faced resistance from the state government. Mohan Bhagwat's rally in January 2017 did not get police permission until the court intervened. In September 2017, when the Sangh affiliate, Sister Nivedita Mission Trust, planned to organize a function on Swami Vivekananda's disciple Nivedita's role in the Indian freedom movement, the authorities of the venue, Mahajati Sadan, withdrew permission to use the hall.

'Through its activities, the RSS, its affiliates and sister organizations like Bajrang Dal, VHP could make their presence felt in the state. Whenever there was communal tension in the state, these organizations were there to support the Hindus,' says an RSS volunteer. 'This sense of protection under the Sangh helped its political offshoot BJP to gain electorally.'

Saffron flags in remote villages and, most importantly, in minority-dominated areas showed how these organizations helped mobilize Hindus, irrespective of caste and creed, in Bengal. The BJP, in a way, reaped the benefits of the work these social organizations had done.

5

Decline of the Left Front

To the surprise of many journalists, at a closed-door 'off-the-record' meeting held just before the 2016 assembly elections in Bengal, a senior RSS functionary said, 'Left is our biggest enemy.' The comment flummoxed many. Wasn't the saffron camp aiming at eroding some of Mamata Banerjee's popularity and plotting the decimation of Trinamool? The truth is that the Left has always been a bigger enemy of the RSS–BJP than the TMC. 'With the Trinamool, we hardly have any ideological battle. We are more concerned with the Left, as their ideology has permeated the state due to the long rule,' added the senior RSS leader.

In the last 20 odd years, when the RSS–BJP combine had the option of aggressively taking on the Left, they chose not to make much effort to dislodge the communist government in Bengal. It was clear that they had neither a strong organization nor intention. Instead, they concentrated on silently expanding the activities of their fringe organizations and subtly supported Mamata Banerjee in overthrowing the Left regime in the state. Not only did the people of Bengal adore Mamata, but they also supported her in her fight against the Left rule. She was hugely popular and the TMC had emerged as the main anti-Left force since its inception in 1998.

The BJP utilized her popularity to fully decimate the Left in Bengal. 'They knew Mamata is an easier enemy to conquer than the Left,' says Biswajit Bhattacharya. 'Bringing the Left forces down was the BJP's only goal. Once that was done, they could take Mamata head-on.' The RSS–BJP top brass must have rejoiced the Left Front drawing a blank in the 2019 Lok Sabha elections in Bengal more than the TMC being reduced to 22 MPs from 34.

Why is the BJP organically opposed to the Left? The question is perhaps answered in second sarsanghchalak 'Guruji' M.S. Golwalkar's book *A Bunch of Thoughts*. The fight between the Sangh's nationalism and the communists' internationalism is the core of this ideological divide. Golwalkar writes, 'The present state of strife and wars resulting in human destruction and misery has led many thinkers to conclude that the sentiment of nationalism which nourishes exclusive self-interest is the major obstacle in the way of world unity and human welfare. They, therefore, declare that nationalism should be rooted out from the minds of men all over the world. The Communist ideology which claims internationalism as its sheet anchor often talks in this strain.'[1]

The RSS and the BJP believe in Hindu nationalism which, they think, is deeply rooted in this country and is based on Hindu culture, which could not be erased even after the 200-year British rule and the establishment of constitutional nationalism post-Independence. The RSS has been opposing the culture of Karl Marx and Macaulay in India. If Marxism talks about a stateless society as the culmination of class struggle and instilling a sense of internationalism

[1] Golwalkar, M.S. *Bunch of Thoughts*. Sahitya Sindhu Prakashan 1996.

Macaulay, a British bureaucrat, introduced English education in India in place of Sanskrit and Persian in the 1830s, the saffron camp believes both these 'foreign elements' have destroyed Hindu culture. They don't want Left ideology to come in between their brand of territorial nationalism and the goal of setting up a Hindu Rashtra in India. They think Marxists and communists are the main hindrances in achieving this goal. Golwalkar also vehemently criticizes communists in his book. 'A person can either be a Hindu or a Communist. He cannot be both,' he writes.

This guiding literature sets the tone for RSS-BJP combine not only in Bengal but in the whole country. They believe that Nehru's constitutional nationalism is an offshoot of the so-called modern, Western, socialist ideology. So, the Modi-Shah duo is as active in destroying Nehruvian thoughts as they are in diluting the Leftist ideology from the country. The attack on JNU (either by bringing in sedition charges against its students for shouting 'anti-national' slogans or branding it as the hub of Left politics and the students as 'urban Naxals'), fighting the Left Democratic Front (LDF) government in Kerala, defeating the Left in the tiny North-Eastern state of Tripura and supporting Mamata to decimate the Left in Bengal, all can be seen through the same prism of ideological war. On social media too, the Rightist forces attack the 'Left Liberals' more than those who support the Congress or Trinamool. It is in this light that the BJP's fight against the Left in Bengal should be viewed and analysed.

In 2006, when the Singur movement was at its peak, a senior union minister, who was a BJP spokesperson during the UPA's rule, visited the area. Mamata was agitating against the acquisition of farmland for the Tata

Nano car factory. 'One day, he told me he wanted to go to Singur and didn't want any media focus. He wanted to go there privately,' says a senior Bengal BJP leader. 'I took him there. He got off the car with a notebook and pen. He started touring the affected villages on foot and talking to the villagers. He took notes as he was asking them about their plight.'

The BJP leader further adds his senior colleague from Delhi was collecting first-hand information only to corner the Left at the national level. 'He told me, we may be a marginal force in Bengal [at that time], but we are the main Opposition at the national level. This is our opportunity to attack the Left there in Delhi. This ground-level information will help us clear our understanding and sharpen our attack,' the BJP leader says.

The BJP did not have to do much to defeat the Left in Bengal. This was partly to Mamata Banerjee's credit and partly to the Left's inability to guard their fort. The BJP simply filled the void the Left created in Bengal politics especially after 2011.

THE LEFT'S DECLINE SINCE 2011

While trying to reach the remote village of Jakri, Khanakul, in Hooghly district in 2009 to investigate the reports of violence where the Left and the TMC workers had clashed, I asked a passer-by for directions. Google Maps doesn't work here, neither does GPS, so you are at the sole mercy of locals for directions. A man on a cycle stopped and, while trying to help, started telling tales of how CPIM leaders were unleashing terror in his area and how the Left Front government had failed them. I met at least five persons on the road to the remote village. To my utter surprise, they kept narrating the same story of the Left's misrule. No prodding was needed. All they wanted was to share their sorry state of affairs and they had understood I was a journalist.

They said that till the late 1980s, the Left Front rule was beneficial. They got their right to land and livelihood even though they were the marginal rural population in the state. Things changed during the Left's third term; who started undermining the common man. In many parts of the state, the Left cadres did not allow the common man to exercise their fundamental right—the right to vote. The villagers complained that they were not allowed to vote and party cadres would cast votes on their behalf. This caused huge resentment among the villagers. Those who tried to oppose the Left leaders were attacked. In the process, the villagers lost their voice and were at the mercy of the ruling party cadres.

Khanakul falls under the Arambag parliamentary constituency from where former CPIM MP Anil Basu had won with a record margin of nearly six lakh votes in 2004 Lok Sabha elections, the highest margin in the country till then. This result was attributed to the 'terror' of the Left party in the area. It was alleged that genuine voters could not go to the polling booths to exercise their democratic right of choosing their representative through a secret ballot. The ruling party allegedly manipulated the polling.

In many areas, the Opposition polled zero votes in a number of booths. The ruling party turned arrogant and started terrorizing common people and interfering in the private lives of individuals. Any family dispute would have to get resolved at the local CPIM party office. Terms like Local Committee (LC), Local Committee Member (LCM), Local Committee Secretary (LCS) became popular among the people. The LC offices were almost the administrative, judicial and executive headquarters in the area. In the name of party's growth in the state, the CPIM leadership let the local satraps rule. Nothing could pass without the approval of the LCS.

On the other hand, when 'Licence Raj' was removed through the New Economic Policy of the P.V. Narasimha Rao government at the Centre in 1991, the Left, as a whole and the trade unions, in particular, kept resisting the economic reforms. Many industrial units had to shut down in Bengal due to aggressive trade unionism. 'The degeneration of the Left Front or, to be specific, the CPIM began with the entry of businessmen, promoters, goons into the party since 1987, after the Left Front came to power for the third time. There was no filter to induct new members. In a bid to form a mass party, the Left tried to extend the party's control over all aspects of society. A new class of "political dadas" emerged in Bengal and they turned out to be the local satraps with the full backing of the Communist Party,' says journalist Biswajit Bhattacharyya, who covered the Left for a long time.

The CPIM leadership soon realized that 'alien influences and trends'[2] had penetrated the party and affected its membership. CPIM politburo member Md Salim admits that inertia had set in the organization after being in power for 10 years and unwanted elements (persons and activities) had crept into the party. The Central Committee of the CPIM in 1996 had adopted a 'Rectification Document' to launch an intra-party campaign to do away with these 'alien' forces. They attributed the influence to the setback of socialism and the existence of the party in the semi-feudal, petty-bourgeois society. The CPIM leadership accepted that there were adjustments by the party to accommodate itself with the 'existing bourgeois order'. The document

[2] Central Committee, The Marxist CPI(M). 2009. 'On Rectification Campaign: Edited version of the Resolution adopted by the Central Committee', XXVI 1, January–March 2010.

mentions that 'a large number of entrants into the Party have not acquired the basic understanding of the Party and its programmatic objectives... The tactical alliance with bourgeois parties particularly electoral alliances have led to the possibilities for the penetration of the bourgeois style of functioning within the Party.' The document also proved that there was hardly any ideological training of the new comrades they welcomed to the CPIM.

Ironically, the West Bengal unit of the CPIM did not pay much heed to the rectification campaign. Rather, when the then land and land reforms minister, Binay Krishna Chowdhury, had said '*gaach, machh* and contractors' are going to kill the party, he was vehemently criticized by his colleagues. He meant that the timber mafia, the fight over the ownership of fish ponds (known as *bheri* in Bengali), and the contractor raj were dominating party affairs. In January 1996, Chowdhury had said at a party function in his home district Burdwan, 'The government is corrupt. After 18 years in power, we have fallen prey to corruption. I may be called mad for saying so, but this is the bitter truth.'[3]

The CPIM leaders were defensive, but when asked for his reaction on Binay Chowdhury's comment, the then chief minister, Jyoti Basu, told journalists, 'If he thinks the government is corrupt, why is he continuing to be in the government?'[4]

Binay Chowdhury, who had a clean image as a communist leader and had led the land reforms movement in the late 1970s and early 1980s, was rebutted by his own party leaders. It showed the arrogance of the CPIM leadership in the face of the

[3] Banerjee, R. *India Today*. 'Left Front Government of West Bengal is corrupt: Benoy Chowdhury'. 15 January 1996.

[4] Ibid.

party's growing influence in the state and an absence of any formidable Opposition. The political vacuum in the Opposition space in the state had helped them grow in electoral numbers as well. But the damage was done. While the Left leaders were happy with the growth of the party, they cared little about the quality of cadres and the arrogance of their leaders. The CPIM started to rot in the presence of a cadre-base which was neither trained in the party's ideology nor in its objectives. They clung on to power and people experienced atrocities like those in Khanakul. The ruling party cadres often terrorized the people and made them act according to their commands in many ways. The people had to turn to the party leaders to resolve even family disputes and the leaders' verdict was final. People had to make a beeline at the party office to avail social welfare benefits. If someone was opposed to the Left, the person was ostracized in the community. The Opposition's political workers or supporters were attacked if they tried to exert influence in the area. Starting from hiring the labourers for harvesting the crop in the villages to setting up any business venture, nothing could be done without the permission of the local *dadas* (big brothers).

In 2008, the Rectification Document was once again discussed in Coimbatore. The CPIM leadership, which since 1996 had claimed that 'rectification is a continuous process', admitted that there has not been any significant change in the party's condition in terms of 'wrong trends within the party'. It recorded that 'not enough is done to go to the roots and take systematic steps, political, ideological and organizational to deal with the fundamental sources of the problems'. This trend of inviting members and supporters to the party without any ideological training diluted the communist ideology of the CPIM.

However, it was the year 2006 that proved to be the turning point for the Left in Bengal in many ways. The Left Front came to power with a massive mandate of 235 seats in the 294-seat-strong West Bengal assembly in 2006. Their leaders thought they had got the mandate to implement their electoral slogan—*Krishi amader bhitti, Shilpa amader bhabishyot* (Agriculture is our base, industry is our future). The idea was to send out a message that they were changing their stance. The Left Front government—which carried out the land reforms process and handed over the ownership of land to landless farmers, worked hard to improve the agricultural production—would now concentrate on inviting investment for setting up industrial units, thereby, they would create jobs for the unemployed youth. The hurry with which the then chief minister, Buddhadeb Bhattacharjee, tried to bring big industries to the state rang the first alarm bells for the Left Front government.

The goal of the seventh Left Front government was determined the day Bhattacharjee took oath as the chief minister in 2006. He had invited top industrialists to the ceremony at Raj Bhavan. The next day he, along with his industry minister, Nirupam Sen, held a meeting with the industrialists at the state CPIM headquarters. Soon after taking over as chief minister, Bhattacharjee in a joint press conference on 18 May 2006 with the Tata Group chairman, Ratan Tata, announced that they were going to set up a ₹1 lakh-car project in Singur in the Hooghly district. He would need about 700 acres of land to set up the main factory and in the rest of the 300 acres, there would be ancillary units.

The CPIM's industrialization bid was nothing new. Former chief minister Jyoti Basu too had tried to woo industrialists with his controversial annual 'business trips' abroad. The Opposition claimed that these business trips bore no fruit and brought no investment. In 1994, amid a lot of debate and discussion within the party, Jyoti Basu had announced his industrial policy and crowned his colleague, Lok Sabha MP Somnath Chatterjee, as the head of the West Bengal Industrial Development Corporation. In 2001, when Buddhadeb Bhattacharjee took over the baton from Basu, he appointed former Burdwan district secretary of the CPIM, Nirupam Sen, as his industry minister. This was a significant decision. So far, the commerce and industry departments were allocated to a minister from a smaller party of the Left Front. This was the first time that a senior leader of the 'big brother' CPIM was given the charge of the industry department. Sen, who had never been a part of the Left Front cabinet, got this responsibility with the endorsement of the leadership to carry forward the industrialization drive. Following the liberal economic policies of the 1990s, the new industry minister initiated the process of divesting the sick public sector units in the state and took a loan from British government's Department for International Development (DFID) to take up reform measures and invite industries to set up their units in the state. Despite hiccups, Sen was operating at a slow but steady pace.

There was a significant change in the Left Front government's approach towards industrialization in 2006 with two flagship projects. On the one hand, the government invited the Tatas to set up their Nano car factory, and on the other, the chief minister laid out the red carpet for the Indonesian Beni Santosa's Salim

Group to set up a chemical hub along with a few other infrastructure projects. While the government had acquired 1,000 acres of farmland in Singur for the Tata factory, they had planned to take over 5,000 acres of land in Nandigram for the chemical hub. The Salim Group was also attempting to buy land for various infrastructure projects like a highway connecting North 24 Parganas to East Midnapore with a bridge to Nayachar, an island and a proposed industrial hub.

The seed of resentment among the farmers was sowed with the announcement of the Singur project. On 25 May 2006, when Tata officials went to inspect the land for the proposed car factory, they faced the wrath of the locals. The officials had to run away from Singur due to the violent protests from villagers, who were not ready to give up their farmland and demanded job assurance.

Former chief minister Jyoti Basu realized the core problem of the Left government's approach towards industrialization was not taking the party workers and supporters in confidence before initiating this policy change. While he was always in favour of a connection between the leaders and workers, the industrialization drive of 2006 lacked this approach. Apparently, he told his party colleagues the same and asked them to rectify this mistake. When Basu was coming out of the first CPIM secretariat meeting after the Tata officials were attacked by the Singur villagers, he was asked for his reaction by the journalists. Basu in his nonchalant way answered, 'I have asked Buddha why precautions were not taken before the Tata officials went to the spot. I heard our Krishak Sabha president did not know about their visit. He was taking an afternoon siesta then.'

By saying that the Krishak Sabha president was taking an afternoon siesta and was not aware of the

Tata officials' visit, the veteran communist leader made it clear that the local party functionaries were not consulted when the project was planned and the decision to acquire farmland was taken. Buddhadeb Bhattacharjee, in his bid to initiate industrialization in the state, had ignored the importance of his own party workers; instead, he had depended on bureaucrats and some of the top-rung leaders of the party. This was the core mistake of his policy change. 'Both Buddhadeb Bhattacharjee and Nirupam Sen led the industrialization drive ignoring the regimentation of a communist party. They depended much on bureaucrats. They did not feel the necessity of sending out the message to the grassroots level before implementing any policy. The duo acted more as social democrats deviating from the original ideologies of communism. Their alibi was that the Communist Party needs to be pragmatic drawing from the experiences in China for the economic development of the state,' says Biswajit Bhattacharya.

On the contrary, when their colleague Gautam Deb had acquired thousands of acres of land in Rajarhat to set up a satellite township, Newtown, adjacent to Kolkata, he had carried out the process over years and by taking all the stakeholders, including the local Opposition leaders, on board. The mistake in Singur, however, could not be rectified despite Jyoti Basu and a few other CPIM leaders' warnings. The Buddhadeb Bhattacharjee government was in a hurry for industrialization and the creation of jobs for the young. They did not want to put a brake on his 'well-intentioned' but 'wrongly-implemented' industrial development plan. Mamata Banerjee used this opportunity and launched a massive movement.

'I would say Singur and Nandigram worked just as a catalyst for the fall of the Left Front government. The signs of its demise were in the offing. If malpractices among the party's rank and file was one side of the story, the other side was the mismanagement of the industrialization drive. It only accelerated the process of their fall from power. The Left—known for standing by the poor, farmers and labourers, and famous for their flagship land reforms—was now acquiring agricultural land from farmers. The local party leaders and workers were not taken into confidence most of the time.

Way back in 2003, a senior CPIM leader from South 24 Parganas district had told me the government officials had come directly to villages to measure and dig up land for laying the pipe for a drinking water project. The villagers were angry apprehending the government would acquire their land. The local party had no information and they had a hard time to convince the agitating villagers as they were unaware of such administrative decisions. This approach of directly using the administration bypassing the local party leaders grew with time. The transformation from land reforms to land acquisition was shocking for people to accept. This message went out like wildfire across the state, especially in the rural areas, that the Left Front government would now grab agricultural land. Mamata Banerjee utilized this issue and emerged as a messiah of the poor and farmers. She did not have to look back,' says Biswajit Bhattacharya.

Since September 2006, Mamata's graph went up and the Left's was in the decline. The police firing on the farmers of Nandigram on 14 March 2007 killing 14 villagers was the final nail in the Left Front's coffin.

For the next four years, Buddhadeb Bhattacharjee led a virtually 'lame-duck government'. The police and administration turned out to be inactive, the industrialization process hit a roadblock due to Mamata Banerjee's movement in Singur and Nandigram, Maoist insurgency in Junglemahal resurfaced in a new avatar, and a breakaway faction of Gorkha National Liberation Front relaunched their violent agitation demanding a separate state of Gorkhaland. The Opposition forces, under the leadership of Mamata Banerjee, created tremendous pressure on the Left Front government. Over and above administrative logjams and failures, the common people, who had suffered due to the arrogance of the Left leaders, got a voice against the CPIM. The balance of power started shifting from the Left to the Centre with the TMC taking over the reins. In 2008, the Left, under the leadership of the then CPIM general secretary, Prakash Karat, withdrew support from the UPA I government in Delhi on the issue of signing civil nuclear agreement treaty with the USA. It did not bring down the Manmohan Singh government, but rather caused problems for the Left, especially in Bengal.

'It was a huge blunder for the Left. The decision to withdraw support from the central government on an ideological issue that could hardly be explained to the common people actually isolated the Left in the country. This decision also paved the way for the Congress to come closer to Mamata Banerjee in Bengal to teach a lesson to the CPIM,' says Biswajit Bhattacharya.

If the 2008 panchayat elections were an indicator of the Left's decline, they also showed that Mamata Banerjee was invading CPIM's rural bastion. In the panchayat elections, the Trinamool bagged two zila parishads in South 24 Parganas and East Midnapore.

Allying with the Congress and garnering the support of all anti-Left Front forces, Mamata Banerjee dislodged the 34-year-old Left Front government.

There has been no turning around for the Left since 2011. Be it Buddhadeb Bhattacharjee himself or other senior Left leaders, no one could come up with a concrete plan to revamp the party. Md Salim, a CPIM politburo member, explains that there was a grand alliance against the Left. 'From known Naxalites to Maoists to SUCI to the Congress—everyone went with TMC in the name of strengthening the democracy, which was said to be in danger under the Left rule,' he says 'Our mistake was we allowed the grand alliance to grow, both nationally and at the state level. We thought like "*bhadralok*" that people would understand the mistake they were making by supporting Mamata Banerjee. The media projected her as the "better Left", which has been proved wrong.'

The Left leadership waited for an organic reaction from the people in bringing down the TMC-led grand alliance. 'But the number game went against us when the anti-Left forces across the country started uniting against us,' says Mohammad Salim.

At the national level, the party was in an embarrassing position as their withdrawal of support from the first Manmohan Singh government could not make much impact. The UPA-I government did not fall. At the state level, the administrative decisions of the Left Front government had further isolated them. The Nandigram police firing and a subsequent bid by the CPIM to reclaim lost ground through an alleged armed retaliation in November 2007 made things worse for the Left. The TMC's dominance in Bengal's political space grew as Mamata Banerjee's followers started to assert themselves and so did the disgruntled Left workers and supporters. The change in this balance of power led to large-scale political violence in various parts of the state. The Left leaders and workers were shunted out of the area where they had worked for long. The political turf-war between the TMC and the Left intensified. In the face of political onslaught, the Left leaders were rendered clueless about how to protect their party cadres. This helplessness was visible as early as 2008–09 when the Left government was still in power but fast losing its political direction.

THE LEFT'S FAILURE TO PROTECT ITS CADRES

During the 2009 Lok Sabha elections, a group of journalists tried to catch the outgoing MP and CPIM leader, Sujan Chakraborty, for a sound bite on the polling day. After several calls, we were asked to wait in front of a school, a polling booth, in Bhangar in South 24 Parganas. He was seeking re-nomination from Jadavpur constituency. While waiting for him to reach the polling booth, we hardly saw any Left cadres or flags in the vicinity. After a long time, he reached in a car with his polling agent. However, he did not wait there for long and asked us to follow his car. We followed Sujan Chakraborty's car until he stopped in a 'no man's land' in the middle of the road. He got off the car and in an open area with no CPIM supporters or flags, he agreed to answer our questions. There were reasons for him to allege that TMC leaders were scaring off CPIM polling agents in the area. We also found that a few CPIM party offices were under lock and key in Bhangar. He did not want to invite the attention of the TMC workers and thus trouble by talking to the media in a crowded place.

This was not only about Bhangar or Sujan Chakraborty. A similar situation prevailed in most parts of the state and kept getting worse over the years. With the balance of power tilting, CPIM leaders were now pariahs in the localities they once considered their kingdoms. Many CPIM leaders, cadres and supporters had to leave their residences and take shelter in other parts of the state. Those who could resist the onslaught or switch sides survived. Many comrades of the CPIM from a few districts alleged that they did not receive any help from the state leadership to either resist the assault or fight a legal battle when they were accused in false cases and, sometimes, even arrested by their own government's police.

During her 2011 poll campaign, Mamata Banerjee's clarion call was 'We want change, not revenge'. It is true that Bengal did not witness large-scale violence post the 2011 election results as many had anticipated. Still, there were backlashes in several parts; CPIM supporters were attacked and their houses ransacked. This was perhaps a natural backlash keeping in mind that these people had to suffer the terror of the Left parties for so long.

'My mother who was a CPIM women's wing leader had to go in hiding for months. Several false cases were slapped against her and other comrades of the locality after the 2011 assembly elections. Our houses were ransacked and sitting in Kolkata, I could not get much help either from the ruling party or CPIM party leaders,' says a broadcast journalist who hails from Burdwan district and works in Kolkata.

The TMC not only targeted the Left's grassroots workers and supporters, but the police—under the new government—also went after their leaders at the local level or in Kolkata. Many Left regional big guns such as Tapan Ghosh, Sukur Ali, Sushanta Ghosh and Lakshman Seth were accused in old political murder cases and arrested.

In June 2011, soon after the change of guard, a few skeletons were unearthed from a pit near former Garbeta MLA Susanta Ghosh's ancestral home in Benachapra. The villagers of Piyasala claimed these were the skeletons of five TMC workers who had allegedly been killed in broad daylight in September 2002 by CPIM goons at the insistence of Ghosh. Susanta's name topped the list of 40 accused in the murder case. On 11 August, in the evening, after long arguments and counter-arguments in a small courtroom packed with journalists, lawyers and supporters of the former minister, the court ordered his arrest. It was unbelievable that such a powerful leader in the area could be arrested on the charges of political murder! Once known as the 'King of Garbeta', Ghosh was being dragged by the police and pushed into a CID van in the same West Midnapore area that he once dominated. As cameras flashed, Ghosh, known to keep his cool, shouted that it was all a conspiracy. Initially, former chief minister Buddhadeb Bhattacharjee stood by him saying it was vendetta politics by Mamata Banerjee, but soon the party deserted him. He was in jail for nearly a year. A few youth wing supporters of the Left went to receive Ghosh from the Alipore Central Jail when he got bail. He remained the party MLA from Garbeta till 2016, after which he was denied a ticket in the next assembly elections and dropped from the state committee as well.

In East Midnapore, the 'King of Haldia', Lakshman Seth, also had to face the same fate. In January 2012, the CID filed a charge sheet against Lakshman Seth and 87 others. They were booked under Sections 302 (murder) and 120 (B) (Criminal conspiracy). The CID said that six villagers of Nandigram had been abducted and killed by the CPIM goons, their bodies dumped in a river. After an arrest warrant was issued against him in February 2012, he went into hiding. Seth was arrested by the CID from a guest house in Mumbai in March 2012. Along with him, two local CPIM leaders, who had led the party in Nandigram, Amiya Sahoo and Ashok Guria, were also arrested. Seth was also shunted out by the party and two years later in 2014, he was expelled for anti-party activities. He accused the party of conspiring to throw him out.

In 2011, senior CPIM leader and MP Mohammed Salim was forced to move out of the 3,400-square-feet quarter he and his wife, Rosina Khatun, enjoyed as part of her government job as an anaesthetist in Chittaranjan Sishu Sadan in Bhabanipur area of Kolkata. In June that year, the Mamata Banerjee government found that Rosina was not entitled to such a big quarter and should have been allotted a 700-square-feet accommodation instead. The government alleged that due to her husband's political influence she had been allotted the huge space on the top floor of a state-run hospital.

The government's anti-corruption branch also accused former health minister and the then leader of the Opposition Surya Kanta Mishra's wife, Usha Mishra, and her relatives for financial irregularities in the funds given to her NGO, Bhagavati Devi Nari Kalyan Samiti. In 2015, it was alleged that Usha's NGO had received ₹30.85 lakh between 2007 and 2011 from National AIDS Control Organization (NACO) through West Bengal State Aids Prevention & Control Society to spread AIDS awareness. The NGO's office was raided and Usha Mishra had to surrender in a local court to obtain bail.

These cases represented the situation of Left leaders in West Bengal post 2011. Most were struggling to fight criminal cases lodged against them and were not able to support their party cadres at the grassroots level. Also, there was hardly any public sympathy for these CPIM leaders. Their backbones broke in the face of such backlash. Former chief minister Buddhadeb Bhattacharjee gave a call for 'turning around once again', but it did not elicit a response.

ORGANIZATIONAL AND IDEOLOGICAL CRISIS

After their defeat in 2011, the next crucial election was in 2014. It saw a further decline in the Left's vote share from around 40 per cent in the 2011 assembly elections to 29.95 per cent with the CPIM polling 22.96 per cent of votes; there was also a significant rise in BJP's share of votes from 4.06 per cent in the 2011 assembly elections to 17.02 per cent in 2014. Though the BJP could not topple the Left as the main Opposition in 2014, the trend was alarming for the CPIM. They only had two MPs from West Bengal. Organizationally, the CPIM was in such a poor condition that during the state conference in 2016, they had decided to wind up several branch committees due to lack of support and leadership and merge them to form area committees.

Looking at the dangerous trend of organizational decline in West Bengal, the CPIM leadership held a plenum on organization at the end of 2015 to examine their flaws and find ways to recover. The five-day plenum between 27 and 31 December took resolutions on various points. While blaming the decline in the organizational strength mostly on the defeat in the 2011 election, the plenum said it was 'followed by unprecedented terror unleashed by the ruling TMC with the connivance of the police in the last four and half years'. According to CPIM's claim, 'The Party has lost 163 leaders, cadres and supporters out of

170 martyrs of the Left Front. More than one lakh cadres are facing severe political repression.'[5]

The CPIM was trying to regroup and relaunch. They had organized campaigns and strikes, mainly through the mass frontal organizations they had. The peasant front had organized a Krishak Jatha (peasants' march) in various parts of the state, the worker front called for a general strike and a strike with the teagardens' workers for the poor condition there, mainly in the closed tea-garden. The workers were also denied basic facilities in most of the cases. The CPIM as the parent organization also organized the 'March to Nabanna' (state secretariat), which was intercepted by the police and the Left supporters had to face the police's lathi-charge. These showed that the Left supporters were waiting in the wings, but the lack of leadership and a clear political plan were the reasons the party found it hard to motivate its supporters.

There was a lack of a mass leader in the CPIM. Former chief minister Buddhadeb Bhattacharjee had to limit his political activities due to his poor health. Though he was no match for Jyoti Basu's mass leadership and statesmanship, Buddhadeb Bhattacharjee's clean, honest, *bhadralok*, intellectual, culture-savvy image, despite his administrative failure, had made him popular among the CPIM supporters and workers. Even after the Left's defeat and on the eve of the 2019 Lok Sabha elections, his presence at a public meeting meant a lot to the Left supporters. Apart from him, the CPIM lacked a mass leader who could draw the crowds. Biman Bose, who too had a clean image, could not lead the party to fight against the ruling party or the BJP. In Surja Kanta Mishra's elevation to the position of the leader of the

[5] CPI(M). 'Plenum: Report on Organisation'. CPI(M), 27–31 December 2015.

Opposition first and then the state secretary, the CPIM found new potential, but he too failed to put the party together. Leaders like the present Left Legislative Party chief Sujan Chakraborty and Md Salim, who clung on to win Raiganj Lok Sabha seat in 2014, also could not have much impact on the party's rank and file.

The party decided to focus on recruiting young cadres and drop inactive workers from all committees and also decided to drop the ageing members. However, there was no second-rung leadership in the CPIM. The young student leader and Rajya Sabha member Ritabrata Banerjee, considered to be a potential leader who could hold the party's reins in future, was expelled after there were allegations of sexual harassment against him. He was also accused of misusing his power as an MP and threatening a party supporter who had questioned his lifestyle. There was an open spat between Ritabrata and Md Salim, who was part of the disciplinary committee that recommended Ritabrata's expulsion. Another youth leader Koustav Mukherjee was also accused of sexual harassment.

'It is not true that we did not try to put in place the second-generation leaders. Leadership growth is an organic process. There are some organizational principles. Media attention is not there on young leaders until they are at the helm of affairs. If there is no student movement, student unions are depoliticized, elections to the student bodies are suspended, how will leaders come up? They wanted to cut off a generation with the Left. It is a challenge. If we cannot bring up campus-centric leaders, we have to change our tactics,' says Md Salim.

At the same time, the influence of other Left Front partners also started declining in the pockets they ruled. Be it the Revolutionary Socialist Party, All India

Forward Bloc or Communist Party of India—all seemed to be in hibernation. The Left MLAs' defection to the TMC was also surprising to many. CPIM's Chhaya Dolui, who won in 2011 from Chandrakona assembly constituency, RSP's Anantadeb Adhikari and Dasarath Tirkey, and Forward Bloc's Sunil Mandal and Udayan Guha joined Mamata's party in 2014; some of them like Dasarath and Sunil also got elected to the Lok Sabha on a TMC ticket in 2014 itself. When the CPIM and other Left parties failed to arrest this exodus at the state level, it's obvious they failed at the grassroots level too. Many blame it on the CPIM's lack of ideological training while the Left leadership puts the blame squarely on Mamata's politics of absolutism.

Along with their organizational crisis, the CPIM also lost focus on its political tactical line. In the late 1980s and early 1990s, the party decided to oppose both the Congress and the BJP depending on the situation; the party did grow but only in three states—Kerala, Tripura and West Bengal. The CPIM leadership credits its workers' front for consolidating the class struggle against the bourgeois liberal economic policies. In 1998, the CPIM leadership called for a 'third alternative' with the non-Congress, non-BJP secular parties. Still, the majority of the CPIM's highest policy-making body, the central committee, voted against the proposal of nominating veteran Left leader Jyoti Basu to the post of prime minister in 1998. Jyoti Basu had termed the decision of the central committee meeting, held in Kolkata's Nazrul Manch, as a 'historical blunder'. The idea of a third alternative also failed and the CPIM leadership realized that regional parties have their own agenda and can switch sides when required. Their experiences with political parties like Mulayam

Singh's Samajwadi Party, Mayawati's Bahujan Samaj Party and Chandrababu Naidu's Telugu Desam Party were bitter. So, again at the 2012 Party Congress at Kozhikode, the CPIM dropped the idea of a third alternative and stressed on allying with other 'secular parties'. The Political Resolution adopted in the 20th Party Congress held in April 2012 had clearly laid down the following Political Line:[6]

> 2.137 The CPI(M) has to politically fight the Congress and the BJP. Both are parties which represent the big bourgeois landlord order which perpetuates class exploitation and is responsible for the social oppression of various sections of the people. They pursue neo-liberal policies and advocate a pro-US foreign policy. Defeating the Congress and UPA government is imperative given the crushing burden of price rise, unemployment, suffering of the farmers and workers on the one hand and the brazen corruption and big sops to big business and the wealthy sections. Isolating the BJP and countering its communal and Right-wing agenda is necessary and important for the advance of the Left, democratic and secular forces.
>
> 2.138 As against the Congress and BJP, the CPI(M) puts forth the Left and democratic alternative. Only a Left and democratic platform can be the alternative to the bourgeois-landlord rule. This alternative needs to be built up through a process of movements and struggles and the emergence of a political alliance of the Left and democratic forces. In the course of these efforts, it may be necessary to rally those non-Congress, non-BJP forces which can play a

[6] CPI(M). 'Political Resolution: Adopted at the 20th Congress'. CPI(M), 30 April 2012.

> role in defence of democracy, national sovereignty, secularism, federalism and defence of the people's livelihood and rights. The emergence of such joint platforms should help the process of building the alliance of the Left and democratic forces.

However, it left the door open for 'suitable electoral tactics in the states for understanding with the regional parties' with a caveat that it should be 'done within the framework of the overall P-TL (Political-Tactical line) and it should be governed by the party's interests and the requirement of rallying the Left and democratic forces'. Three years later, the CPIM once again changed its tactical line and in the Vishakhapatnam Party Congress in 2015, it called for a Left democratic alliance. The Left did realize the threat of communalism and the Right-wing Hindutva agenda. They thought the impact of the neoliberal economic policies should be integrated with the threat of communalism to draw the masses into their fold. In the same resolution, they blamed the Congress for pursuing neoliberal economic policies and decided to oppose them. Though they had taken up an eight-point agenda to fight the BJP—RSS combine at its 21st Party Congress, this could hardly be seen being executed on the ground in Bengal.

Despite the rejection of the political line taken up in 2015 Party Congress that CPIM would not ally with Congress, on the eve of the 2016 assembly elections, the CPIM leadership in Bengal was busy chalking out a plan for allying with the Congress, their arch-rival since the inception of the party in 1964. The calculation of the two decaying forces in West Bengal was that if they contested together, according to the 2014 Lok Sabha elections, the alliance might get 98 seats. With the Left winning 68 seats and Congress 30 seats, this Left–Congress alliance could be a face-saver. In fact, the 2014 Lok Sabha elections showed that the Left–Congress combined vote share of 39.72 was marginally ahead of the TMC vote share of 39.64 per cent. They hoped to replicate the same arithmetic in the 2016 assembly elections, which would put the alliance above the TMC. They also expected the BJP vote share to drop in the 2016 assembly elections as it was a state-level election where the Modi-magic wouldn't work. They thought a part of the BJP's votes would come to their kitty. However, there were divisions within the Left and the CPIM regarding the alliance with the Congress. The Left Front partners, like the Forward Bloc and the Revolutionary Socialist Party opposed the move and openly criticized it.

Within the CPIM, a large section of leaders from the districts and in Kolkata opposed the decision to go for an alliance, even as the CPIM politburo maintained that there should be an alliance with the Congress. The Kerala lobby of the CPIM, which leads the Left Democratic Front there, had to face the Congress as their main enemy. So, they were naturally opposed to the alliance. Still, party patriarch, Buddhadeb Bhattacharjee, and general secretary, Sitaram Yechury, went ahead with the plan. It did not have the official approval of the Central Committee, the highest decision-making body of the party. Rather than calling it an 'alliance', they called it 'an understanding'. While the CPIM's top leaders in the state wanted a face-saver, the Congress, which had influence in a few districts like Murshidabad, Malda and North Dinajpur, wanted to cash in on CPIM support to save their party 'signboard' or show the sign of their survival. Since the alliance did not have an official stamp from the central leadership, the discomfort of the CPIM leaders was evident when Sitaram Yechury avoided sharing the stage with the state Congress president, Adhir

Chowdhury, in Singur.[7] Adhir was waiting for Sitaram to arrive and in his speech, he was upfront about the '*jote*' (alliance) with the Left and compared the alliance with former US president Barack Obama shaking hands with former Cuban President Fidel Castro. Despite such a call, Sitaram took the stage after Adhir had left and did not mention anything about the alliance. Rather he said, 'There is nothing official about it [the alliance].' The CPIM leaders time and again wanted to hammer the point that the alliance was a demand of the grassroots workers of both the parties and not the leadership.

While Sitaram played hide-and-seek, the CPIM leadership in favour of the alliance went ahead with it. Former chief minister Buddhadeb Bhattacharjee shared the dais with Congress Vice President Rahul Gandhi at Kolkata's Park Circus Maidan. The scene was unprecedented and made headlines. However, this half-hearted effort by both camps did not yield much result. Even after the controversy over the Narada investigation made a sudden appearance during the 2016 assembly elections campaign, none of the Opposition parties could capitalize on the issue and the TMC came back to power with an increased majority despite fighting the election alone.

'The Left, they took a short cut. They allied with the Congress without any programmatic alternative. If there was any historic blunder they committed, it was this alliance. Subsequent events have proved that the people rejected the opportunistic alliance,' says political activist Prasenjit Bose.

In 2016, their calculation went terribly wrong and the Congress–Left alliance got 76 seats out which 44 went to the Congress while CPIM got 26, RSP 3,

---

[7] Roy, R. *Catchnews*. 'Rare moment of camarederie: Rahul and Buddhadeb share in Kolkata'. (Updated) 10 February 2017.

Forward Bloc 2 and CPI only 1 seat. The TMC came back to power with an increased margin. From 184 seats in 2011, the TMC went to 216 in 2016. 'The Left transferred its vote to the Congress candidates across the state, but the Congress supporters did not vote for the Left,' says Biswajit Bhattacharya. The fallacy of the alliance was that the Congress had its support base in certain pockets of North Bengal and Murshidabad but they did not have much of a vote bank in South Bengal. In reality, the Congress did not have the power to transfer its vote to the CPIM, which still had some influence in the southern part of the state.

A post-poll survey by CSDS-Lokniti[8] showed that many anti-TMC voters did not find the Left–Congress alliance a credible one. Out of all those who voted for the Left Front in 2014, 88 per cent voted for the alliance and only 9 per cent cast their vote in favour of the TMC in 2016. Whereas out of those who voted for the Congress in 2014, 73 per cent voted for the Congress and 24 per cent voted for the TMC.

Interestingly, according to the survey, 51 per cent of the BJP vote share in the 2014 Lok Sabha elections got divided almost equally between the TMC and the Left–Congress alliance. While 26 per cent went to the alliance, 25 per cent had gone to the TMC in 2016. The result had shown that there was a decline in the support base of the Left Front. The TMC had emerged as the 'New Left' winning these supporters. The BJP could not make its mark in 2016.

Thus, the assessment that an alliance with the Congress in 2016 was a face-saver was a fallacy. 'If there was a historic blunder it was the Left allying with the Congress. You see in the Opposition space, the Left came

[8] 'West Bengal Postpoll Assembly Election 2016–Survey Findings'.

third and Congress came up as the main Opposition. That sounded the death knell for the CPIM in West Bengal,' says Prasenjit Bose.

However, the Left leaders still felt that this was not a setback for the Left–Congress alliance. They blamed the media and the TMC–RSS's 'secret pact'. Md Salim says, 'In 2016, there was a constituency-wise targeted vote transfer and a systematic arrangement between the RSS and TMC. I won't say BJP. Dilip Ghosh claimed that in 100 seats, BJP voted for TMC. We are saying in 25 seats, TMC voted for BJP. That helped them. BJP did not do it out of mercy for TMC. If the Left–Congress combine were to make a comeback, then the stage would be set for the Left, which the BJP never wanted. TMC also wanted to undo a Left comeback.'

The CPIM being in denial also damaged the political space they enjoyed in Bengal. Though the CPIM leaders claimed that the media had put the Left and the Congress in the same bracket and created a narrative about them being finished, the truth was that neither the Left nor the Congress leadership was confident of the alliance. 'We have been saying that it was not an alliance. Congress leadership also calls for joint programmes. But remember we have done some "seat adjustment",' says Md Salim. The Left's failure to justify the move to join hands with the Congress not only disillusioned the common people but also frustrated the grassroots Left workers and supporters.

As the Left's support base further declined, the anti-TMC space was being filled up by the BJP. The Basirhat assembly by-election in September 2014 was a shocker for the Left as the BJP candidate Samik Bhattacharya won the seat making an entry into the West Bengal Vidhansabha as the sole MLA from the saffron camp. In the 2016 Cooch Behar by-election, which was necessitated due to the death of TMC MP Renuka Sinha, the BJP came up as number two, pushing the Forward Bloc candidate to third position. The election, which took place on 19 November 2016, just after demonetisation, also showed that the anti-TMC vote was going to the BJP. The trend continued in Contai (South) assembly and Uluberia parliamentary by-elections. The BJP came up as number two in the state, replacing the Left and the Congress. The Left could not revive itself and resorted to their previous strategy of allying with the Congress in 2019's general elections as well.

'The Left had run a government for three decades. There have been ideological changes and that reflected in the party's organization. They were thrown out of power and there were reasons behind it. There were no changes in its programme. The Congress–Left combine could not come up with any alternative,' says Prasenjit Bose.

Since there was no strong opposition to the BJP and the Congress, and the Left leaders were confused about the alliance before the 2019 elections, they could not convince people that they could put up a fight against the TMC or the BJP. Rather than increasing their own strength, the Left leaders carried on a futile exercise of waiting for the Congress leaders to respond. They had demanded that Raiganj and Murshidabad, where the CPIM had won in 2014, should be left to them. In Raiganj, former MP Deepa Dasmunshi was a contender for a Congress nomination. The CPIM had also demanded a few seats for its allies RSP and Forward Bloc. The Congress, however, was not ready to listen. Left Front Chairman Biman Basu announced Md Salim as their candidate in Raiganj even before the negotiations started. When the Congress leaders still did not respond, the Left Front chairman declared the name, of a few more candidates, keeping a few seats vacant for the Congress. But, it seemed that the state Congress leadership was not interested in joining hands with the Left.

Though the Left leaders claimed to be uniting the anti-TMC and anti-BJP votes, they could not clarify whether they would join the government if the NDA fell short of a majority and the Congress, or any other regional party, let alone the TMC, led the 'secular' government. They also could not come up with an alternative programme or concrete plan for the Lok Sabha elections, which were to elect the government at the Centre and not the state.

The 2019 Lok Sabha results showed that, in terms of vote share, the Left came down from 29 per cent in 2014 and 26 per cent in 2016 to just 7 per cent; they drew a blank from the state. The BJP now occupied the Opposition space. Those who were opposed to the TMC voted for the BJP. A large section of the Left's Hindu vote went to the BJP and the minorities sided with the TMC apparently in the hope of being protected in the face of the RSS–BJP Hindu onslaught.

For example, in Basirhat constituency in North 24 Parganas, the Left's vote share went down by 25 per cent compared to 2014. The BJP gained 11 per cent votes in this constituency. The TMC got 39 per cent vote in 2014 and in 2016, its vote share had gone up to 55 per cent. The increase of 16 per cent came from the Left vote bank.

In Joynagar constituency in South 24 Parganas, the TMC vote share increased by 11 per cent whereas the Left's dropped by 5 per cent more than the BJP's increase in vote share. Here too, the Left votes had shifted to the TMC.

Both these constituencies are dominated by minorities and scheduled castes. In Dum Dum constituency, increase in BJP's vote share is same as the drop in Left's vote percentage.

There has been a huge shift of the Left support base towards the BJP. A rough calculation shows that around 1 crore Left supporters shifted their votes to the BJP in 2019. In the 2014 Lok Sabha elections, the Left bagged 1.52 crore votes in Bengal. In the 2016 assembly elections, the vote share came down to 1.43 crore and in 2019, the number was 42.51 lakh.

The CPIM state committee has detected that a large section of the local leadership worked in favour of the BJP to transfer the Left vote to the BJP's kitty as there had been a perception that the Left was not strong enough, organizationally, to fight Mamata Banerjee. 'This is an RSS ploy to rally a section of the Left to the BJP by spreading a rumour that the Left cannot take on TMC and we cannot put the corrupt TMC leaders, including the "aunt-nephew" duo, behind the bars. It has been done tactically. There have been local arrangements since the panchayat polls,' admits Md Salim.

A former MP from North 24 Parganas has been accused of helping a BJP candidate win from the industrial belt. The CPIM leader did not want to take any names but accepted that they have identified the 'rebel' leaders in the party. 'We had detected who sabotaged and we are taking action against them,' says Md Salim. Still, the CPIM leadership decided not to go all out against the rogue elements in the party. 'We have started taking action. But we are not going to take action everywhere. We will have to look at it futuristically,' adds Salim.

With such an exodus of its support base to the BJP and some of its leaders secretly allying with the Rightist force in the name of overthrowing Mamata Banerjee's government, the Left will increasingly lose its relevance in the state politics. The binary of Mamata versus the

BJP has already been created in Bengal. The Left as well as the Congress are marginal players now. The Left has the compulsion of fighting both the BJP and the TMC in the same breath, otherwise, in the national politics, they will lose more relevance. In fact, the Left could emerge as the principal Opposition to the BJP at the national level if they have a proper strategy and mass base in place. In Bengal, the Left leaders are a little clueless and the Left cadres are divided on the question of the 'main enemy': is it the TMC or the BJP? Will attacking the TMC help the BJP more in Bengal politics? There is a theory in the Left circle '*aage Ram, pore baam*', which means let 'Ram' or the saffron camp decimate the TMC in the state and then '*baam*' or the Left will emerge as the principal Opposition party in the state. The Left believes that only they could take on the RSS-BJP ideology. So, they will fight it out 'one-on-one' against the BJP after the TMC's destruction and come back to power once again. Neither the Left leaders nor the political analysts have any timeline for this change to happen, if it does at all. For the time being, the Left is allying with the Congress to stay afloat in the political arena and gain whatever they can in the electoral politics. Unless the Left can devise a strategy to revive their organization and existing support base a part of which is shifting to the Right, they have no political future in Bengal, at least in the near future.

6

Run-up to the 2019 Lok Sabha Elections

On 12 March 2019, soon after the Election Commission had declared the dates for the general elections in the country, Mamata Banerjee called a press conference to announce the list of candidates for the Lok Sabha elections. It's well known that the mercurial Mamata has peculiar preferences, such as using her residence to announce the candidate list, always on a Friday. Even after the TMC built its office known as the 'Trinamool Bhavan' off EM Bypass in Topsia, Mamata has not used it to announce her candidate lists (except on one occasion), preferring to use her residence to do the same. So, there was nothing unnatural about the choice of the venue, the same old 30B Harish Chatterjee Street. However, the difference was that it was not a Friday; it was a Tuesday. This press conference turned out to be one of the most bizarre conferences that the Bengal chief minister and TMC chief has held to date.

The room adjacent to the office at her residence was readied for the press conference[1] and Mamata Banerjee was flanked by Subrata Bakshi, the all India general

[1] AITC Official. 2019. 'Mamata Banerjee announces list of candidates for the 2019 Lok Sabha elections'. YouTube, 12 March. Available at: https://www.youtube.com/watch?v=d14W4upMlQk

secretary of TMC; behind her were her trusted ministers, Arup Biswas and Firhad Hakim. Interestingly, seated next to Mamata were Sandhya Roy and Uma Soren, the outgoing TMC MPs. The party's secretary-general, Partha Chatterjee, had not got a seat next to the party chief and was seated next to Uma.

Mamata began the presser in her Didi-esque manner by apologizing for not being able to accommodate all the media persons in the briefing room, 'We had said we would start at 3:30 p.m. It is just 3:30. Many of you came early. I am sorry for the pain you had to take and I could not accommodate you in the room. Forgive me if there is any mistake on our part.' It was nothing new, Mamata has always been cordial with the media on such occasions. However, the next few minutes saw something unprecedented unfold.

Explaining the situation in the country, she said, 'Let me first tell you that some are not contesting the elections. I tell you their names first. This is a matter of expressing my gratitude. Harvard professor Sugata Bose called me to inform that he did not get permission to contest the election. The university has formulated a policy. He has told me "I am with you and I will be with you, but I am not getting permission. If I get permission, I will contest again".'

She turned to the lady sitting next to her, Sandhya Roy, a film star and the outgoing MP from Midnapore. 'She has done the [party's assignments in] Parliament seriously. Since she wants to do some other work and cannot run around, it would be easier for her if she could do something sitting in one place.'

Turning to Jhargram MP Uma Soren, she said, 'She told me she wants to work for the party and asked me to nominate someone in her place. She assured she would work for the party anywhere.'

This was unprecedented. Never in the history of the TMC, had Mamata Banerjee had to rally behind MPs or MLAs who were denied tickets. It had always been her unilateral decision to nominate or drop names from the candidates list. On earlier occasions, journalists had seen nomination-seekers waiting outside the press conference hall at Mamata Banerjee's Kalighat residence simply to see their names on the list. Never had Mamata had to give explanations in public.

Be it Sugata Bose or Uma Soren or Sandhya Roy—none of them was a mass leader or important enough in the TMC organization that Mamata Banerjee had to clarify why they were denied tickets. Even for the outgoing MP from Basirhat, Idris Ali, Mamata had to explain that he could not be given a ticket and would be nominated for the assembly by-elections to Uluberia. 'We have spoken to him and he was convinced,' said Mamata.

Many in the media refused to acknowledge the underlying meaning of Mamata Banerjee's gesture at the press conference. The media was busy with the news that two Tollywood actors, Nusrat Jahan and Mimi Chakraborty, were nominated by the TMC chief. Surprise nominations from the film fraternity have been the TMC chief's trump card. She had earlier fielded actors such as Tapas Pal, Shatabdi Roy, Debashri Roy, Moonmoon Sen, Sandhya Roy, Dev and Mithun Chakraborty in the Parliament or assembly elections. In some cases, the nominations came as a surprise to the film stars themselves. In a way, Mamata almost forced some of these actors to contest the elections.

It has been Mamata Banerjee's strategy to field such 'neutral' or 'celebrity' candidates wherever there is factionalism within the party. For example, Jadavpur constituency, which is is made up of parts of southern fringes of Kolkata and parts of South 24 Parganas district, has never got a hardcore political candidate. Bhangar, a block which falls in Jadavpur constituency, is infamous for the factional feud between two groups within the TMC, and nominating a political candidate would mean one faction wouldn't campaign for him or her. Perhaps, there would be sabotage in the election by the TMC's own men. So, In 1999 and 2004, Krishna Bose, a professor and member of Netaji Subhas Chandra Bose's family, got the TMC nomination. In 2009, the nomination was given to singer Kabir Suman. Sugato Bose, Krishna Bose's son and professor of History at Harvard University, was nominated in 2014. In 2019, it went to film actor Mimi Chakraborty.

The same rule applied in the case of Asansol constituency. This time Moonmoon Sen, the outgoing MP from Bankura, was taken out of her old constituency, apparently due to resentment among the workers because of her absence from Bankura after she was elected. She was nominated from Asansol as the two opposing camps locked horns there. Mamata had always tasted success with this formula and she reapplied it in 2019 as well.

Thus, nominating Tollywood actors was not a new move, yet the local media went gaga over it. Earlier, despite so much tension in the party ranks and files, Mamata had never clarified why she was putting up a 'celebrity' or an 'apolitical' candidate nor did she bring up the issue of the internal feud in the party. However, this time, before the 2019 Lok Sabha elections, this point-by-point 'clarification' over dropping candidates at the press conference was indeed new and it was clear as daylight that she was under pressure. She was indeed losing her grip over her own party with the Modi–BJP wave looming large. This was apparent a little later in the presser.

While announcing the candidate from Cooch Behar, she made an unexpected comment. 'In Cooch Behar, our candidate is Paresh Chandra Adhikari,' she said. He was a minister in the Left Front cabinet and a Forward Bloc MLA, who had switched over to the TMC a few months before the Lok Sabha elections. After a pause, Mamata continued, 'We could not nominate Partha [Partha Pratim Roy], the young boy. He contested the by-election. We will utilize him in party work if he remains in the party or if he wants to work. My good wishes will be with him if he remains in the party. Some people, not all, go here and there if they are denied tickets. So those who will be with the party, we will treat them with respect. But the party has to be choosy in a lot of things.'

Partha Pratim Roy had won the Cooch Behar Lok Sabha by-election defeating BJP's Hemchandra Burman in 2016 and had pushed the Forward Bloc to third position. Roy had increased the party's victory margin from 38,000 votes in 2014 to 4.9 lakh in the 2016 by-polls. However, since his election, he had grown distant from the party's Cooch Behar district president, Rabindra Nath Ghosh. Though Partha was a prominent youth leader, due to the power struggle within the party, he was denied the nomination in 2019.

Throughout the conference, it was clearly visible that Mamata was unsure whether those who had been denied tickets, such as Partha, would switch over to the BJP. Just before the election dates were announced, TMC MPs Anupam Hazra from Bolpur and Soumitra Khan from Bishnupur had joined the saffron camp. Though it did not immediately hamper the TMC's electoral position as neither Anupam nor Soumitra were big leaders in the ruling party's hierarchy, it definitely created political pressure on Mamata to hold her flock together before the crucial Lok Sabha elections.

Rallying behind the outgoing MPs who had been denied tickets was not the only sign of Mamata's nervousness; there was another significant characteristic of the TMC candidates list. Unlike previous occasions, Mamata's 2019 candidate list was full of political personalities. Except for Nusrat and Mimi, businessman Khalilur Rahman in Jangipur and deceased TMC MLA Satyajit Biswas's wife, Rupali, there was no political novice in the list. In 2014, the TMC chief had sent singer (now Mamata's cabinet minister) Indranil Sen to fight the Congress heavyweight Adhir Ranjan Chowdhury in Beharampore. At that time, Indranil had no experience in electoral politics. Five years down the line, Mamata fielded a former Adhir-aide and Congress MLA Apurba David Sarkar to fight it out in Beharampore. In place of Sandhya Roy, former state Congress president and present TMC Rajya Sabha MP Manas Bhunia was fielded from Midnapore seat against state BJP president Dilip Ghosh. Last time, she had nominated actor Moonmoon Sen from Bankura, but in 2019, Mamata sent veteran minister Subrata Mukherjee to contest against the BJP's state vice president Subhash Sarkar. These nominations demonstrated Mamata was serious in fighting a political battle against the BJP and had accepted that 'this is a challenging election'.

Though she claimed in the press conference that the list was ratified by the steering committee of the party in presence of all the state presidents, the list underlined the fact that Mamata had the last word in picking the candidates. She wanted to ensure that she held the leash over the party's nominations; in some cases, her nephew's choices had also been turned down. A TMC insider says, 'Even Abhishek Banerjee, considered to be the heir apparent, did not have any say in the candidate list. Didn't you see he was not even present at the press conference?' Denying a ticket to Partha Pratim Roy was an example of Abhishek being snubbed by his aunt. Partha, considered close to Abhishek, was also the youth TMC president in Cooch Behar. Apparently, Abhishek wanted to nominate a few more candidates of his choice which Mamata had rejected at the last moment.

However, these careful calculations also could not prevent defections from the TMC to the BJP. The day after Mamata Banerjee announced her candidate list, Bhatpara MLA Arjun Singh, who wanted a nomination from Barackpore constituency replacing two-time TMC MP and former railway minister, Dinesh Trivedi, came to attend a meeting at Mamata's Kalighat residence. There were rumours that Arjun might join the BJP since he had been denied the ticket he wanted. During the meeting, as Mamata came face-to-face with Arjun, she apparently told him, '*Ja toke mukto kore dilam* (Go, I am setting you free).'

In the meeting with the MPs and MLAs to decide the strategy for the Lok Sabha election campaign, Mamata Banerjee said, 'One or two persons are greedy about nominations. I will be happy if they leave. I am least bothered about those who leave and those who take them. I have told many, go, I am setting you free.' Not only was this an attempt to put a brave face in front of her party colleagues, but also a way to gauge who would stay with her and who would leave.

Within a week, Arjun Singh jumped ship and joined the BJP and bagged a nomination from his original choice, the Barackpore constituency. Arjun Singh, who was once miffed with Mukul Roy's influence in the party, had joined the saffron camp in Mukul's presence. When Mukul had joined the BJP, Arjun Singh had said, 'Mukul Roy is a traitor.' But after he himself joined the BJP, Singh clarified that he had used the words at the behest of the TMC. Arjun Singh, who had once been seen on the streets of Kankinara in his constituency combating communal riots and abusing the BJP, openly praised Narendra Modi's nationalistic approach and criticized Mamata for not supporting the country's prime minister during the Balakot strike. Explaining the reason for his decision to cutoff ties with Mamata Banerjee after 30 years, he said, 'When the Indian army under the leadership of Modiji took action against terrorists, some comments from Mamata Banerjee were regrettable. I was pained at what Mamata had said. I decided to leave the party after the incident. I understood that it was not possible to work with this party.'

He put out an open challenge to Dinesh Trivedi. Without Arjun's support, it was indeed difficult for Dinesh to sail through the elections as the Bhatpara MLA exerted influence in at least four assembly constituencies in the Barackpore industrial belt. Mukul Roy's son was the MLA of Bijpur constituency and, apparently, Mukul had assured a lead of about 50,000 votes from Bijpur in favour of Arjun.

Neither Anupam Hazra nor Saumitra Khan was as influential as Arjun Singh in their respective constituencies, but Arjun was a good catch compared to others. The general perception was that Mukul Roy had negotiated with Arjun to take him in to the BJP, but a BJP insider claims, 'One of Arjun's relatives in Uttar Pradesh is in our party and Arjun got in touch with him to reach out to the top leadership. Mukul Roy had nothing much to do about it except being present in Delhi on the day Arjun joined.'

Mukul Roy did not stop with Singh; he kept mounting pressure on the TMC chief. He even threatened that about 40 MLAs from Mamata's camp were in touch with the BJP. None of the MLAs, apart from Arjun, switched sides before the elections, but breakaway TMC leaders like Nishith Pramanik of Cooch Behar came to the BJP with Mukul Roy's help and bagged a nomination. There were many criminal cases against Nishith, which he claimed to be false, and there was some resentment among the local BJP leadership, but the state leadership went ahead with Mukul's decision.

Similarly, former TMC minister Manjul Krishna Thakur's son Shantanu Thakur was nominated from Bongaon constituency. An alleged leaked tape,[2] much before the elections, claimed that Mukul Roy was trying to convince the party's observer Kailash Vijayvargiya that Shantanu could be an asset to the BJP. This nomination was crucial as he represented the Matuas (a Hindu sect comprising mostly *namashudra* Dalit immigrants from erstwhile East Pakistan, now Bangladesh)who followed the preaching of Thakur Guruchand, the grandfather of Shantanu Thakur. Earlier, the Left Front partner, Forward Bloc, exerted influence on this politically influential community. Later, the TMC had taken over and Mamata was considered close to Guruchand's wife and the matriarch of the Matuas, Binapani Devi. Just a month before the demise of Binapani Devi on 6 March 2019, Prime Minister Narendra Modi visited her at her Thakurnagar residence in North 24 Parganas and the BJP was able to capture the imagination of this politically divided community. Mamata's sitting MP and Binapani Devi's daughter-in-law Mamata Bala Thakur could not save the TMC vote bank among the Matuas. Neither could the district TMC president and one of Mamata Banerjee's most trusted aides, Jyotipriyo Mullick.

---

[2] *The Indian Affairs*. 'Political Score Fixing Of The Alleged Audio Tape Of A Big BJP Leader With Mukul Roy Is Going Viral Again In Bengal'. 5 February 2019.

Apart from garnering support from these small groups with subtle political power, such as the Matuas in North 24 Parganas and Kurmi tribals in Junglemahal, Mamata's former strategist Mukul Roy had also successfully spread the fear of defection among the TMC leaders before the Lok Sabha elections. 'Though a professional agency had done a survey in the constituencies in West Bengal on who could be the best nominees for BJP, Mukul Roy had his say in some of the constituencies and fielded his own candidates,' says a BJP insider. It was difficult for Mamata to gauge who could sabotage the party from the inside and help the BJP sail through this crucial election. The BJP had won half the battle by rattling the ranks and files of Mamata's camp. Not only the TMC, but defections also hit the CPIM when its MLA from Habibpur in Malda, Khagen Murmu, joined the BJP before the elections. Murmu was nominated from Malda North constituency.

THE INFLUENCE OF NARENDRA MODI AND AMIT SHAH

As TMC's rank and file tried to put up a brave front despite the saffron-pressure, Prime Minister Narendra Modi and the BJP's national president, Amit Shah, launched a fierce election campaign in Bengal as early as January–February 2019. Mamata Banerjee had set a '42 out of 42' target for her party in the Lok Sabha polls, and the Modi–Shah duo wanted at least 23 seats from Bengal. They had given the target to the state leadership a year and a half before the elections. It was unprecedented that both the leaders together held more than 30 rallies in the state in a seven-phase election. It almost seemed that Bengal was heading towards assembly elections and not Lok Sabha polls.

In the rest of the country, the Modi-Shah duo cited the Balakot strike in their list of achievements and took credit for the targeted attack on terrorists along the Line of Control in Pakistan; but, in West Bengal, the BJP's top leadership adopted a completely different approach. Instead of a hyper-nationalistic pitch, the Modi–Shah duo set their campaign agenda in four different strands:

(a) implementation of NRC and the Citizenship Bill particularly focusing on Bengal, (b) fighting the corruption and 'syndicate raj' unleashed by TMC top brass, (c) the anti-Hindu image of Mamata Banerjee and (d) Mamata Banerjee's reluctance to implement the central government's schemes like Ayushman Bharat Yojana, PM Kisan Samman Nidhi, etc.

'Though they did not unfold their hard Hindutva and anti-Muslim image in front of the Bengal voters, raising the NRC[3] and Citizenship Bill[4] issues were aimed at the Bangladeshi Muslim infiltrators and a veiled attack on the minorities in the state,' says Suvashis Maitra.

Infiltration through the porous Indo-Bangla border was nothing new. In fact, during the Left rule, Mamata Banerjee was vocal on the issue and alleged that the Left Front used illegal migrants from Bangladesh as its vote bank. Mamata Banerjee, on 4 August 2005, had thrown a sheaf of papers at the deputy speaker Charanjit Singh Atwal for not allowing her to raise the Bangladeshi

[3] NRC is the National Register of Citizens, a process aimed at removing illegal immigrants from India. The NRC process was recently completed in Assam. However, Union Home Minister Amit Shah announced in the Parliament in November 2019 that the NRC would? be implemented across India.

[4] The Citizenship Bill, which has been passed in the Indian Parliament in December 2019, will be known as the Citizenship Amendment Act (CAA). It will allow citizenship to Hindu, Buddhist, Sikh, Jain, Christian and Parsi minorities from Pakistan, Afghanistan and Bangladesh who faced persecution on the basis of religion. Those who entered India on or before 31 December 2014 will be granted citizenship or those who, under these categories, had been living in India for six years will be eligible for Indian citizenship under the provisions of CAA.

infiltration issue on the floor of the Lok Sabha. The then Lok Sabha speaker, Somnath Chatterjee, had disallowed her notice. Outraged, Mamata had resigned from the Lok Sabha. 'Illegal migrants from Bangladesh are also part of the voters list in West Bengal. The state government has done nothing about it. Therefore, the issue must be discussed,' she had said.[5] Though her 'conditional' resignation letter was not accepted by the speaker due to procedural reasons; the same issue came back to haunt her 14 years later. The prime minister and the BJP president both attacked Mamata Banerjee for forgetting the 'old issue' and supporting Bangladeshi infiltrators for vote-bank politics.

As mentioned briefly in Chapter Three, in the run-up to the 2014 Lok Sabha election campaign, at a rally in Serampore in Hooghly district, the then prime ministerial candidate, Narendra Modi, had set the same pitch. However, at that time the rhetoric did not work well in favour of the BJP. Referring to Bangladeshi infiltrators, he had told the rally organized for BJP candidate Bappi Lahiri, 'You can write it down. After 16 May, these Bangladeshis better be prepared with their bags.'[6]

Modi's speech garnered a negative reaction as Serampore constituency has a huge population of people who came from East Pakistan during the Partition; since then, there has been a huge influx of Hindu Bangladeshis to Bengal. Though Modi and the BJP clarified that they were in favour of giving shelter to Hindus who were being persecuted in Bangladesh or other parts of the world, the narrative that the BJP wanted to throw out

---

[5] *The Telegraph Online*. 'Mamata casts shame at House Paper throw at Speaker'. 4 August 2005.

[6] Narendra Modi. 2014. 'Srirampur (West Bengal): Shri Narendra Modi addresses a Public Meeting'. YouTube, 27 April. Available at: https://www.youtube.com/watch?v=0t4bvXY1m8I

the *bangals,* or those who came from East Pakistan, was already built.

Mamata Banerjee stood by the '*bangals*' and dared Modi to touch them. The voters were miffed with Modi's pitch in 2014. However, in 2019, the BJP leaders were well prepared and they had the case study of NRC in Assam to fall back on. They could show how they had initiated the process of identifying the illegal immigrants from Bangladesh, mainly Muslims, under the NRC in Assam. This time they were clear in building the narrative that Narendra Modi's government would throw out only illegal Muslim immigrants and that Hindu minorities from Bangladesh would be given Indian citizenship through the proposed Citizenship Amendment Bill. BJP projected that they were ready to implement the NRC in Bengal. During the election campaign, Amit Shah, at a rally in Bankura district of West Bengal, asked the gathering, 'Tell me clearly, should infiltrators be thrown out of Bengal?' The crowd cheered in the affirmative. 'We will throw out the infiltrators, but first, we will accord Indian citizenship to the refugees, be it Hindu, Sikh, Buddhist, Jains or Christians who have come from Bangladesh. They are our people. They have come here after being terrorized. Modiji has brought the Citizenship Amendment Bill in which there is a provision to grant citizenship to refugees,' added Shah. Even though he did not name the community that would suffer because of the amended Citizenship Act, he sent out a clear message to the minorities.

The NRC campaign was gaining momentum. On the one hand, it was consolidating the minority votes in favour of Mamata Banerjee as they found her to be a trusted shelter and, on the other, a section of the population, especially in the bordering districts, was not ready to buy Mamata Banerjee's argument of blocking the NRC in Bengal. A senior TV journalist, while covering the election campaign met a voter in Nadia district's Mahakhol village[7], which borders Bangladesh, who said, 'Those coming from Bangladesh are better educated than us. They are getting good jobs and we are not.' The locals alleged that the Bangladeshi infiltrators were bribing administrative officials to get their passport and voter IDs done. 'Earlier, you needed land deeds and other documents to get a passport. Now, a Bangladeshi man, who has been living here for some time, simply pays and procures these documents. In fact, now we are compelled to pay for these documents, which should have come to us in due process.' This resentment indeed divided the voters.

In another minority-dominated village in Cooch Behar, which borders Bangladesh, the villagers said, 'We are Indians. No one has the right to evict us. Only Allah can do it.' The NRC pitch clicked with the voters. The BJP got support from Hindu Bengali refugees who had migrated to West Bengal after the Partition. 'Even refugee colonies in Nadia or North Bengal which had supported the Left for long found a new ally in the BJP. The same reason why the Matuas rallied behind Narendra Modi in this election,' says Biswajit Bhattacharya. The results also showed that the BJP did well in Nadia, Malda, North and South Dinajpur, Cooch Behar and Jalpaiguri, which has a sizeable population of Bangladeshi refugees.

The BJP's ground-level surveys had also indicated that people's resentment over the local-level corruption was growing. The party sent out a message that Narendra Modi was someone who could take action against TMC

---

[7] Zee 24 Ghanta. 2019. 'Aapnar Ray: Krishnagar'. *YouTube*, 17 April. Available at: https://www.youtube.com/watch?v=KeTapX8YSwM&list=PLw4Ml54l0Jfa-mIKzuXvO6slFOWXRSbQsZ&index=7

leaders. Narendra Modi at an election rally in Bolpur[8] raised the issue of infiltration and the TMC's *dadagiri* in the same breath, saying, 'After suffering under the Left and Congress rule for so many decades, you had reposed your faith in Didi. But what has Didi given you? She put infiltration and *dadagiri* in top gear and put a speed breaker on development in West Bengal. You tell me is it possible to do any work in Bengal without giving their share to the dadas and tolabaji [extortion]?' Modi even coined the term 'Speed Breaker Didi' to accuse Mamata of playing with the present and future of Bengal allowing extortion rackets to grow. Modi also accused Mamata of not allowing central projects to be implemented properly in the state. He hit out at the state government, saying, 'Central government sends funds for various projects. But there is *tolabaji* over that money as well. TMC's tolabaji doesn't even spare the ration given to the poor.'

At the same Bolpur rally, Narendra Modi also mixed the Bengali sentiment related to Rabindranath Tagore and the TMC's corruption. Since Tagore's Shantiniketan is in Bolpur, Modi invoked the great poet and raised the issue of 'syndicate raj' in his speech. 'Gurudev Rabindranath did not imagine a Bengal where you would have to stand with folded hands in front of the syndicate raj to build or even rent a house or flat,' Modi said. Earlier, the TMC leaders had replied to the 'syndicate raj' rhetoric with the 'syndicate of lynching' narrative, but this time the syndicatepitch put them on the backfoot. In July 2018, from the Kishan Kalyan rally in Midnapore town[9], Prime Minister Narendra Modi

---

[8] Narendra Modi. 2019. 'PM Modi addresses Public Meeting at Bolpur, West Bengal'. *YouTube*, 24 April. Available at: https://www.youtube.com/watch?v=ZVz6mcqghDs

[9] Narendra Modi. 2018. 'PM Modi addresses Kisan Kalyan Rally at Medinipur, West Bengal'. *YouTube*, 16 July. Available at: https://www.youtube.com/watch?v=v-stGNH6WFE

launched the same attack on TMC. Amidst a cheering crowd, he said, 'The syndicate and the true face of those who spoke about Ma-Mati-Manush have been exposed in [the last] eight years. This syndicate is of extortion, snatching benefits from farmers, conspiring to kill the Opposition, atrocities against the poor, [and] sticking to the power by hook or crook.'

The BJP also rampantly used the '*bua-bhatija*' barb, which was originally coined for the alliance between Bahujan Samaj Party's '*bua*' Mayawati and Samajwadi Party's '*bhatija*' Akhilesh Yadav, to attack another set of '*bua-bhatija*', that is, Mamata Banerjee and her nephew Abhishek Banerjee. They were connected to the 'syndicate raj', which the BJP leaders alleged was 'government-sponsored' in many cases. Much before the Lok Sabha elections, Amit Shah received a legal notice from Abhishek Banerjee after he accused both Mamata and Abhishek of running illegal syndicates and endorsing scams in Bengal. At a BJP Yuva Morcha rally on 11 August 2018 at Kolkata's Mayo Road, Amit Shah had said, 'Mamatadi came to power opposing corruption, fighting against the law and order situation. But since the TMC government was formed, she has presented a series of scams, Narada, Saradha, Rose Valley, corruption of syndicate, corruption of the nephew [Abhishek Banerjee]. The whole of Bengal has been gripped by the port mafia, coal mafia and cattle mafia. You can get rid of this corruption if Narendra Modi led BJP government comes to power in Bengal.'

'After the NDA government came to power, the central government sanctioned ₹3,59,000 crore for Bengal. I want to ask the villagers of Bengal, has the money reached your villages? Where has it gone? Modiji had sent it, but where has it gone? It has gone as gifts to *bhatije* and syndicate, the corruption of TMC,' Shah told the rally.[10] Abhishek Banerjee, through legal notice, asked the BJP national president to prove the charges he had made or apologize within a day. The matter went to court. The legal procedure did not deter the top BJP leaders from bringing up the issue of the syndicate raj and connect it with the 'bua-bhatija' in Bengal during the election campaign. The BJP leaders continued with their attack on Mamata Banerjee's bid to push Abhishek at the helm of affairs. They equated Mamata's move with the Gandhi family's dynastic politics. Narendra Modi, at a rally in Abhishek Banerjee's constituency Diamond Harbour in the last phase of the poll campaign, said, '*Iss baar Didi ke bhajite ka dabba gul hai*. After the election results, the office of the nephew will get locked. I have been told that keeping with TMC tradition, the nephew's office has also been built by capturing the road.' Then, Modi asked the crowd, 'Hasn't it been constructed like that? Isn't it illegal encroachment? Didi, your party has collected so much money using extortion money. Why have you encroached upon the road?'[11] Modi also cited his own example of how he had demolished his own election office in Gujarat when he got to know that it was built illegally.

These constant attacks on Mamata and Abhishek Banerjee were well calculated. 'Narendra Modi and Amit Shah created a sense among the people of Bengal that they would put both Mamata and Abhishek in jail for all their misdeeds,' says CPIM leader Md Salim, who adds, 'People believed in this chest-thumping false rhetoric.'

---

[10] Bharatiya Janata Party. 2018. 'Shri Amit Shah addresses 'Yuva Swabhiman Samavesh Rally' in Kolkata, West Bengal'. YouTube, 11 August. Available at: https://www.youtube.com/watch?v=0u46_tS7rUw

[11] Bharatiya Janata Party. 2019. 'PM Shri Narendra Modi addresses a public meeting in Diamond Harbour, West Bengal'. YouTube, 15 May. Available at: https://www.youtube.com/watch?v=qtvSEqw3d-U

The BJP top leadership's continuous attack on 'syndicate raj', and on Mamata and Abhishek helped in mobilizing people's support. The grassroots level voters, who could not stand up against the extortion of the local ruling party leaders for long, found confidence in the narrative built by the BJP in the run-up to the elections.

The BJP also successfully created an anti-Hindu image of Mamata Banerjee by harping on two incidents—the controversy surrounding the refusal to grant permission to organize Saraswati Puja in Tehatta High School in Howrah's Uluberia, and the district administration's denial of permission to hold Durga Puja in Kanglapahari village—as described in detail in Chapter 3.

At all rallies, both Amit Shah and the PM harped on the point that Mamata Banerjee did not allow Saraswati Puja and Durga Puja in Bengal. This pitch helped polarize the electorate in the state. If the sporadic communal riots in the state had helped the saffron camp mobilize the Hindus to come under their umbrella, irrespective of party lines in the riot-hit areas, the accusation that Mamata was anti-Hindu gave the majority community a voice to express their grudge against the minorities. 'This evoked the anti-Muslim sentiment among the Bengalis, who for long had successfully evaded the communal trap under the Left rule,' says Suvashis Maitra.

MAMATA ON THE DEFENSIVE

Since 2018, much before the Lok Sabha election poll bugle was sounded, Mamata Banerjee wanted to forge a national alliance against Narendra Modi. As early as March 2018, Mamata met NCP chief, Sharad Pawar, Shiv Sena's Sanjay Raut, RJD's Misa Bharti and disgruntled BJP leaders Shatrughan Sinha, Yashwant Sinha and Arun Shourie in Delhi. The meeting was held in order to formulate a strategy for fighting the Narendra Modi government. She was also in touch with Telugu Desam Party's (TDP) Chandrababu Naidu and also met Telangana Rashtra Samiti head and Telangana Chief Minister K. Chandrashekhar Rao. Mamata was also willing to fly to Uttar Pradesh to meet Bahujan Samaj Party chief, Mayawati and Samajwadi Party leader Akhilesh Yadav to discuss the alliance. Though the Congress was not too keen to leave the alliance to Mamata's hands, they were, nonetheless, interested to join this Opposition movement against Modi.

'A narrative was being built and many newsroom managers also seriously discussed if the Opposition parties come together before the 2019 Lok Sabha elections, they can put up a good fight against Narendra Modi,' says a senior journalist from Delhi, Jayanta Bhattacharya. 'And Mamata took a lead as she perhaps wanted to play an important role in national politics.'

TMC insiders close to Mamata claimed she might not have uttered the words herself, but she wanted to be the prime ministerial candidate if the situation had demanded so. There was no doubt that if not the prime ministerial candidate, Mamata Banerjee wanted to be the kingmaker in national politics. The Opposition's movement against the Modi government got a boost with the Karnataka Assembly election result in May 2018. There Janata Dal (Secular) and Congress alliance formed the government. The oath-taking ceremony of Karnataka Chief Minister H.D. Kumaraswamy turned out to be a show of Opposition unity. Later, the result of Chhattisgarh, Rajasthan and Madhya Pradesh elections in November 2018 came as a further boost. In all the three states, the Congress had overthrown the BJP governments. The Congress put up a good fight in Gujarat assembly elections at the same time.

While the Congress desperately tried their hand at shaping the anti-Modi brigade by organizing the United India rally in Kolkata's Brigade Parade Ground in January 2019, bringing top leaders of the regional parties opposed to Narendra Modi, the Bengal chief minister had set the tone for the Lok Sabha elections. Even though Congress President Rahul Gandhi was not keen on sharing the stage, he had sent a letter of support along with the then leader of the Opposition in Lok Sabha Mallikarjun Kharge to attend Mamata's rally in Kolkata. The former prime minister and JD (S) leader H.D. Deve Gowda, his son and the then chief minister of Karnataka, H.D. Kumaraswamy, Delhi chief minister Arvind Kejriwal, NCP leader Sharad Pawar, Andhra Pradesh Chief Minister and TDP leader N. Chandrababu Naidu, Samajwadi Party's Akhilesh Yadav, DMK's M.K. Stalin, National Conference leader Farooq Abdullah, unhappy BJP leaders Shatrughan Sinha and Yashwant Sinha—all attended the rally. The Left, for the obvious reason of the long-standing rivalry, could not join the TMC chief in Bengal. Another significant absentee was the BSP's Mayawati. The gathering of 23 Opposition parties and about 30 leaders created a sense of hope that the Opposition was uniting against Modi. The United India Alliance was unveiled at the Kolkata rally and Mamata said, 'There will be no "*achche din*" for BJP. I am not concerned about who becomes the PM, I just want the BJP to go.'

The rallying of the Opposition leaders was based on only one agenda—dethrone Modi. The whole Opposition movement was centred around Narendra Modi and his decisions of demonetization or implementing flawed GST or the attack on the minorities and the Dalits or how he was using central agencies against the Opposition. Repeatedly, Mamata

Banerjee and other leaders were asked who would be the prime minister if the Opposition could muster a majority. No one had a definite answer; Mamata echoed the standard response, 'This meeting has been forced by historical necessity. You ask who the leader of the Opposition is. There are so many people on the stage. Can't you see? We have many leaders.' They promised the country that the prime minister would be nominated from the Opposition camp only after the elections. This is where the Opposition lagged behind; they did not have a face to counter the mighty image of Narendra Modi in national politics. This sense of uncertainty over the leadership as well as the agenda of the alliance helped the BJP turn the tide in their favour.

The regional Opposition parties could not get the larger picture of the RSS–BJP politics. Mob lynching by gau rakshaks, isolating Muslims, the imposition of Hindu majoritarian nationalism, using armed forces and keeping Pakistan in focus while building a rhetoric of strong leadership and robust nationalism, breaching people's privacy by strengthening the use of surveillance through tools like Aadhaar, gagging the media, not stoppering attacks on the Dalits, undermining constitutional institutions, massive unemployment and crony capitalism dominated the election campaign by the Opposition camp. But, they still failed to win the hearts of the majority of Indians. As mentioned earlier, what the Opposition leaders perhaps failed to realize (or formulate a strong counter-strategy) was that it was not a battle of these issues in isolation and it could not be fought with traditional politicking. This was a battle of ideology. They could not identify that there was an organization called Rashtriya Swayamsevak Sangh that had a deep-rooted ideological plan for India, which their political arm, that is BJP, has been implementing meticulously. They want to rewrite the history of India since and before Independence. The idea is to erase the Nehruvian constitutional secular nationalism, which, they believe, is liberal in nature and influenced by Western philosophy. Their aim is to establish a narrative that is rooted in Indian Hindu culture. This was gaining popularity among the masses and the resounding victory of Modi was proof of the fact. This aspect was ignored by the Opposition leaders, including Mamata Banerjee. A fractured, half-hearted, agenda-less effort by multiple Opposition leaders could not fight the BJP wave.

In the initial period of the election campaigning before she launched her own election rallies in Bengal, Mamata Banerjee did visit Vishakhapatnam on 31 March 2019 to attend a rally organized by TDP Chief Chandrababu Naidu. Mamata tried to prove her connect with the people of Andhra Pradesh, 'I have come here earlier when Balayogiji was the speaker. I had also come to Ramoji Rao's studio.' Then she spoke a few lines in scripted Telugu. Only Mamata Banerjee and Arvind Kejriwal participated in this rally. No other Opposition leader was seen on the dais. Mamata's speech, as usual, centred around Modi and his 'revenge politics' against the regional leaders. Perhaps she realized that the United India Alliance was not working out with Rahul Gandhi's reluctance to join hands with the regional parties and Akhilesh–Mayawati keeping the Congress out of their alliance. So, like other regional parties, by the beginning of April 2019, Mamata was also back to square one, fighting her own battle on her own turf as a lone warrior.

She was under such pressure that she had to travel across the state to rectify the mistakes of her workers and attend to organizational issues she had ignored for long. Mamata planned to address around 100 rallies and roadshows in the run-up to the 2019 Lok Sabha elections. Like the 2016 assembly elections in Bengal, she once again tried to project herself as the 'candidate' in all 42 seats. Previously, she had appealed to the people to vote for her in all 294 constituencies. It had worked then, but in 2019, it was a difficult task for Mamata. That time, there had been no prominent face against her in the state. However, in 2019, there was Narendra Modi. She had made it a battle between herself and the prime minister.

This mood also reflected in the campaign strategy. She did not want to leave even an inch to the BJP leadership. Mamata had apparently advanced the launch of her campaign from 4 April to 3 April in North Bengal only to compete with the prime minister. Narendra Modi had a rally on 3 April in Siliguri's Baghajatin Park and another in Kolkata's Brigade Parade Ground. She camped in North Bengal for the first phase of polls and stayed there for over a week to address back-to-back rallies. On an average, she was addressing three rallies in various constituencies in North Bengal every day.

In the first election rally in West Bengal, Narendra Modi had called Mamata Banerjee 'Speed Breaker Didi' for stalling central government schemes in Bengal; in reply to that jibe, Mamata at the first rally in Cooch Behar on the same day called Narendra Modi 'expiry babu'. She told the gathering, 'From now on, I will call him expiry babu, the "expiry prime minister".' It essentially meant the prime minister was running a caretaker government after the election dates were announced and she did not recognize Narendra Modi as the country's prime minister any more. She also replied to Modi's charge that the Bengal government had stalled the process of implementation of central schemes in the state. 'Expiry babu, you have said in Siliguri today that our government does not work for the poor. What have you done in five years? Answer this.

If you think what you said was true, then come for a direct debate with me. You will question me and I will reply. I will give you proof. Don't lie every day. Lying is not your job, Mr Prime Minister.'

Apart from defending her party's stand in the face of the BJP's onslaught, Mamata was also desperate for an image makeover. She spoke less about the minorities and more about her Hindu identity. She chanted the Gayatri Mantra, verses of Chandi and said, 'I do Kali Puja at home. I visit Durga Puja pandals the way I attend Eid and Christmas celebrations.' She had to raise her pitch to debunk BJP leaders' claim that Mamata Banerjee did not allow Durga Puja and Saraswati Puja in Bengal. In rally after rally she asked the gathering more in Narendra Modi-style, 'They say, here I don't allow you to do Durga Puja or Saraswati Puja. What do you say, my mothers and sisters? You tell me, does Durga Puja take place here? Does Lakshmi Puja take place here? Does Saraswati Puja take place?' When the crowd cheered in affirmation, she continued, 'Do you have Eid Mubarak here? Do you celebrate Christmas here? So you could understand, they lie continuously.' She criticized the BJP leaders for 'spreading lies'. Expressions like 'inshallah' vanished from her speeches. In fact, the minorities almost vanished from her poll speeches, except in the minority-dominated areas. TMC leaders were happier being photographed at temples than at mazaars. Abhishek Banerjee was seen visiting the Barakachhari Kali temple in his constituency and Mamata started visiting temples regularly to project her Hindu identity.

'Mamata Banerjee's understanding of secularism and its translation into policy level is deeply problematic. Her moves to introduce *imam bhata* or asking Muslim clerics to attend her rallies diluted her secular principles and helped BJP polarize the state communally,' says economist Prasenjit Bose. Except for raising their voice against the Election Commission's decision to hold elections during the month of Ramzan, TMC leaders were not keen to project the plight of minorities in this polarized election. 'Can't you see Mamata Banerjee is not highlighting the work she has done for the Muslims in her speeches? We are living under fear. But we will vote for TMC as they have protected us in times of turmoil,' said Imran Ali, a farmer from Uluberia, the constituency where Mamata Banerjee's party increased their vote share in the by-election.

The sorry state of affairs at Mamata Banerjee's rallies was evident as the crowds got thinner. This avatar of Mamata Banerjee, who was seen waiting for the ground to fill up before starting her speech, was unknown to political observers. Didi was always seen with a sea of people accompanying her. This was not the case in most of North Bengal. She had lost the charisma of drawing crowds. In her heydays, the vehicular movement had to be stopped for at least two to three hours before she reached the venue and took the stage.

Though she did not say anything openly, but she expressed her anger and anguish to the local party leaders on certain occasions. Like in Mamata's first election rally at Dinhata in Cooch Behar on 3 April 2019 or the Rasmela Maidan in the same district or in Baghajatin Park in Siliguri, the crowd was not as large as expected. Rather, the parallel meetings addressed by Narendra Modi drew more crowds. The local leaders were blamed for not mobilizing the supporters. Mamata Banerjee tried to cover up the organizational and political loopholes with highlighting the developmental work she had carried out. However, in Darjeeling, North Bengal and Junglemahal, instead of mentioning the developmental projects that she had taken up, she almost pleaded with the voters to forgive the TMC's mistakes. Some bought it but most didn't.

In the last leg of campaigning, Mamata was heard saying at a rally in Belpahari, 'Whatever punishment you wanted to give me, you have given during the panchayat elections. We have taken action. Now, please vote for us.' She was now in apology mode, but it was difficult for her to fight a lonely battle. 'Even if you slap TMC, the party will still be lying at your feet. Remember, we do not run away or create riots...sometimes being upset with some local TMC leaders you vote for the BJP. But in TMC, we have never let any local leader take money for doing the poor people's work. Some have done it. The leaders who took money have been removed. We take action against them. Do you think I am a thief or Partha Chatterjee is a thief or Sukumar Hansda is a thief? There are both good and bad people in politics, but not all are bad.'

She also had to defend her decision to induct her nephew Abhishek Banerjee into the party fold. 'When Indira Gandhi lost the elections, the CPIM cadres used to threaten us. I was adamant. At that time, all my siblings used to take part in marches. So it's nothing new, my family has been involved in politics from the beginning... He [Abhishek] did not want to join politics. I had told him, see if you, the young generation, don't come forward, then who would be in politics?' she told a rally in Belpahari on 5 May.[12] She also cited examples of West Bengal minister Suvendu Adhikari and former prime minister Rajiv Gandhi to explain how some children from political families join politics. 'When I was assaulted and suffered a head injury in 1990, I was

[12] AITC Official. 2019. 'Mamata Banerjee addresses a public meeting at Belpahari'. YouTube, 8 May. Available at: https://www.youtube.com/watch?v=3HNkoGWB44k

in the hospital for three months. Abhishek had seen my bloodied pictures. He was around two then and used to get scared looking at my bandaged body. He would raise the flag and say, "Jyotibabu answer why did you assault Didi?" He had then made up his mind to be with me. There are thousands of boys and girls in politics and he is one of them... We have about 200 leaders like Suvendu, Arup, Bobby, Parthada, Subrata Bakshi at this level.'

Mamata made her battle more difficult with a strategic call to her party colleagues. In an election-related preparatory meeting with the elected TMC councillors, Mamata Banerjee warned them and the elected representatives that those who were unable to get a lead in the number of votes for the Lok Sabha candidate from their municipal ward wouldn't get the nomination in the next civic polls.

A week before the elections, I met a couple of TMC leaders at a lunch invitation, which had no political connection. The attendance of these TMC leaders at the lunch at a time when they were supposed to be engrossed in poll planning and campaigning for their candidates was indeed surprising. When I asked one of the leaders of the party about this, he said, 'Didi has committed a mistake by asking the councillors to get leads for the party candidate. The councillor may try to garner votes in favour of the party nominee, but their rival camp [within TMC] won't let it happen. If the councillor fails to get a lead, the leader of the rival camp will stand a chance to get the nomination in the next civic polls. He would, therefore, try to sabotage.' This prophecy turned out to be true in many seats. In Balurghat seat in South Dinajpur, the TMC's sitting MP Arpita Ghosh lost to the BJP candidate. In Malda North, Congress sitting MP-turned TMC-candidate, Mausam Benazir Noor, lost to the BJP candidate. In the Hooghly seat, the sitting MP Ratna

De Nag lost to the BJP Mahila Morcha president and actor, Locket Chatterjee. In all these seats and in Purulia, there were allegations of sabotage by the local leaders that brought misfortune to the sitting MPs. In none of the seats were the local leaders happy with the nominations.

In the last leg of the elections, Mamata Banerjee perhaps could feel the pulse of the electorate. She stressed more on roadshows connecting with the people on the streets than rallies delivering speeches from the dais. People got a glimpse of the old Mamata Banerjee, who could reach out to the masses easily and mix with them while walking in political marches.

There were also instances when Mamata lost her cool and the BJP used it to attack her. While travelling to West Midnapore through Chandrakona, Mamata Banerjee reacted sharply to the chanting of 'Jai Shri Ram' by local youths. She got off the car and chased them and used abusive language. This was not how a chief minister was supposed to behave. The BJP IT cell got the footage and made it go viral on social media. Soon, the BJP leaders used this incident to paint Mamata as anti-Hindu. Be it Amit Shah or Narendra Modi, all the top leaders of the BJP kept attacking Mamata on the 'Jai Shri Ram' issue. They asked the crowd at an election rally, 'Is it a crime to take the name of Ram in Bengal? Why should someone be jailed for chanting Jai Shri Ram?' The BJP leaders chanted 'Ram Naam' at rallies and dared Mamata to arrest them.

While it turned out to be a joke for a large section of the people in Bengal to chant 'Jai Shri Ram' and tease their friends and TMC supporters, the BJP encashed on it to make it an assertion on the Hindus in Bengal. They created a narrative where it was a criminal act to chant 'Ram Naam' in the West Bengal led by Mamata Banerjee, and Hindus in the state were supposed to challenge her.

Soon the Hindutva narrative that was built up by the saffron camp changed to Bengali versus non-Bengali, thanks to a ruckus between TMC and BJP workers during Amit Shah's roadshow in Kolkata that led to the desecration of Iswarchandra Vidyasagar's bust. An iconic figure of Bengal renaissance and a renowned educationist, Vidyasagar has a high place in every Bengali's heart. Anyone who learns the Bengali alphabet begins the journey with Vidyasagar's *Barnaparichay* (introduction to the alphabet). On 15 May, when BJP President Amit Shah's roadshow started from Esplanade and reached Calcutta University, a group of TMC students' wing supporters were present there chanting anti-BJP slogans. There was a skirmish in front of the university. About a kilometre ahead, in front of Vidyasagar College on 17 Bidhan Sarani, the incident went out of control. There was an open clash between the TMC and BJP activists. BJP activists allegedly stormed into the college and took out the bust of Vidyasagar and destroyed it. Though the Special Investigating Team of Kolkata Police could not come up with any specific proof against any particular party, the blame game between the Mamata and Modi camps began. Several amateur videos surfaced on social media, but none could definitely prove which camp had desecrated the bust.

It helped Mamata to accuse BJP of disrespecting Bengal's iconic figure and thereby the cultural heritage of the state. Modi's 'Jai Shri Ram' narrative, which was imported from North India, lost its sheen after this incident. The violence forced the Election Commission to come up with a controversial decision. They curtailed the campaigning hours by a day and asked all parties to conclude their rallies and roadshows by 10 p.m. on 15 May instead of 5 p.m. the next day. There was no clarification about why the decision to bring forward the deadline in such a manner was taken. It deviated from the normal practice of not allowing any campaign meeting by political parties during the period of 48 hours ending with the hour fixed for the closing of the polls. The TMC leaders alleged that it was to make way for the prime minister to conclude his election campaign in Bengal. Narendra Modi was scheduled to address election reallies in Bengal on that day.

The Lok Sabha elections, which were supposed to be UP-centric, turned out to be focused on Bengal. The electoral battle, which should have been a Rahul Gandhi versus Narendra Modi duel, ended up being a bitter battle between Modi and Mamata. The BJP, in the last leg of the elections, was branded as an anti-Bengali party. The pride of Bengali culture dominated the political discussion much to Mamata's favour. So, from Hindu majority versus Muslim minorities to the assertion of Hindu identity through the 'Jai Shri Ram' chant, the narrative of Bengal-being-disrespected-by-the-BJP captured the imagination of voters. Ironically, the BJP could not win any of the Bengal's nine seats that went to the polls in the final phase of the 2019 elections.

POLLING DAY SHOCKERS

While in Junglemahal, the presence of the BJP or fringe Hindu organizations was visible either through saffron flags or posters and graffiti, there were a lot of areas where the BJP's presence was not felt on the surface. A journalist friend, Debamoy Ghosh, called me a few days before the polling day in Ranaghat constituency in Nadia district and told me, 'I don't know how the BJP is claiming that they will win the seat. I took a walk from Nabadwip station and went a few kilometres inside the town; I could hardly see any BJP posters.' It was a correct observation. But, beneath the surface, the people were preparing to assert their voice. The BJP's

Jagannath Sarkar won the Ranaghat constituency by over two lakh votes. In many constituencies, the ruling party failed to feel the pulse of the people. A large number of voters have always participated in exercising their franchise, but this time a number of silent voters made the difference for the TMC. They got a chance to express their angst against the ruling party through the ballot.

There were alarming signs for the ruling party in the state on the polling day. So far, the Opposition parties had demanded deployment of central forces in polling booths to run free and fair elections. They did not have much faith in the state police. In 2019, a new phenomenon emerged in Bengal. The polling officials demanded deployment of central forces at the polling booth. It was significant as polling officials were state government employees or the teachers in schools and colleges. The first agitation was reported in North Bengal's Cooch Behar, Alipurduar, Raiganj and afterwards, it spread across the state even reaching Kolkata.

'We demanded deployment of central forces for our security. From our experience, we have seen how the ruling party workers and leaders threaten us inside the polling booth. You have no way of protesting. We have families and we need to get back home,' said a polling officer who was posted in Krishnanagar. He went on to narrate the horrors of polling booths, 'During the by-election in Noapara, the ruling party cadres came inside the polling booth and asked us to hand over the operation of the EVMs. One of us tried to protest. We were told this was their area. No one can disobey their diktat. We had to surrender. Some of them were probably carrying weapons. We did not dare challenge them.' Incidentally, a polling officer, Rajkumar Roy, a teacher by profession, was found dead near a railway track in Raiganj during the panchayat elections. His colleagues alleged that he was killed.

During the Lok Sabha elections, when the state government employees asked for central forces for their protection, it put the Mamata Banerjee government in an embarrassing situation. But, this move showed how the people in Bengal were getting a chance to raise their voice against the political misdeeds of the ruling party. Never before had polling officials voiced their concern so loudly through demonstrations; in some cases, they went on a strike refusing to draw polling materials before going to the polling booth. 'The state government employees largely belonged to the Left Coordination Committee and since 2011 their voice has been suppressed under the TMC rule. Now, they can assert their demands against the ruling government in the changing political scenarios,' said a TMC leader from North Bengal. 'Whatever be the case, the fact that the state government employees could raise their voice against the government despite the fear of getting punished by the Election Commission, was a big shift in Bengal's political stage,' says a state government employee in the cooperative department who was on poll duty.

Political violence is nothing new in Bengal. The TMC and the Left workers regularly clashed on polling days. But this time, another dangerous trend emerged during the elections. A section of voters in North Bengal's Raiganj claimed that they were not being allowed to vote as they were Hindus. A woman claimed on camera, 'Partisan politics has divided the village between Hindu and Muslims. Now, we are not allowed to vote.' When asked if they were not allowed to vote because they were Hindus, she said, 'Yes.'

Party politics and division between the supporters of two parties, irrespective of their caste and creed or religion, is an accepted practice in Bengal elections.

Every election, a section of voters allege that either their votes had been cast before they went to the polling booth or they were intercepted on their way to the polling booths. But, never before had Bengal seen such division on religious lines. A video claiming that Hindus were being evicted from the Diamond Harbour constituency had gone viral. Though the video could not be verified, the BJP took advantage of the allegations to hammer home the point of how Hindus were being deprived of their rights to vote in Bengal.

The behaviour of some leaders of the ruling party also proved that the TMC was on the back foot. North Bengal Development Minister Rabindranath Ghosh, an aggressive leader of Cooch Behar, alleged a conspiracy between the election observers and the BJP within a few hours of polling. 'Since morning, I was getting reports that there is mismanagement, EVM machines are not working. People were waiting for long. They are going home. The observers are missing and could not be reached on phone. Now, I am getting news that security forces from the border are going inside the booths to influence the voters. There is a conspiracy to disturb the elections,' Ghosh told journalists around 10 a.m. on 11 April 2019. He was also caught in a confrontation with the CRPF jawans at a polling booth. A top minister in the Mamata government alleging misconduct in the elections within three hours of the beginning of the polling process was alarming for the ruling party. It was almost like conceding defeat even before the game had begun.

In Barrackpore constituency, breakaway TMC MLA Arjun Singh, who was contesting on a BJP ticket, had some other plans. On the day of the poll, he was seen visiting different booths in TMC's stronghold Amdanaga. It was not unusual for a candidate to visit his constituency on polling day. However, he was surrounded by TMC supporters on a couple of occasions and even got into a scuffle with them. While chasing TMC supporters, he stumbled and fell on the road and injured himself. His security guards and BJP supporters were seen running behind agitating TMC workers in Amdanga's Tentulia village.

'The TMC leadership thought that Arjun was on the backfoot. What they perhaps could not see is that the BJP candidate was concentrating only on areas he had a lesser support base and keeping the TMC workers under pressure. But in the assembly segments like Naihati, Bhatpara, Jagaddal he did not have to put much effort. His supporters and workers were taking care of the polling booths there,' says a TV journalist who was following Arjun Singh's cavalcade on the polling day. 'So those who thought Arjun was under pressure and might lose the elections were found to be wrong as the result came in.'

The BJP candidate defeated TMC heavyweight Dinesh Trivedi with a huge margin. This once again proved that Mamata's magic was not the only factor in winning elections, the local satraps too had a role to play. Year after year, the TMC had managed to win Barackpore constituency, but Arjun Singh, a local MLA, managed to snatch the seat with a BJP ticket. His son Pawan Singh also won the assembly by-election of the Bhatpara constituency a few days later. Mamata, even by putting up her trump card, former minister Madan Mitra, could not retain the seat.

Lack of local leaders, dwindling control over the party organization, sabotage by own workers, 'carpet-bombing' by Modi–Shah rallies and their high octave electoral pitch made the election more challenging for Mamata Banerjee. On the other hand, strategic thrust on Bengal, utilizing people's anger against the TMC local leaders, getting the support of a section of Left vote bank, evoking communal tension and imparting confidence among the Hindu and anti-TMC voters made things easier for the BJP. They almost reached their target of 23 seats, set by Amit Shah, by winning 18 seats. Mamata was reduced to just 22 from 34 and the Congress won 2 seats while the Left drew a blank for the first time in the state.

7

Post-election Bengal's Political Future

'Jai Shri Ram!'

In Bengal, this chant had become more a way to tease the TMC supporters than a real assertion of the might of the Rightist force or simply a way to remember the Lord. However, what no one had ever imagined was that West Bengal Chief Minister Mamata Banerjee would stop her white SUV and get off to confront the crowd chanting the slogan.

A week after the Lok Sabha election results were announced, the industrial belt in North 24 Paragans district along the Ganga River was on the boil. Communal tension had flared up with TMC-MLA-turned-BJP-MP Arjun Singh exerting his power. On 30 May 2019, Mamata had been visiting the trouble-torn areas in Bhatpara in North 24 Parganas, nearly 35 kilometres from Kolkata, to take stock of the situation and was in a foul mood.

'Come here. If you have the guts, face me. You, BJP goons,' Mamata shouted at the crowd. Her security personnel surrounded her, but she kept chasing the Ram-chanting gang. 'You are surviving because of us. I can drive you out of here tomorrow. I will see which dada or which *mastan* [goon] saves you. You are eating and living here, and you are attacking the motorcade. I will get you skinned.'[1]

In a way, she indicated that those chanting Ram slogans were 'outsiders'. A large section of the residents in this belt come from North India or Bihar mainly to work in the jute mills. A lot of them have been living here for two or three generations. Clearly, this section had voted for the BJP in the 2019 Lok Sabha elections to send breakaway TMC MLA Arjun Singh to parliament and invoked the wrath of the chief minister. She asked her director (security), Vineet Goyal, to conduct raids. 'I want every house to be checked,' she instructed the police.

The most shocking scene had, however, yet to unfold. A moment after the chief minister went back to her car and the cavalcade started moving, the crowd again chanted 'Jai Shri Ram'. Mamata Banerjee stopped her car and got off. This time the DGP, Veerendra, was behind her. She shouted, 'Come. Come and face me if you can. You criminals.' Neither did the crowd disperse nor did the slogan-chanting gang come forward. Mamata moved to the media persons and said, 'See, there is a limit to being gentle. I was going in my car. How dare they abuse me by sporting BJP flags? They are outsiders, and we have taken care of them. They are not Bengal's local people.'

Mamata Banerjee had reacted in a similar fashion during her election campaign in West Midnapore when a group of men chanted 'Jai Shri Ram'. This was no more a mere slogan, but a strong indicator of the cultural transformation in Bengal. As Monobina

---

[1] *India Today*. 2019. 'Mamata Banerjee Loses Cool After People Chant 'Jai Shri Ram'. YouTube, 30 May. Available at: https://www.youtube.com/watch?v=jz-9tA_w9g3c

Gupta, a senior journalist and author, wrote during the Lok Sabha election campaign, 'A slogan coined by the Bhartiya Janata Party (BJP) currently doing the WhatsApp rounds—"Tomar Naam, Amar Naam, Jai Shri Ram, Jai Shri Ram (your name, my name [is], Jai Shri Ram, Jai Shri Ram)"—is symbolic of the political and cultural transformations underway in Bengal. Over the last six decades, the slogan has evolved as political realities have morphed in the state.'[2] The original slogan 'Tomar Naam, Amar Naam, Vietnam' was coined during the 1960s as the Left dominated Bengal politics, with the Congress weakening, and garnered the support of Bengali radicals for Vietnam's fight against US aggression. The same slogan transformed into 'Tomar Naam, Amar Naam, Nandigram, Nandigram' during the Nandigram-Singur peasant movement against forceful farmland acquisition by the Left government. Mamata Banerjee was then leading the fight against the Left. The popularity of the Ram slogan in 2019 marked another transition in the state politics, as Gupta wrote, 'The state once known to be Communist/Left bastion—is leaning towards the untested saffron party.'[3]

Post the election results, the knee-jerk reaction from the incumbent chief minister, who has been the messiah of the state, created a ripple in the political circles and social spheres of the state. This reaction showed her anger over the rise of the BJP in the state in electoral numbers. Though the TMC had increased its vote percentage compared to the 2014 Lok Sabha elections, it had lost its ground in a large portion of the state in terms of the number of Lok Sabha seats. But, more

---

[2] Gupta, M. *The Wire*. 'From "Vietnam" to "Jai Shri Ram": The Slogan Capturing Bengal's Shift from Left to Right'. 10 May 2019.

[3] Ibid.

than the loss of the number of seats, Mamata Banerjee's fall from grace was a significant development in West Bengal politics in the last 10 years. Mamata alone could not win elections any more.

TABLE 7.1: Lok Sabha Election Results 2014 vs 2019

Party	2019 LS Seats	Vote Percentage	2014 LS Seats	Vote Percentage
TMC	22	43.28	34	39.79
BJP	18	40.25	2	17.02
Left	0	7.46	2	29.95
Congress	2	5.61	4	9.69

Source: Election Commission of India

TABLE 7.2: Lok Sabha 2019 vs Vidhan Sabha 2016 Results

Party	2019 Vote Percentage	2016 Vote Percentage
TMC	43.28	44.91
BJP	40.25	10.16
Left	7.46	25.69
Congress	5.61	12.25

The slogan-chanting crowd in Bhatpara also showed how people had dared to take on the administrative chief and top officials of her administration. They did not hesitate to chant 'Jai Shri Ram' the second time even after the chief minister got out of the car and chased them in the presence of senior police officers, including the DGP of the state. This incident was the manifestation of two things—the people had begun to protest even in front of the chief of the ruling party, maybe drawing courage from the rise of the BJP in the state; and Mamata was losing her cool as the TMC and the administration went rudderless in the aftermath of the election results.

MAMATA'S WOES

The 2019 Lok Sabha elections have shown that Bengal is no longer a citadel of Left progressive politics. It is crystal clear with the invasion of the saffron camp into the red bastion. Welfare politics, which had paid dividends not only for the Left Front for 34 years but also Mamata Banerjee, who was projected as 'more Left than the Left', has taken a sharp turn in the last decade. The state has been polarized on communal lines, witnessed a new kind of identity politics and people in different strata of the society have started looking for an alternative which they got in Narendra Modi's BJP.

The most prominent cry for asylum has come from Bengali Hindus. The festering wound of Bengal's partition, when it was divided into East Pakistan and West Bengal on religious lines, still pains many in the state. Many have had to flee to West Bengal from East Pakistan (now Bangladesh) in the face of atrocities committed against them by the Muslims there. The sentiment of a communal divide between Hindus and Muslims, nurtured by the colonial rulers, still exists in almost every Bengali household. Some, like economist Prasenjit Bose, may say, 'I don't think the people of Bengal are communal in nature.' Congress leader Abdul Mannan may claim that 'the culture BJP is bringing to the state is not our culture'. But, one thing that cannot be denied is the fact that Bengal politics has taken a sharp turn towards the Right. The election results are a testimony to that fact. If the Left could keep this communal sentiment doused by dividing the state according to political affiliation, the Left versus Congress or Left versus TMC binary, Mamata has scratched that festering wound with her appeasement politics. This flare-up has also been aided by a few incidents of communal tension in certain parts of the state. Prasenjit Bose says, 'This was systematic. Planned riots in targeted pockets in the state and BJP made the best use of this situation.'

As it has been observed, Amit Shah and Narendra Modi continuously attacked Mamata Banerjee for not allowing Durga Puja and Saraswati Puja in Bengal. They evoked the fear of Muslim aggression in the state. BJP State President Dilip Ghosh explains, 'People were apprehensive if there would be another partition and if the Hindus would have to be refugees once again.' With the promise of NRC, the new Citizenship Bill, and driving out Bangladeshi Muslim infiltrators, the BJP leadership carried out a veiled attack against Muslims and assured a safe haven to the Bengali Hindus.

Mamata's reaction to the 'Jai Shri Ram' slogan made the situation worse. Despite her clarification at each and every election rally, she could not build a credible pro-Hindu or secular image. The result shows that people, mostly the Hindus, were looking up to the BJP for 'shelter' against minority aggression. The voting pattern, too, proves it. While the TMC retained its vote share in minority-dominated areas such as Park Circus, Metiabruz, Khiderpore, Basirhat and South 24 Parganas, the BJP fared well in Asansol, Malda and both North and South Dinajpur where the communal sentiment is high. However, TMC Secretary-General Partha Chatterjee refuses to accept this explanation. 'Muslims did not vote for us entirely. Otherwise, we could have won seats in Murshidabad or Malda.' He might be right as the Congress polled the Muslim votes in districts where they have a strong base. Chatterjee confesses, 'We had taken it for granted that the 70 per cent non-minority votes would come to us. We had also expected that 30 per cent of minority votes would come to us. It was not right. Even now, I would say this calculation is wrong. There is a debate inside the party on this as well. Here, people have seen who is powerful in the area, is it Congress or the Left or the BJP and those opposed to TMC voted for them. The anti-BJP votes came to us where we have been strong.'

People also seem to be looking for an alternative in the BJP to teach a lesson to the TMC for the local leaders' atrocities, extortion and corruption. The way people shifted their allegiance from the Left to Mamata Banerjee in 2008, the same way, the voters shifted their support to the BJP in 2019. In every conversation I had in the rural areas, the majority said they were angry with the local TMC leaders and not with Mamata. They wanted to express their anger against them. 'In certain areas, the lifestyle of the local leaders and the mismanagement of the gram panchayat and panchayat samitis deprived people the benefits of government schemes, and they were misused. This is one of the biggest reasons behind our defeat,' says Partha Chatterjee. At the same time, he blames the Left and the Congress for not being able to hold on to their vote bank. 'Can you imagine the Left has come down to 5 per cent? Even during the 1972 elections, they did not perform this poorly. Congress is completely flattened. You will see where the Left and the Congress has done well, the BJP has not been able to win seats.'

Even though the Left leaders are not ready to accept the fact that their supporters are shifting allegiance to the BJP, the vote share figures reveal a different picture. The BJP has gained from an eroding Left vote bank. Since 2011, Left workers and supporters have been hounded out by TMC workers. The elected representatives of the Left were forced to change camps at all levels in the state. The state or politburo leadership of the Left could not stand by their supporters and workers in their hour of need. Today, they want to find shelter in the BJP against the atrocities of the ruling party.

The marginalized and Adivasi population of Bengal are also looking up to the BJP. The TMC's rout in North Bengal tea gardens and Junglemahal, which have SC- and ST- dominated seats, shows Mamata Banerjee could not stand up to the expectations of identity politics of this section of the people. The same applies to the demand for a separate state of Gorkhaland in Darjeeling. She poured funds for infrastructure development in these backward areas, but her party men kept taking 'cut money' (bribe or commission). Despite the BJP's anti-Dalit image, these tribals reposed their faith in the saffron party. The saffron camp won five out of the ten constituencies (Cooch Behar, Jalpaiguri, Ranaghat, Bishnupur, Bongaon) reserved for Scheduled Caste candidates and two out of two constituencies reserved for the Scheduled Tribes, (Jhagram and Alipurduars).

The side-lined TMC workers too have been trying to find their next political destination in the BJP. Though TMC leaders refuse to accept it in the open but after Abhishek Banerjee's youth wing floated a virtual parallel organization within the TMC as TMC youth wing chief, those who could not be a part of this gang subtly worked for the BJP in this election. Former TMC leader Mukul Roy, who is now with the BJP, made judicious use of these estranged workers at the local level. There will always be an opportunistic individual who will try to stay close to the power centre and swiftly shift their loyalties to the saffron camp. Dilip Ghosh says, 'There are some who loved the BJP but thought what was the point joining a losing party. After the election results showed signs of hope, BJP's success has given confidence to them to join us.' The BJP makes no bones about welcoming anyone who comes to them after deserting the TMC.

It took 34 years for the people to throw out the Left government in Bengal. For Mamata, the shockwaves have been felt in just eight years. The situation only went from bad to worse for Mamata after the elections. She had to ban victory rallies because of simmering tension between TMC and BJP activists. The winds of change started blowing perilously close to Kolkata. Communal violence in North 24 Parganas's Kankinara–Bhatpara was a direct outcome of the shift in the balance of power. The area is dominated by migrant workers and is crime-prone. 'Areas such as Kankinara and Jagaddal in Bhatpara constituency are full of goons consisting mainly of migrant workers from Bihar and UP. It is infamous for hooliganism, bomb-making, adulteration, etc. Now, as these goons are divided into two groups after the Lok Sabha elections [in which local satrap and former TMC MLA Arjun Singh came victorious], there is more violence,' says a woman living in Bhatpara.

In late June, when a street food vendor, Dharamveer Shaw, was killed in firing between miscreants and the police, the situation took an ugly turn. Taking advantage of what had happened, the BJP and its newly elected MP Arjun Singh tried to create pressure on the TMC government. The BJP sent its parliamentary team to the area to take stock of the situation, but they were prevented by both administration and the local TMC workers from visiting the troubled site. 'BJP was trying to create pressure on our government. They did not understand that Mamata Banerjee's government is an elected government by the people for five years,' said TMC minister Tapas Roy. However, it took two quick changes of commissioners of police at the Barrackpore

Commissionerate (in which Bhatpara falls) to take control of the situation.

When faced with a sudden surge in the BJP's electoral strength, Mamata did feel nervous. Not only in Barrackpore, but a post-election political clash in South 24 Parganas's Sandeshkhali also witnessed the killing of three BJP and one TMC activist. The fight apparently broke out over the removal of BJP flags. There were allegations and incidents of TMC party offices being captured overnight and painted saffron. The killing in Sandeshkhali soon took a communal colour. The names of the deceased evoked tension. The BJP claimed that four of their workers, Sukanta Mondal, Pradip Mandal, Tapan Mandal and Debadas Mondal, were killed in the clash. In contrast, the TMC claimed that their supporter twenty-six-year-old Qayyum Mollah was first hacked up and then shot at by the BJP goons. Debadas Mondal's body could not be traced immediately after the incident. Pradip's wife, Padma Mondal, told journalists, 'Our only fault is that we support the BJP in our area. My husband asked TMC workers to remove their flag from his shop and he was brutally killed. For God's sake, please let peace prevail and Bengal see "unnayan" [development] and not bloodshed.' On the other hand, Qayyum's father, Liyaqat Ali Mollah, alleged that the BJP workers had first killed his son and in retaliation, the villagers launched an attack.

Though the BJP had lost the Basirhat parliamentary seat, under which Sandeshkhali falls, local BJP leaders claimed that the balance of power in this tiny hamlet close to Sundarbans was shifting. In the Bhangipara booth, the BJP had a lead and it might have worried the local TMC leaders. The TMC block president, Sheikh Shajahan, was accused of spearheading the violence. There were allegations that the clash had been triggered by the fear of losing control over the (*bheri*) [fishing pond], a source of income for the political outfits and the local leaders.

The BJP did not want to lose out on a chance to take political mileage out of the incident. Led by senior BJP leaders such as Rahul Sinha and Mukul Roy, the party tried to bring bodies to Kolkata to stage a protest exactly like the dharnas Mamata Banerjee had organized during the Left rule. It was a spectacle, with the police trying to stop the cavalcade of the BJP leaders with mortuary vans. After a few who-blinks-first moments, the BJP leaders relented and sent the bodies back to the village for cremation.

However, the pressure kept mounting on the Mamata Banerjee government. Soon after the Sandeshkhali incident, the strike by junior doctors at Nil Ratan Sircar Medical College and Hospital (which began on 11 June 2019) created another embarrassing moment for the chief minister.

On 10 June 2019, a truck full of nearly 200 outsiders had attacked a section of junior doctors at the government-run medical college after the death of a 75-year old patient, Mohammad Sayeed. Two junior doctors had to be admitted to the hospital with head injuries. One of them, Dr Paribaha Mukhopadhyay, suffered a serious skull injury as he was hit with a brick by the hooligans. He had to be shifted to a private hospital and undergo surgery. His colleagues refused to work citing lack of security in the government hospital. Doctors from other government medical colleges also joined the strike and the government healthcare service across the state came to a virtual halt for the next two–three days. They were demanding that the government make proper security arrangements for doctors at government-run hospitals.

Unfortunately, in Bengal, nothing remains a simple law-and-order issue, quickly taking a political turn;

and, especially after the 2019 Lok Sabha elections, most of the time, it takes a communal hue. The BJP tried to look at the NRS incident through a communal prism too. BJP leader Mukul Roy, while expressing solidarity, told the media, '*Ekta bishesh sampradayer lokjon hamla chaliyechhe. Tara Trinamool korey... ei hamlay Trinamool jorito. Ar akranto, chikitsak* Paribaha Mukherjee [the people of a particular community carried out the attack. They belong to Trinamool. The doctor who has been attacked is Paribaha Mukherjee].'[4] It was not a slip of the tongue. He later clarified his reference to the communal narrative, saying, 'Such an attack on [Dr Paribaha] Mukherjee and his colleagues cannot be taken lightly. It is a planned move by a particular community and the ruling party patronised the attackers.'[5]

This was condemned by many, but the narrative touched a chord with those who had supported the BJP in the Lok Sabha elections. Mamata's pro-minority image was exploited by the saffron camp once again. On 26 May, at her first press conference after the 2019 Lok Sabha polls, Mamata had said, 'I appease Muslims, no? I will go there [Iftar party] a hundred times. *Je goru dudh dei tar lathio khete hoi* [if a cow gives milk, one must be ready to get kicked by it too].'[6] Mamata knew that the minorities had voted for the TMC in large numbers hoping for security from the onslaught of the Rightist forces in a highly polarized state. Though she practised soft Hindutva during the election campaign, she did not want to lose the vote bank she had nurtured for long. The BJP exploited this too and forced people

[4] TT Bureau. *The Telegraph Online*. 12 June 2019. 'Calcutta doctors attacked, BJP leader blames a particular community'. 12 June 2019.

[5] Ibid.

[6] *India Today*. 'Will attend Iftar 100 times: Mamata over Muslim appeasement allegations'. 26 May 2019.

to look at a simple political incident or law and order situation through the prism of religious communities.

Frustrated with the narrative that Mamata government is soft on minorities and refused to take action if anyone from the minority community was involved in a crime, a section of eminent Muslims in Kolkata wrote an open letter to the chief minister asking her to take stringent action if there was violation of law and order irrespective of religion. Urging the chief minister to increase more engagement with the minority community on the issues of gender sensitization, civic consciousness, law compliance, they wrote, 'Bring the assailants to book, not just these two incidents but every single instance where Muslims are involved. They should not be allowed to get away scot-free because they happen to be Muslims (as is a growing perception).'

Mamata mishandled the situation arising out of the junior doctors' strike simply by being stubborn. There was pressure on her government from all quarters. The intellectuals, who had once hit the streets of Kolkata in solidarity with the people of Nandigram against the Left Front government in 2008, had now apparently turned against Mamata. People like Aparna Sen, Kousik Sen and other ultra-Left activists came forward to express solidarity with the junior doctors. Aparna Sen, in an interview to NDTV on 4 June 2019,[7] had already said, 'Mamata is turning her voters against her. She is digging her own grave!' Though this specific comment's point of reference was the chief minister's 'knee-jerk' reaction to the 'Jai Shri Ram' slogan, it is important to note that intellectuals representing civil society were raising their voice against the TMC government. Despite expressing her worries over

[7] *NDTV*. 'Mamata Banerjee "Digging Her Own Grave": Aparna Sen On "Jai Shri Ram" Row'. 4 June 2019.

the BJP's Savarkar brand of Hindu nationalism, the filmmaker said, 'Civilized, urban, elite middle class are all pro-BJP now.' She called the civil society activists to act as an Opposition.

As the pressure started building on Mamata over the doctors' strike, she sent her junior minister for health Chandrima Bhattacharya and Kolkata CP Anuj Sharma to negotiate with the junior doctors; however, they refused to speak to her emissaries. Their demand was that the chief minister should come to the hospital and meet the agitating doctors. Soon, senior doctors from other government-run medical colleges and hospitals also extended their support. Mamata aggravated the already-complicated situation by visiting another government hospital, SSKM, on the third day of the strike, branding the agitating doctors as 'BJP' and 'outsiders'. She made a sudden visit and waded through the crowd chanting 'We want justice' to take the mic and said, 'They are outsiders [the agitators]. The government will not support them in any way. I condemn the doctors who have gone on strike. Policemen die in the line of duty but the police don't go on a strike.' She also gave an ultimatum to the doctors and warned them of strict action if they did not resume duty within four hours. 'Those who don't join the duty will have to vacate the hostel,' she stated. To her dismay, the doctors did not listen to her diktat and knocked on the doors of the Raj Bhavan. This showed how helpless Mamata was and none of her doctor-leaders, like MLA Nirmal Majhi or Rajya Sabha MP Shantanu Sen, could help to resolve the crisis. Support for junior doctors started pouring in from all over India and it kept Mamata's West Bengal in national headlines.

At first, Mamata remained adamant and refused to relent to the doctors' demand, but gradually she softened her stand. She took control of the situation by appealing to the agitating doctors three days after the incident, that is, on 14 June 2019, to come to the state secretariat, Nabanna, to hold a dialogue to resolve the crisis. The doctors refused to do that. On the fifth day of the strike, Mamata, through some senior doctors of the city, arranged for a meeting with the agitators' delegation. The junior doctors did not turn up. She told the media persons that she would not take action against the protesting doctors or impose the Essential Services Maintenance Act. She regretted the fact that she waited for the junior doctors but they did not come to the state secretariat. 'They cannot decide where the government will hold the meeting. I think the state secretariat is the best place to hold such talks,' Mamata told the journalists.

This led to a new turn of events and public sympathy suddenly shifted towards Mamata and against the agitating doctors. Many on social media condemned the junior doctors' refusal to meet the chief minister at the state secretariat holding entire health services to ransom. On the seventh day of the strike, on 17 June 2019, the doctors relented and agreed to meet the chief minister at Nabanna but with a rider—it would not be a closed-door meeting and would be televised. Mamata agreed.

So, on 17 June, the government sent a bus to the NRS Medical College and Hospital to ferry the representatives of the junior doctors from each medical college across the state. Mamata took full advantage of the televised meeting and behaved like an elder sister. The junior doctors did not protest and the strike was called off after she assured them security.

THE PK EFFECT

After the doctors' strike was called off, Mamata slowly seemed to be getting back control over the messy political and administrative situation in the state. Many wondered how Mamata calmed down and negotiated with the agitating doctors whom she had branded as BJP activists and 'outsiders' just a few days back. How could she take control of the situation and turn the tide? How could she come out stronger when almost everyone thought Mamata Banerjee's government and administration would collapse soon? Many predicted that Mamata's administration would remain as a 'lame duck' government under the onslaught of the BJP. But, that did not happen.

It is believed this was poll strategist Prashant Kishor's effect on Mamata. On 4 June 2019, a surprise meeting between the chief minister and Prashant Kishor, attended by Youth TMC Chief Abhishek Banerjee, changed the party's attitude. The man, who was behind the success of Narendra Modi's campaign in 2014, Nitish Kumar's Bihar campaign in 2015 and Jaganmohan Reddy's victory in 2019 assembly elections in Andhra Pradesh, had now taken up Mamata's brief. Unconfirmed sources claimed that the TMC had to pay around ₹400 crore to Kishor-backed Indian Political Action Committee (IPAC), but Mamata denied such reports and counter-claimed that IPAC was doing it as a CSR project. This was, however, a huge development in West Bengal politics and a big step by Mamata. Faced with the BJP's challenge, Mamata had to take professional help to set things right before the assembly elections in 2021. 'I would say it was a decision taken on two counts—blood and water! Blood as in relation. Mamata Banerjee's nephew Abhishek Banerjee had taken the initiative to bring Prashant Kishor to help TMC. Similar efforts were made before the 2016 assembly elections when PK met Mamata Banerjee in TMC Bhavan. But at that time, PK was busy with other briefs and TMC apparently did not have so much money to spend on PK's team. Now, Mamata relented first by listening to her nephew and second, she wanted to test the water of taking the help of professionals after shocking results in the Lok Sabha elections,' says Jayanta Bhattacharya.

In fact, there was no other option for Mamata but to seek professional advice to counter 'corporate BJP', which had a proper hierarchical organization and division of labour and strategy. The decision paid off. It was not just the NRS junior-doctors' strike, PK also helped Mamata rebuild her image and refurbish the party organization in a structured way. Both were under question after the 2019 Lok Sabha elections. 'PK had to deal with countering BJP's organization as well as the traditional TMC organization which was mainly local leader-driven,' says Jayanta Bhattacharya.

For about a month after the election, Mamata looked rattled with more and more TMC MLAs joining the saffron party. Mukul Roy's son Subhranshu Roy, TMC MLA from Bijpur, and Tushar Bhattacharya, MLA from Bishnupur, also joined the BJP days after the results were out. Kalchini TMC MLA Wilson Champari jumped ship and joined the BJP along with Sunil Singh of Noapara. BJP leaders claimed that they had the support of over 100 MLAs. Veteran TMC leader Biplab Mitra from South Dinajpur, who had been with the party since day one, also changed sides. Councillors from different TMC-run municipalities like Bhatpara, Halishahar, Bongaon and Balurghat joined the BJP, making the ruling party a minority there. The BJP was able to create a sense of panic in TMC.

In the middle of this exodus, Mamata made an interesting move. This too was attributed to PK's strategy. A day after resolving the doctors' strike, on

18 June 2019, a confident TMC chief met councillors of TMC-run civic bodies across the state. She alleged that those who were corrupt were joining the BJP. It essentially meant that the BJP was accepting corrupt leaders from her party. 'No one can protect them,' she said. Realizing that her voters were angry with the grassroots TMC workers, she addressed the local body representatives. The chief minister reminded them that unlike MLAs and MPs, the councillors got government money to carry out developmental projects at the grassroots and they should take the job seriously. At the same time, Mamata put up a brave face, 'If 10 to 15 councillors go in lieu of money, I don't care. I will give tickets to new people. Those who want to leave the party, please do so early so that I can give a chance to the young brothers.' To stop the exodus, she hinted that workers and leaders who were with the party would get a chance if they stuck with the TMC as 'those who have left the party, should not be taken back'.[8]

She also regretted giving the nomination to Arjun Singh's relative Sunil Singh in the Noapara by-election and Subhranshu in Bijpur. 'Only workers don't commit mistakes. We [leaders] also do it,' Mamata told a cheering crowd.

However, her masterstroke was yet to come. She asked her councillors to return the 'cut money' they had extorted from the beneficiaries of the government schemes. 'It will not be tolerated that you will help them get benefits under the House for All scheme and then receive a 25 per cent commission. You will take ₹25,000 from the poor in the name of Banglar Bari project! This

---

[8] IANS. 2019. 'Won't allow thieves to stay in party, says Mamata amid defections'. *Outlook India*, 18 June. Available at: https://www.outlookindia.com/newsscroll/wont-allow-thieves-to-stay-in-party-says-mamata-amid-defections/1557494

cannot go on. We have already formed the economic offences wing and asked people to complain directly.'

This 'cut money' debate changed the ball game in West Bengal politics post the Lok Sabha elections. 'Mamata did two things by asking her party men to return cut money. She stopped the exodus as many TMC councillors or workers could not change sides. If the BJP takes them, the saffron camp will then be branded as a party full of corrupt leaders and workers. The entire political body of the state was busy fighting the cut money allegations and the attention shifted from religious polarization and Jai Shri Ram chants,' says Rantidev Sengupta. The attempt met success. Across the state, TMC workers were seen busy defending the 'cut money' issue and the Opposition was busy staging agitations against the ruling party activists who took 'cut money'.

However, this created a sense of resentment among the grassroots level TMC workers. It now seemed like the local leaders were dishonest and top-level leaders were clean. But the 'cut money' debate helped in changing the narrative of Bengal politics and Mamata took control of this situation despite demonstrations against the ruling party workers at several places.

Prashant Kishor designed various campaigns for the TMC to revamp both Mamata's image and the party's. In tune with the 'cut-money' narrative, the first flagship public relations campaign was 'Didike Bolo' (Tell Didi). On 29 July 2019, she announced the programme in which anyone could register a complaint or give a suggestion directly by calling up a phone number the chief minister shared. A website, www.didikebolo.com, was also launched. Anyone could register themselves and lodge a complaint on the website as well. The CMO also opened a grievance cell and this campaign was an extension of the platform through party apparatus.

There were a few significant changes in Mamata's presentation as well. While unveiling the Didike Bolo campaign's logo, Mamata came to the dais alone, probably for the first time. No other leaders were seen jostling to share the frame with Mamata. There was only one chair and a glass full of water and the fiery lady of Bengal read out a written statement. Mamata Banerjee, who has always been considered to be an impulsive leader, suddenly turned into a 'disciplined' one. When asked about the change she said, 'This is the modernization of TMC and we want to use modern methods.'

The chief minister assured action on the issues raised by the common people. 'We are launching this campaign to know about their problems and reach out to them directly,' Mamata told journalists. Within a day of launching the campaign, Didike Bolo social media handles claimed they received one lakh calls and there were about 50 thousand complaints on the website.

The 2019 Lok Sabha elections have also shown that people are annoyed with the local TMC leaders' and workers' corruption. Mamata has tried to address the grievances through Didike Bolo programme. 'This is a Prashant Kishor brainchild. Wherever he worked, he tried to connect with the masses. If you remember, in Bihar he used the colour red to design the RJD–JDU alliance in the 2015 assembly elections whereas Lalu Prasad Yadav's RJD uses blue and Nitish Kumar's JDU has green in their flag. Then why did he use red? It was to connect with the people across Bihar where all forms of Leftist political outfits—socialists, communists, Maoists, ultra or progressive Left—had their influence plus both Lalu and Nitish came out of Jayprakash Narayan's movement of the 1970s. Similarly, PK wanted to brand Mamata. Look at the words carefully. It is not CM'ke Bolun or Didike Bolun. The campaign was Didike Bolo.

Didi is the elder sister in Bengali and people call Mamata as Didi and "bolo" is "tell me". In Bengali, this is the term used for addressing someone close to each other. Bolun is more formal. This campaign was to rebuild the connect Mamata had with the masses and bring the people and the leader closer to each other,' says Jayanta Bhattacharya. It basically meant that the people aggrieved by the local TMC leaders or administrative officials could now directly reach out to the chief minister. The programme also generated massive data as demographic details were sought from each caller when they tried to register any complaint.

As an extension of the same programme, over 1,000 TMC public representatives and office-bearers were instructed to visit villages and towns and spend at least a night with the locals and speak to them and the grassroots workers. They were also asked to have at least one meal with the booth-level workers. The idea was also to reach out to 10,000 villages over 100 days.

It was clear that Prashant Kishor's goal was to replicate the organizational strategy BJP had adopted before the Lok Sabha elections. Sending public representatives and office-bearers to villages and towns was to counter the BJP's Vistarak Yojona, in which BJP workers go to villages and spend a fortnight to two years to build the organization. So, for Mamata, this was a chance to monitor and detect loopholes in her collapsing organization and connect with the people. In the Didike Bolo launch programme, Mamata had admitted, 'We are not an organized party.'

Earlier, Mamata used to announce a series of programme, for the TMC workers, but there was hardly any mechanism to closely monitor the implementation of those activities. Now, not just the implementation but the impact was also monitored by a professional team of poll strategists. Team PK started taking care of turning the TMC into an organized party. The team members were surveying the ground realities. They analysed the data received from the Didike Bolo complaints, spoke to various people other than the party members at the grassroots level and prepared reports.

Several block-level leaders got calls from PK's team members who monitored the execution of the Didike Bolo campaign minutely. Block president of Goaltore, Bhaskar Chakraborty, got the shock of his life when Prashant Kishor directly called him and asked about the progress of the campaign. Almost all block presidents got regular calls from the members of PK's team, which was operating out of a Salt Lake office. 'Prashant Kishor's team members regularly call and suggest whom we should meet and speak to in a village and who are the persons we need to reach out to,' said a block president in a Junglemahal district. They were identifying influential people in the village or town and asking TMC leaders and workers to reach out to these opinion-makers of the area.

Prashant Kishor himself attended TMC's party meeting with the district president and gave a pep talk urging the party's leaders to bring back confidence in the rank and file. Each MLA was asked to suggest four names for each constituency who would be responsible for the organizational work and social media in that area. The team also wanted names of at least three persons in each booth to be promoted as the faces of the area in the run-up to the assembly elections in 2021. Apart from these campaigns, there were a series of meetings held with specific groups of public representatives and leaders, including SC/STs and the tribal community, to understand the dynamics of each section and point them towards rebuilding the party's image in their respective communities.

On 2 March 2020, Mamata Banerjee launched another campaign called 'Banglar Gorbo Mamata' (Bengal's Pride Mamata). This huge outreach activity was aimed at promoting Mamata's image as 'one of the fiercest protectors and guardians of the ideals of Justice, Liberty, Equality and Fraternity, as enshrined in the Preamble of the Constitution, a passionate proponent and the true custodian of Bengal's culture, dignity, and pride, the principal architect working tirelessly to restore Bengal's past glory and steering it towards its brighter and prosperous future'.[9] This was particularly aimed at consolidating an ideological pitch for Mamata Banerjee and the TMC.

Under three phases of this programme, there were plans to assemble a constituency-wise TMC workers' meet, Jolojoge Jogajog, in which key party leaders in each assembly constituency would meet and interact with the local media over a meal, Swikriti Sammelan, to facilitate 10,000 old and inactive party workers for their contribution in building the TMC. Mamata felt that many of her old workers had distanced themselves from the party and she kept emphasizing the point of taking them back into the party fold, lest BJP once again exploits this weak point.

There were other elements of the campaign like Bongodhwani Jatra (reaching out to the people and engaging them in different interactive sessions in at least three villages or towns covering 40,000 kilometres across 294 assembly constituencies in 15 days), Sanhati Sabha (community meetings between party leaders and more than 2.5 lakh members of the SC community), Chetona Sabha (community meetings between party leaders and the ST community), Banglar Barta (public meetings in 3,500 panchayat and municipality

[9] https://www.banglargorbomamata.com/register/en/

headquarters), Nobin Baran Sabha (welcoming one lakh young individuals to the TMC across the state), Bishishta Sammelan (felicitating 15,000 influential women and celebrating their association with the party), Trinamooler Sathe Manyojon (one-on-one meetings with party leaders and 25,000 influencers across 294 assembly constituencies), Trinamool Padatik Sammelan (culminating the campaign with a 1,500-kilometre padayatra across the state followed by Booth Karmi Sammelan with five lakh booth workers in each of the 294 assembly constituencies).

These campaigns, which had to be aborted due to the Covid-19 outbreak, were planned to reach out to every important constituent in the state, assembly-wise, including grassroots workers, women, the SC and ST community, old and inactive TMC workers, youth, celebrities and influencers, with Mamata Banerjee's message and also to draw feedback from grassroots up. It was important to rejuvenate the party and engage the party workers in a more constructive and organized way.

In June 2020, the TMC launched their third flagship programme, Banglar Yuva Shakti, again designed by Team PK, during the Covid-19 outbreak. It was 'an initiative to onboard, unite, and join hands with 10 lakh motivated youth who are willing to help the people of Bengal during this time of crisis'. Interestingly, here, for the first time, Abhishek Banerjee's photo appeared along with Mamata Banerjee's in the campaign poster. This indicated a projection of Abhishek as the youth leader and the TMC's second-in-command. Banglar Yuva Shakti invited registration of young people in the age group of 18–35 and take up the responsibility of 10 households each. The participants were not required to be members of TMC or Youth TMC. Anyone with any party affiliation and even apolitical persons were asked to register and help the households under them. Many saw this as a replication of the BJP's 'panna pramukh' strategy in Banglar Yuva Shakti. In the BJP's organizational structure, each panna pramukh is responsible for the voters of one page of a voters list. They are supposed to be in touch with the voters and mobilize them to go to the polling booth and vote for the party on the polling day.

PK's strategy also reflected in reorganizing the party structure and the selection of party office-bearers. Mamata Banerjee accommodated almost all the factions while choosing the district office-bearers and announcing the new names in July 2020. The posts of district chairman and district coordinator were created along with that of district president. The district coordinators were assigned responsibilities of specific areas. She removed the post of district observer, essentially a senior state-level leader who would oversee the organization of the assigned district. Instead, she formed a 21-member state coordination committee and a seven-member steering committee, choosing senior leaders from the state coordination committee.

Most importantly, for the first time, the appointment of block-level presidents had to be ratified by TMC Chief Mamata Banerjee. Earlier, district presidents used to directly appoint block-level presidents and just inform the state leadership. Sources close to the party chief say PK's team also drew up a parallel list of block presidents with inputs from the grassroots workers and prepared reports on the prospective presidents. Mamata decided to cross-check the names and select the block president. Since its inception in 1998, the TMC had never gone ahead with the appointment of its office-bearers in such an organized and uniform manner.

But did Mamata Banerjee need Prashant Kishor to take all these initiatives? The Opposition has been mocking the TMC chief for hiring a professional to help with her politics, which, she has always claimed, has roots in the grassroots. However, TMC Secretary-General Partha Chatterjee says, 'You know, sometimes you need a private tutor even if the guardians can teach a child. The child won't listen to the parents but when a tutor comes every day and teaches him from 6 to 7 in the evening, there is a feeling that "yes, sir had come". Similarly, what PK is saying is nothing new. They have identified certain points where we had gone wrong. They are doing a back-office job, which we could not do. They are giving managerial organizational support.'

PK's micromanagement strategy to mobilize local resources and rake up local issues paid its dividend in the by-elections of three assembly constituencies, Kharagpur, Karimpur and Kaliaganj, held in November 2019; the NRC–CAA issue also played a significant role. In these elections, PK's team helped the TMC release customized manifestos for each constituency. Election machinery was active for door-to-door campaigning exactly in the way RSS–BJP had done before the 2019 Lok Sabha elections. On top of it, the local TMC satraps like minister Suvendu Adhikari worked hard to get the party candidate elected. The TMC had only Karimpur in its basket in the 2016 assembly elections. In the by-elections, they bagged all three. Snatching Kharagpur from the BJP (which was held by state the BJP chief, Dilip Ghosh, before he was elected as an MP) was a big morale-booster for the ruling party. Kaliaganj, which was held by a Congress–Left backed candidate, also went to TMC's kitty.

Though the by-election results cannot guarantee a victory in the full-fledged assembly elections in the state, the result provided much-needed oxygen to Mamata Banerjee. Over the months succeeding the Lok Sabha elections, the TMC chief deliberately changed her stance and brought back her old self who could connect with the common man easily. For the last few years, she generally travelled by chopper to attend the administrative review meetings in the districts and there was hardly any scope for interactions with the common people. However, after the Lok Sabha disaster, she has been seen interacting with slum dwellers and villagers, tea-stall owners in districts like Howrah, Burdwan and East Midnapore. Though, in some cases, she looks a little uncomfortable as people were not as spontaneous as they used to be. Nonetheless, her change of stance is clear.

Another change the TMC chief has brought in her image-makeover has been her visible (and alleged) 'Muslim appeasement' gestures. She has not been uttering 'inshallah' in her speeches as she used to do quite often or seen with Muslim clerics in public meetings. This was a conscious effort to battle her 'pro-Muslim' image as alleged by the BJP. However, this did not deter her from attending namaaz on the day of Eid at Kolkata's iconic Red Road. Just before Durga Puja in 2020, she announced a monthly allowance of ₹1,000 for 8,000 poor Hindu priests and assistance for building houses under Banglar Awas Yojana.

THE NRC AND CAA MOVEMENT

If organizational revamping and image-makeover was her priority, Mamata Banerjee got her mojo back during the movement against the passing of the Citizenship Amendment Act 2019 in the Parliament in the winter session of 2019. Mamata Banerjee had been opposing this bill since its presentation in the Parliament in 2016 (the earlier avatar of Citizenship Amendment Bill which was passed in Lok Sabha but could not be passed in the Rajya Sabha; hence it could not be enacted). She had to face stiff opposition from the BJP in the 2019 Lok Sabha election campaign on the issue of the National Register of Citizens. The TMC chief was opposed to the idea of any NRC in the line of Assam where identifying the Bangladeshis coming to the state after 24 March 1971 was part of the Assam Accord of 1985 signed between the Government of India and the representatives of the Assam movement. During the Lok Sabha campaign, the BJP had branded Mamata as favouring those who wanted Bangladeshi Muslim infiltrators to reside in Bengal. In August 2018, in a rally from Kolkata's Mayo Road, BJP leader Amit Shah had alleged that 'now she wants to keep them [Bangladeshi infiltrators] in Bengal and Assam. Does your country's interest come first or your vote bank? They are making bombs here.'[10] This narrative went well with the BJP's religious polarization efforts in the state. At that time, they tried to defend the Assam NRC list, in which many Hindus were excluded, as a 'draft list'. They promised the excluded names would be there in the final list. Many Bengali Hindus' names were also out of the Assam NRC. Still, Mamata's pitch that BJP is anti-Bengali did not work in the Lok Sabha campaign.

However, when Assam NRC's final list came out on 31 August 2019, it was found that a good number of Hindus were there among the 19 lakh people who could not prove their citizenship claim. 'NRC is not easy to implement here. What happened in Assam? They

[10] The Bengal Story Bureau. *The Bengal Story*. 'Amit Shah says Bangladeshi infiltrators are Mamata's votebank'. 11 August 2018.

excluded 19 lakh people, which include Bengali Hindus. BJP being at the Centre cannot evade the issue. It may turn BJP's core voters against them,' says Prasenjit Bose.

Mamata picked up the issue as the people in Bengal were scared of not being able to prove their citizenship with proper documents. The BJP wanted to hide the issue under the garb of CAA, claiming the Hindus coming from Bangladesh would get citizenship under this act. Though the NRC was supposed to create an atmosphere of fear among the infiltrators, the common Bengali Hindu citizens were also feeling apprehensive. People rushed to government offices to arrange their documents like their Aadhaar card, land deeds, parental lineage, birth certificates, certificates from local public representatives among others. 'My grandson came back from school one afternoon and asked me about the NRC and family history. When I asked why he was asking me these questions, he said his classmates were discussing about it,' says Soumen Nag, 'He is just 10 years old. You can understand how the narrative is catching young minds and what problem it is going to cause.'

Mamata hit the chord and went back to her 'street-fighter' self. She organized protest marches across the state, including in Kolkata, and walked in those protest marches against the implementation of the CAA, NRC and then the National Population Register. While the CAA was termed as anti-constitutional, the NRC was considered as anti-citizen. 'Why would someone have to prove his citizenship after residing in the country for so long?'—this was the question that got a lot of political traction. Soon after the President gave his assent to the act, Mamata Banerjee told a press conference, 'Let's form an alliance. Not a single person should be thrown out of the country. No NRC. There will be no division, no divide and rule.' She also extended her solidarity to the civil society movements against the CAA and NRC in the state and across the country. Unlike the note ban in 2016, spontaneous civil society movements erupted over the CAA–NRC issue across the country. Mamata became the political pivot of the agitation.

The BJP could sense it and attacked her by organizing Abhinandan Yatra in Kolkata. The BJP's then working president, J.P. Nadda, led a march in December 2019 from central Kolkata's Hind Cinema to north Kolkata's Shyambazar. At the end of the march, Nadda addressed a rally and said, 'All she [Mamata Banerjee] knows is appeasement.'

The saffron camp wanted to project it as an act to provide citizenship to the Matua community whose members had come from Bangladesh and took shelter in Bengal's bordering district. Both the TMC and the BJP had vied for the Matua vote bank during the elections. 'This act is to give citizenship not to take citizenship from anyone,' J.P. Nadda told the gathering. 'Among people who crossed over to India for shelter and safety were those from the Matua and Namashudra [both are Hindu Dalit] communities from Bangladesh. Prime Minister Modi has given them citizenship rights. Is that wrong?'[11] Quite significantly, Nadda's rally drew a huge crowd and thereby marked a polarization on the issue in Bengal.

A few sporadic incidents of violence were also reported from some minority-dominated districts or areas. A static train was set on fire in Murshidabad's Lalgola, railway stations were vandalized in Murshidabad, Malda, and several toll plazas were vandalized in Howrah districts. BJP leaders called these rioters anti-national Bangladeshi infiltrators. While Dilip Ghosh accused the Mamata

---

[11] *Hindustan Times*. 'At pro-CAA rally in Bengal, Nadda says "huge" turnout signals change'. 24 December 2019.

Banerjee government of failing to make genuine efforts to stop the violence and destruction of public property, the then BJP national secretary, Rahul Sinha, demanded President's Rule in the state. 'If this continues, there won't be any option but to impose President's Rule in Bengal,' he told the media.

The imposition of President's Rule in order to remove an elected government would have been a disaster for the BJP. So, as in most of the cases, it remained a rhetoric. The localized riots on the NRC issue and outrage over the possible application of President's Rule worked in favour of Mamata. She could consolidate her core support base which was opposed to the BJP. She had found an issue against the BJP to shrug off the wounds of the Lok Sabha elections and hit the streets in her old avatar of 'fiery lady of Bengal'. Mamata's movement resonated with people's sentiment. Those who were apprehensive of the NRC process and proving their citizenship by digging up old documents rallied behind her. At the same time, the liberal Left supporters found someone to follow in Mamata Banerjee who was leading from the front.

Though Mamata gained from the CAA–NRC protest, another threat was looming large on her. Asaduddin Owaisi's All India Majlis-e-Ittehadul Muslimeen (AIMIM) started subtly expanding their base in Muslim-dominated districts. AIMIM's Bengal in-charge Zameerul Hasan claimed their party had a strong presence in at least 55 assembly constituencies in Murshidabad, Malda and North Dinajpur districts where Muslims are a majority. The fear of a swing in the Muslim vote bank and a change in the political equations of the state led Mamata to unleash a veiled attack against the AIMIM. Much before the NRC–CAA agitation erupted, in November 2019, Mamata had said at a public meeting in Murshidabad's

Sagardighi, 'Some will come from outside. We don't tolerate any kind of communalism, be it Muslim or Hindu. Some are coming from Hyderabad with sacks of money and promising that they would fight for the people. How will you fight? You are BJP's biggest agent. You cannot fight. Only we can fight.'[12] She did not name the outfit, but the reference was clear. In fact, Asaduddin Owaisi retaliated. He asked Mamata to concentrate on empowering Muslims in her state rather than appeasing them by attending Iftar parties or namaaz or sporting a hijab. During the anti-CAA protest, the possibility of ceding ground to the AIMIM grew further in the ranks and files of the TMC. As Mamata tried to remake her 'secular image', the fear of losing the Muslim support did not completely vanish from her mind.

THE BJP'S PLIGHT

Soon after the elections, the BJP leadership was upbeat for obvious reasons. They were not only exerting political pressure on the government and Mamata Banerjee's TMC, but they were also on a poaching spree. The BJP headquarters in Delhi was busy welcoming TMC and even CPIM legislatures to the party fold. TMC-turned-BJP leader Mukul Roy was going all out to get TMC councillors to break away from the party and destabilize the civic bodies. The first jolt Mukul Roy received was after inducting Birbhum TMC MLA Manirul Islam. The day Manirul joined, Mukul Roy had said, 'He is not only the MLA from Labhpur, but he is also the vice-chairman of Khadi Gramadyog [West Bengal Khadi & Village Industries Board, a statutory

[12] ABP Ananda. 2019. 'Mamata attacks AIMIM, calls them "BJP's biggest dalaals"'. YouTube, 20 November. Available at: https://www.youtube.com/watch?v=X7sJI-kJujA

board under the government of West Bengal]. This is significant.' Elated, Manirul had praised Narendra Modi, 'I have joined BJP listening to the call by Modiji through the slogan "Sabka Saath, Sabka Vikash, Sabka Biswas".'

But, soon after Manirul joined the saffron camp, there was huge resentment in the BJP rank and files. Even the RSS took up the issue of unfiltered induction of TMC leaders as Manirul was accused of murdering a Congress worker when he was with the Forward Bloc. In an open rally, as a TMC MLA, he had threatened to repeat the act by beheading the Opposition. The BJP and RSS leadership questioned such inductions. Rantidev Sengupta, the editor of RSS's mouthpiece, said, 'It is like making BJP a copybook of TMC. The leadership of the BJP must think if they want to replicate a party like TMC. They need to be careful in welcoming leaders from other parties.' The pressure was so intense that Manirul had to be side-lined and he even said that he would resign if the party wanted him to. Since then, there are checks before inducting TMC workers and leaders.

The BJP received another jolt when former Kolkata mayor Sovan Chatterjee and his friend Baishakhi Banerjee joined the BJP. On the day of their joining, another TMC MLA and former film star Deboshree Roy reached the party headquarters in Delhi. Both Sovan and Baishakhi put their foot down and threatened not to join the BJP if Deboshree was inducted in the party. The BJP leadership did not want to lose the opportunity to bring in a big name like Sovan Chatterjee. They did not take Deboshree. Apparently, under pressure from Baishakhi and Sovan, the BJP leadership had to defer the decision of accepting Deboshree in the party forever. The duo again threatened to walk out of the party when Baishakhi was not given equal importance as Sovan.

Ultimately, both of them became mere wallflowers for the BJP.

'There is tension when a new member comes to the family. But we have to remember that the party has to grow and it will only grow when members from other parties join. This is how we have grown in other parts of the country. While the old members will have to accept and adjust, the new entrants will also have to get absorbed in the party and follow our ideology and principles,' says Dilip Ghosh.

There were allegations of corruption against Mukul Roy and Sovan Chatterjee. Reacting to the allegations, Dilip Ghosh says, 'They will have to take responsibility and come out clean. The party will not take any responsibility on their behalf.' But this unfiltered induction made some BJP leaders, such as the party's state general secretary, Sayantan Basu, express the desire to go back to their parent body, the RSS. 'To be frank, Mukul Roy could not be a Himanta Biswa Sharma. Yes, he helped BJP to mount pressure on Mamata, but he could not literally get 100 MLAs to pull down the TMC government in Bengal,' says Prasenjit Bakshi.

The division the newcomers are creating in the BJP is haunting its leaders. It has been so prominent that a group of youths from east Kolkata's Nonadanga surrounded the party president on the sidelines of an organizational meeting at Kolkata's ICCR and demanded that the new local leader, who had joined the BJP recently and was put at the helm of affairs, be removed. 'We are not getting any importance in the party. Many of our workers are homeless now. No action is being taken to bring them back,' complained a worker. After the BJP state president left in his car, these youth complained before the central observer Arvind Menon, who shifted the responsibility to a state leader and left the venue.

The workers were visibly disheartened. 'Remember in 2011, there was no such factionalism within TMC that would cause serious problems for the party in grabbing power. The main focus was to dislodge the Left Front. Factionalism between adi and nabya TMC cropped up after TMC came to power. In 2019, the BJP is already faction-ridden and there is tension among its workers. When they needed to take on Mamata, they have been wasting time in dealing with the like of Sovan and Baishakhi,' says Prasenjit Bakshi.

There are confusions within the BJP as well. Even the leaders have been looking for a direction to launch a concerted fight against Mamata Banerjee. 'Is there any politics in Bengal? I don't think so. We are doing reactive-politics. We are reacting to what Mamata Banerjee is doing,' says a senior state BJP leader. While it is true that the BJP has not been able to organize a mass movement around the 'cut money' issue, the leadership is concentrating on local-level movements. 'We have been organizing localized movements to get people involved in our activities. We have conducted programmes like "Gherao SP office" or "Gherao BDO office" as well as massive protest marches in Kolkata,' says Dilip Ghosh.

They are also trying to strengthen the booth-level organization, which is not strong in all parts of the state. 'The BJP must remember that they have achieved success in terms of numbers, but it was not the success of BJP's ideology. They simply filled up the vacuum created in the Opposition space,' says Prasenjit Bakshi.

The BJP's major problem in Bengal will be the chief ministerial face for 2021 assembly election in Bengal. There is already an internal feud on this issue. The names of former Indian cricket captain Sourav Ganguly, Rajya Sabha MP and journalist Swapan Dasgupta and even a monk of Ramakrishna Mission, Swami Kripakarananda, have already come up in media reports. Former Governor of Tripura and Meghalaya and former BJP state president, Tathagata Roy, also openly threw his hat in the ring expressing his desire to be the chief ministerial candidate. BJP minder Kailash Vijayvargiya clarified that the party would not go to the 2021 assembly elections with any chief ministerial candidate.

In earlier assembly polls, the BJP achieved success in UP and Maharashtra without projecting any chief ministerial candidates. But will this be possible in West Bengal? In 2021, there will be questions about the face against Mamata Banerjee. 'Moreover, most chief ministers in Bengal have come up through movements and established their position. Bengal's politics is more complicated than Assam or Haryana,' says Prasenjit Bakshi.

The Bengal BJP has no such leader who can match the mass leader that Mamata Banerjee is. The TMC also knows this will be an advantage for them. 'In the 2019 Lok Sabha elections, we, the Opposition, could not be united. We could not put up anyone against Narendra Modi. We have suffered. In 2021 Bengal elections, BJP will have to suffer because of the same reason,' says Partha Chatterjee.

The state BJP president claims they have already started preparing for the assembly elections in 2021 and 'people are determined to dislodge the TMC government'. The TMC is also determined to recover its lost ground and believe they have been able to do so.

There is no doubt that the BJP has increased its tally in the Lok Sabha elections riding on a popular sentiment. They have instilled confidence among the people to raise their voices against the atrocities of the TMC leaders and goons. Still, they need to work hard to turn these negative votes into positive ones. They cannot simply wait for Narendra Modi to lead the assembly election campaign.

While the Left and the Congress show no signs of revival, the BJP is the undisputed principal Opposition party in Bengal. In the middle of 2020, the Bengal BJP seems to be losing the steam. Though journalist Pinakpani Ghosh claims, 'Yes, there are reports of infighting in the BJP and it may make the party look like rudderless at the moment. I still believe that the central leadership is putting its strength behind the state president Dilip Ghosh irrespective of the pressure from different lobbies. In BJP, the party president is all-in-all and he believes if they maintain this stance till the 2021 assembly elections, BJP will be in a position to overthrow the TMC government.' The truth is, many workers and a few leaders, including South Dinajpur's Biplab Mitra or Bankura's Tushar Bhattacharya, who jumped the ship from TMC to BJP post 2019 Lok Sabha election results, have started returning to their old party.

In 2007–11, people in Bengal were discussing about rights and livelihood. The discussion was on the creation of jobs, farmland acquisition for industries and SEZs and investment in the state. In 2019–20, the discussion revolves around religious and social polarization and corruption in the ruling party. There has been a sharp shift from politics over economic policies and livelihood to identity politics in the last decade in West Bengal. Even though Prashant Kishor has been trying his best to revive Mamata's as well as the party's image, corruption at the grassroots level could not be eradicated completely. During cyclone Amphan in May 2020, there were reports of rampant corruption while providing relief from all 16 cyclone-affected districts. The state government announced monetary support of ₹20,000 to those who had lost their home in the cyclone and ₹5,000 to those whose houses got partially damaged. The amount was directly transferred to the victims' bank account. Still, the fake list of beneficiaries created a huge political uproar in the state. Even the TMC's gram panchayat members raised the issue with the administration. Panchla Gram Panchayat chief Muzibar Rahman wrote to the district magistrate of Howrah that 80 per cent of the people whose names were sent to the district administration did not suffer any loss in the cyclone. Chief Minister Mamata Banerjee admitted that there was corruption in Amphan relief. 'In other states, the rate of corruption is at 90 per cent. It is 10 per cent here. Our administration is taking strict action,' Banerjee said at a press conference at Nabanna, the state secretariat.[13] Even though the TMC leadership either suspended or expelled a lot of village-level leaders for the 'Amphan corruption', no legal steps were taken against those who cheated the government. Instead, they were asked to return the money. Many did so, giving a written undertaking of 'committing a mistake' to the district administration. PK's mantra could not eradicate this old disease the TMC suffered from.

On the other hand, when the Covid-19 pandemic broke out in the country, Mamata Banerjee projected herself as the saviour of the people of Bengal. In her own style, she was seen going out in the market and drawing circles in front of the vegetable shops to educate the common man of the importance of social distancing. However, within days, her government was accused of hiding the exact death toll in the guise of comorbidity. Here, too, Prashant Kishore, had to chip in to do some course correction in the party's handling of

---

[13] *Hindustan Times*. '"It is 10% here": Bengal CM on corruption complaints over Amphan relief'. 8 July 2020.

the Covid-19 outbreak in the state. Despite neutralising the situation, it seems Mamata Banerjee will have to carry the baggage of her government's Covid-19 management capabilities to the next elections.

However, there is no absolute way of stating that Mamata has been undone. She is known to be a fighter and definitely possesses the power to bounce back. She was the sole TMC MP in 2004 and within four years she had changed the face of Bengal's politics. She was the one to dislodge the Left Front government and perhaps has the potential to perform a similar miracle once again.

'I won't say 2021 is a settled issue as yet. We will have to wait and see,' says Prasenjit Bose. At the same time, Suvashis Maitra has a different calculation to offer: 'There's speculation that this time the Congress and the Left will come out with an open and strong alliance. If that happens and they can recover at least 3 to 5 per cent of their lost votes from the BJP's kitty, the BJP won't be in a position to form the government in 2021.'

Amit Shah's virtual rally during Covid-19 lockdown and Mamata Banerjee's virtual speech on Shaheed Diwas on 21 July 2020 set the tone of the pitched battle of 2021. While BJP is all set to rake up the issues of TMC's corruption, syndicate raj, bhatija-raj (targeting Abhishek Banerjee), Muslim appeasement and Mamata's opposition to NRC–CAA, Mamata Banerjee is depending on her fighter image and on rousing the Bengali sentiment. She declared from the virtual rally, '*Bohiragotora banglay sarkar chalabe na* (no outsiders will rule the state)!' She wanted to bring home the point that only the TMC, being a Bengal-based political party, has the right to rule the state instead of the Modi–Shah-led BJP. So far they have been relying on Modi's face to win the assembly elections in 2021. However, she still has to face the issue of unemployment in the state and the mismanagement of the Covid-19 situation.

Bengal Governor Jagdeep Dhankhar is also keeping Mamata Banerjee on her toes as he often confronts the Bengal government and the TMC party openly. Be it the issue of meeting the vice-chancellors of the universities or raising his concern on why the state government is not willing to implement central government projects like Ayushman Bharat or Kisan Samman Nidhi or the political violence—the Governor has been at loggerheads with the TMC government at every step.

Most importantly, none of the parties are sure of their electoral positions as the civic body polls of nearly 100 municipalities, including Kolkata Municipal Corporation, could not be held in due time because of the Covid-19 pandemic.

There is no doubt that Amit Shah and Narendra Modi, supported by the RSS apparatus, will exert their full pressure on winning Bengal as it is the last bastion in Eastern India where the BJP could not come to power. Their mature political strategy has dislodged many state governments run by the Opposition parties, and their latest project is Win Bengal. Whatever be the election results, Bengal is going to witness a battle of nerves in 2021. All eyes will be on this eastern Indian state that has already witnessed several political nail-biters in the last couple of years.